SUSQUEHANNA UNIVERSITY STUDIES

# Shakespeare

*Susquehanna University Studies* is an annual interdisciplinary scholarly journal published as part of the Susquehanna University Press. Each issue is devoted to a theme or themes of academic interest. The editors invite manuscript submissions prepared in accordance with the *Chicago Manual of Style*, 13th edition.

## EDITORIAL BOARD

Ronald Dotterer, Editor
Odekhiren Amaize
Jane Barlow
Susan R. Bowers
Frank Fletcher
Gerald Gordon
W. Murray Hunt
Jack Kolbert

Contributors should send manuscripts with a self-addressed, stamped envelope to Editor, *Susquehanna University Studies*, Susquehanna University, Selinsgrove, Pennsylvania 17870.

SUSQUEHANNA UNIVERSITY STUDIES

# SHAKESPEARE

## Text, Subtext, and Context

Edited by
RONALD DOTTERER

FINKELSTEIN
MEMORIAL LIBRARY
SPRING VALLEY, N.Y.

SELINSGROVE: SUSQUEHANNA UNIVERSITY PRESS
LONDON AND TORONTO: ASSOCIATED UNIVERSITY PRESSES

8469

© 1989 by Associated University Presses, Inc.

Associated University Presses
440 Forsgate Drive
Cranbury, NJ 08512

Associated University Presses
25 Sicilian Avenue
London WC1A 2QH, England

Associated University Presses
P.O. Box 488, Port Credit
Mississauga, Ontario
Canada L5G 4M2

The paper used in this publication meets the requirements
of the American National Standard for Permanance of Paper
for Printed Library Materials Z39.48-1984.

The Library of Congress has cataloged this serial
publication as follows:
**Susquehanna University.**
    Susquehanna University studies.  v. 1-  1936–
Selinsgrove, Pa., Susquehanna University Press
[etc.]
    v. diagrs.  23–31 cm.
    Annual.
    Indexes:
    Vols. 1–5, 1936–56, in v. 5; Vols. 1–8, 1936–70, in v. 8.
    ISSN 0361-8250 = Susquehanna University studies

    I. Susquehanna University.  Studies.  II. Title.

LH1.S78S8          082          38-14370
                                MARC-S
Library of Congress      [8708–87]rev2

Printed in the United States of America

**To the memory of**

Arthur H. Wilson, George F. Dunkelberger, George E. Fisher,
Russell Galt, Russell W. Gilbert,
William A. Russ, Jr., G. Morris Smith

founding editors of *Susquehanna University Studies*
and
Frederic Bush, M.D.
its generous early benefactor

# Contents

# Foreword

Shakespeare studies, while almost always diverse and vivid, seem unusually so at the present time. They currently embody not only the traditional modes and topics of scholarly inquiry on the Bard and his works, but also virtually every conceivable current of contemporary critical theory and practice, interdisciplinary methodology, and substantive concern. In fact, one could argue that Shakespeare has become one of the major battlegrounds in which crucial scholarly debates within the increasingly fragmented ranks of humanists are taking place. Enlivening a scene once dominated by philologists, biographers, editors, literary historians and "new" critics is a whole new generation of guests at the endless banquet—deconstructionists, poststructuralists, Lacanian analysts, historicists, feminists, social anthropologists, and more. Given this multiplicity, the decline of what was never more than fragile consensus on a whole range of issues should occasion little surprise.

Under these circumstances, the present volume should serve the useful end of introducing its readers to a representative cross-section of new and traditional approaches to Shakespeare's life, his use of language, dramatic techniques, attitudes toward issues of gender, impact on audiences in his own times as well as in other times and places. One may learn from a distinguished authority many of the salient facts about the physical characteristics of Elizabethan theaters, and the archeological/historical studies that have led to recent reinterpretations. One may see how writers with different interpretive styles and strategies seek to unravel problematical passages in the comedies, tragedies, and histories. There is even a healthy voice of dissent from the usual source: a person of the theater freshly expressing the traditional reservations about the ultimate relevance or importance of Shakespeare scholarship, and reminding us that "the play's the thing."

Well, perhaps. The play's the thing all right, but putting on the play isn't the only thing. In the world of Shakespeare, definitive performances or productions are as rare as definitive works of scholarship. On both sides of the footlights, men and women struggle to interpret and understand one of the few universal minds. On the stage and in the study, they perform in order to offer to their public a new interpretation, a fresh insight. Through energetic dialogue, they seek to preserve,

9

extend, and enhance our own encounters with our greatest writer. The essays assembled here, considered as a group, serve to take us in that direction.

Werner Gundersheimer
Director of the Folger Shakespeare Library
Washington, D.C.

# Preface

Founded in 1936, the *Susquehanna University Studies* has a long history as an annual interdisciplinary journal devoted to original articles and research within a wide range of topics. Begun as a vehicle for fostering and dispersing research done by local faculty, the *Studies* over its first fifty years attracted more and more articles by outside scholars. Today the *Studies* takes its place as one of the longer-running continuously published American academic journals.

As it prepared for its second half-century, the *Studies* and Susquehanna University Press, of which it has always been a part, recognized this development. With this issue, *Susquehanna University Studies* acquires a new format: hard-bound collections of essays on themes of critical interest. Under this more permanent and integrated format, the *Studies* continues its fifty-year-long tradition of having contributors write for a broad, intelligent audience, aiming only for an increasingly larger audience for its contributors.

Discussing several possible topics, the editorial board selected Shakespeare as the topic for the first issue of its second half-century and as a fitting bridge to its past. The *Studies*'s first editor-in-chief, Arthur H. Wilson, was a Shakespearean; Shakespeare has been the most frequent subject in the *Studies*—fourteen articles (two of which are included here) have appeared since 1936. In addition, Susquehanna's Apple-Zimmerman Lectureship, begun in 1981, represents a recent example of scholarship fostered by the University. Four lecturers in that series are among this volume's contributors.

Ronald Dotterer

SUSQUEHANNA UNIVERSITY STUDIES

# Shakespeare

# All That Is Known Concerning Shakespeare

## S. Schoenbaum

Perhaps you will permit a brief very personal prelude to my remarks proper. I am only too sensible of the fact that I present myself to you with what some—many? all?—may regard as an unconscionably cheeky title. *All* that is known concerning Shakespeare in an hour? After centuries of patient study and research, and library shelves groaning with explorations of every aspect of the Bard's career. So I am prepared to endure your howls of execration. How nice if I could turn them to unstinted applause! I am also cheeky enough to think I might, when—in due course—the perfect propriety of my title becomes apparent.

First, though, your speaker's task is to rivet the attention—if such a thing is possible—of this perhaps skeptical throng at the outset. Can a good murder miss? By a good murder I mean, and this will come as no surprise, a particularly revolting one; not one of your fictional murders but one that took place four centuries ago. These are garden paths down which Dame Agatha Christie never strayed. As I proceed, you may well wonder what the crime I propose to describe has to do with the subject of this discourse. Does it have anything to do with that subject? My work is cut out for me.

---

It was my privilege to be invited to deliver the first Apple-Zimmerman lecture at Susquehanna University in April of 1981. My title then was "Who Was Shakespeare?," and the lecture (for me) represented a journey down well-traveled paths. I have been traveling some of the same paths since, for Shakespearean biography has remained one of my scholarly preoccupations; scholarship—as I see it—being process: one continues to peck away at seemingly established truths, and sometimes new information comes to light. I do not, however, subscribe to change for its own sake, and some of my original audience (if this collection comes their way) may recognize in its present cheerfully immodest incarnation as "All That Is Known Concerning Shakespeare," the lineaments, if not always the exact contours, of the lecture I gave at Susquehanna seven years ago.

Copyright © 1985 by S. Schoenbaum

The document relating the event has only recently surfaced; more about that anon. It is a deposition preserved in London in the Public Record Office. In it one Roland Wheler, by occupation a shoemaker, describes a murder he himself witnessed; a murder committed by William Bott, a turbulent figure who attracted his share of notice in Stratford-upon-Avon and its environs in the sixteenth century. This Bott hailed from the Wold in Snitterfield, the village, three miles north of Stratford, where Richard Shakespeare, the poet's grandfather, farmed. The two men knew each other; twice, along with others, they appraised the estates of lately deceased locals. In a suit for slander, Bott declared that since childhood he had lived as a man of great honesty and credit among men both honorable and venerable in the neighborhood, but unfortunately he had lost a lot of cash—*magna ineffabilia lucra*—from yearly gifts, fees, and rewards since the Stratford deputy steward charged him with dishonesty. With John Shakespeare, William's father, Bott served on the Stratford town council. When, in May 1565, he was expelled by the corporation for slanderous remarks about that estimable body, John Shakespeare filled the post vacated by Bott's expulsion. Everybody in Stratford, it seems, had a bad word to say about Bott. According to his son-in-law, John Harper, Bott was "a man clearly void of all honesty, fidelity, or fear of God, and openly detected of divers great and notorious crimes, as, namely, felony, adultery, whoredom, falsehood, and forging, a procurer of the disinherison of divers gentlemen your Majesty's subjects (etc.)." I like to refer to his impact on the community as Bottulism.

Bott secured a marriage between his daughter Isabella and John Harper, described as "a plain and simple-minded man," over his head in debt. By elaborate machinations involving substituted deeds and names and a seal surreptitiously obtained for him by his daughter, Bott assured himself of the lands of his son-in-law in the event that Isabella should die childless. The fact that Harper was a minor at the time facilitated Bott's machinations. The stage was now set for the murder described by the witness in the dry legal phraseology common to depositions; phraseology which, by its very impersonal matter-of-factness, inadvertently succeeds in making the event described—an event that had taken place eight years previously—seem more, rather than less, harrowing:

the said Bott having in this wise forged the said deed and so conveyed the said lands, the said Bott's daughter, wife of the said John Harper, did die suddenly and was poisoned with ratsbane, and therewith swelled to death. And this deponent knoweth the same to be true, for that he did see the wife of the said Bott in the presence of the same Bott deliver to the said Harper's wife in a spoon mixed with drink the said poison of ratsbane to drink, which poison she did drink in this deponent's presence, the same William Bott by and at that time leaning to the bed's feet. And this deponent saith that after the wife of the said William Bott had so given the said drink to the said Harper's wife, the said Harper and this deponent did see her lay a thing under a green carpet.

This "thing" was the deadly ratsbane. The Stratford parish register records the burial of Isabella, wife of John Harper, on 7 May 1563. So, according to Roland Wheler, William Bott murdered his own daughter. Incidentally, Mrs. Bott, her husband's willing accomplice, was not Isabella's mother but a second wife. As Wheler deposes, "He knew William Bott to have two wives alive at one time." The first wife Wheler had taken in behalf of Bott to Thorne near Lichfield. The young wife's mother was safely away from the premises when the murder took place. The other Mrs. Bott was dead by the time Wheler deposed, and the bereaved widower had taken a third bride.

What does all this have to do with William Shakespeare, who (after all) had not even been born in 1563? The connection is to be found in the house where the poison was allegedly hidden under a green carpet. For in 1563 William Clopton, a young gentleman newly come into his patrimony and pressed for money, gave up the title of New Place to William Bott. The latter had resided at New Place for several years before acquiring it. The murder, if Wheler's is a true account, almost certainly took place there. It is a murder of kin, by poison for the estate, and so has some of the mythic resonance of *Hamlet*. The handsome five-gabled house, called New Place, the second-finest in Stratford, was purchased some thirty years afterward by a playwright of rising prosperity. Shakespeare bought New Place in 1597. It had by then long since passed from Bott to the Underhill family. In July the seller, William Underhill—"a subtle, covetous, and crafty man," as a contemporary summed him up—died mysteriously at Fillongley, not far from Stratford, after orally bequeathing "all his lands" to his first-born son Fulke. In 1599 this Fulke Underhill, still a minor, was hanged at Warwick for poisoning his father. Thus, associated with the fortunes of New Place, Shakespeare's house—we twice have murder of kin—a father of his daughter, and a son of his father—by poison for the estate.

So one wonders: during one of his periodic flights from the busy life of the capital and its Bankside theaters, as Shakespeare tended the flourishing vines in the Great Garden of New Place, and *Hamlet* was beginning subliminally to take form in his brain, did he ever pause to think of his house and its heritage?

Things unexpectedly come an author's way; that is one of the great pleasures and rewards of the biographer's essentially solitary life. The Bott connection has been public knowledge for only a decade. E. Tangye

Lean had been working on a book on Shakespeare in his Warwickshire context when he died suddenly, leaving behind a great mass of notes and papers. He was not known to me as a Shakespeare scholar, nor was he a trained paleographer—I think I know who helped Lean with transcriptions of Elizabethan hands. His widow Doreen was understandably eager not to have her husband's researches go to waste, and at her invitation arranged through the good offices of my publisher, Oxford University Press, I hastily perused the Lean papers one afternoon in London in 1976. One transcription, uncommented upon, led me to the volume of depositions, "together with numerous letters, briefs informations, &c., on both sides" in a suit among the State Papers Domestic for June 1571 at the Public Record Office; a "confused and intricate case," as it is described in the published calendar. Here I came upon the deposition of the Stratford shoemaker, and I went on to publish an account of the case. Mrs. Lean has since, at my suggestion, donated her late husband's papers to the Birthplace Records Office at Stratford, where students may consult them. Who knows what leads these materials will provide?

Some have written off the possibility of new information about Shakespeare's life surfacing after so much has been picked over. In his little volume for the *English Men of Letters* series, Walter Raleigh offered little hope of new documentary finds about Shakespeare. "It is just possible," he wrote,

> that the store of facts concerning him may yet be increased. But it is not likely; now that antiquaries and scholars have toiled for generations, with an industry beyond all praise, in search for lost memorials. These are the diligent workers among the ruins, who, when the fabric of our knowledge has crumbled to atoms, still
> As for seed of stars, stoop for the sands,
> And by incessant labour gather all . . .
>
> By these ungrudging labours all that we are entitled to hope for has been achieved, and the Life of Shakespeare begins to assume the appearance of a scrapheap of respectable size.

Once more unto the scrapheap! Raleigh's *Shakespeare* appeared in 1907; so such pessimism is nothing new.

Three years after he wrote, an American from Missouri, Charles William Wallace, offered to the world "Shakespeare as a Man among Men"—so runs the title of the article he published in *Harper's Magazine*. The article recounts Wallace's discovery, among the bundles of uncalendared, unindexed, and for three hundred years unperused bundles of documents comprising the Court of Requests holdings at the Public Record Office, of Shakespeare's signed deposition in the case of Stephen

Belott *vs.* Christopher Mountjoy; one of six authenticated signatures which have survived for the poet. "That Shakespeare lived with a hard working family," wrote Wallace, his own ideology molded by a capitalistic democracy, "shared in their daily life, and even lent his help with the hope of making two young people happy marks him as the world would gladly know him, an unpretentious, sympathetic, thoroughly human Man." One may forgive the naively sentimental popularizing excesses of Wallace's prose; after all, he *had* made the Shakespearean discovery of the century.

Or the century so far. For, astonishingly, new information continues to turn up; the quatercentenary year, 1964, saw the announcement of the first notice of Susanna Shakespeare, the poet's elder daughter, after the entry for her christening in the Stratford parish register in May 1583. Along with twenty others, Susanna was cited in May 1606 in the act book of the ecclesiastical court for having failed to receive the sacrament the preceding Easter. A trifling transgression, it might seem, and ordinarily it was, but not in 1606, just before Susanna's twenty-third birthday.

Six months previously, a small band of fanatical Catholics had sought by violence to overthrow the government of England; the episode known to history as the Gunpowder Plot. In no mood for religious toleration, Parliament passed a number of vengeful statutes aimed at persons "popishly affected"; citizens who, in accordance with prescript, occasionally attended church but avoided Anglican communion. Church papists, they were called, and they were subject to heavy fines. Despite a summons, Susanna failed to show in the vicar's court, but eventually the case was dismissed. Presumably, she had meanwhile received the Eucharist. Were her sympathies, then, Catholic, and, if so, were her father's as well? A question of some critical, as well as biographical, interest, and one which has been much debated. The issue is too complex to be more than broached here, but it may be worth mentioning that when Susanna married the next year, the husband she chose, John Hall, was, besides being an eminent Stratford physician, a Puritan as well. Hall would give Holy Trinity a carved pulpit, and serve as churchwarden. He zealously censured parishioners who came late to church, slept through services, swore, wore hats, or put their hands in ladies' plackets. Dr. Hall allied himself with vicar Thomas Wilson, who had antagonized the Stratford corporation with his Puritanical views. How did the good doctor feel about the life-style of his father-in-law, the famous playwright of London? On such matters the documentary record is silent.

It is not silent on Shakespeare's own faith. The first reference comes in a tersely worded note set down by an obscure clergyman, Richard Davies, sometime chaplain of Corpus Christi College, Oxford, in the late

seventeenth century. "He died a papist," Davies says of Shakespeare.
The embers of an old debate have lately been once again stirred over
Shakespeare's name for his fat knight in *I Henry IV*. Originally, his creator
had dubbed him not Falstaff but Oldcastle. The historical Sir John
Oldcastle, Lord Cobham, was a Protestant martyr who denounced the
Pope as anti-Christ, and was hanged and burnt for his heretical faith.
Complaints about the slur on a name revered by Protestants were
lodged, probably by one of Oldcastle's influential descendants, and
Shakespeare made the change to Falstaff. This was, after all, a censored
drama. In his *Church History of Britain: from the Birth of Jesus Christ, until
the year 1648*, Thomas Fuller sternly writes,

> Stage-poets have themselves been very bold with, and others very
> merry at, the memory of Sir John Oldcastle, whom they have fancied a
> boon companion, a jovial roister, and yet a coward to boot, contrary to
> the credit of all chronicles, owning him a martial man of merit. The
> best is, Sir John Falstaffe hath relieved the memory of Sir John Oldcas-
> tle, and of late is substituted buffoon in his place, but it matters as little
> what petulant poets, as what malicious papists, have written against
> him.

It may be worth noting here that in the new Oxford edition of *I Henry IV*,
in *The Complete Works* recently published, Shakespeare's original name
for his boon companion has been restored, and that Oldcastle, not
Falstaff, counterfeits death on Shrewsbury field.

A word about the most recent recovery of all, made public only
recently. It concerns not the dramatist but his father. Four times in the
early 1570s, it seems, John Shakespeare faced prosecution in the Exeche-
quer. Two of the cases brought against him involved offenses against the
statute restricting the buying of wool to manufacturers and merchants of
the staple. Apparently John settled out of court. He was, then, a wool
dealer as well as glover, as was long thought without certain proof. The
other cases involved the lending of money at interest—steep interest.
Although trade in the sixteenth century, as today, depended upon
credit, the anachronistic law of the land declared usury wrong in principle, "a vice most odious and detestable"—so the statute read. To enforce
unworkable legislation the Crown depended upon informers to report
violations to the royal courts, and for their services they were rewarded
with half the penalties levied against the offenders. Twice John Shakespeare was charged with usury. In one case he was fined, and in the
other probably compounded with the informant. His dramatist son
would hold an older view of profiting from barren metal when Shylock,
with a scale ready for his pound of flesh, faced Antonio in a Venetian
court of law in *The Merchant of Venice*.

What revelations remain for future toilers to unearth? Prediction has not had a very happy history ever since Apollo bestowed the gift of prophecy upon Priam's daughter Cassandra, but, undaunted, I'll have a go. Shakespeare's son-in-law, Dr. Hall, treated the whole gamut of human ills from measles to melancholy. We know because he kept a medical diary recording, in Latin, case histories. When his wife Susanna lay "miserably tormented with the colic"—a severe spasmodic griping pain in her belly—Hall gave her an enema, concocted from a pint of hot sack, or sherry, which "Presently brought forth a great deal of wind, and freed her from all pain." I quote from Hall's casebook. His daughter Elizabeth—Shakespeare's one surviving grandchild—Dr. Hall in 1624 successfully treated for a "convulsion of the mouth" and "an erratic fever": "sometimes she was hot, by and by sweating, again cold, all in the space of half an hour, and there she was vexed oft in a day." Her father purged Elizabeth and anointed her spine. She responded to his care. "Thus," he concludes, "was she delivered from death, and deadly diseases, and was well for many years."

Hall's fame as a practitioner prompted James Cooke of nearby Warwick to translate his medical colleague's memoranda; the English version, *Select Observations on English Bodies*, was printed in 1657. The original, neatly kept, small octavo autograph volume came into the possession of the British Museum in 1868. I have consulted it there. Hall may well have ministered to his father-in-law as the latter lay dying, but the extant notebook begins with the year after Shakespeare's death. Did Dr. Hall keep a medical diary for the earlier period of his practice? Reports that a Hall manuscript may be extant in Scotland led me, about twenty years ago, to make enquiries at Register House in Edinburgh and elsewhere. No luck. The casebook which Cooke translated belonged in the nineteenth century to a Scot, Alexander Jackson of 9 India Street in Edinburgh. At the Edinburgh University Library I came upon a letter dated 24 June 1864, the tercentenary year, and addressed by William Oakes Hunt, the Stratford town clerk, to the eminent Victorian Shakespeare biographer James Orchard Halliwell, later Halliwell-Phillipps. Hunt writes, "I forget if I told you that Dr. Hall's maniscript book of cases is in the possession of a Gentleman in Scotland, a friend of Dr. Thomson, who I believe saw them. . . ." Is this the British Library manuscript, or another Hall casebook? (I note that in referring to the item Hunt says not *it* but *them*.) I'd like to track Alexander Jackson down; maybe one day I will. Who was the Scottish gentleman Hunt refers to? I don't yet have the answers to these questions.

There is nothing inherently improbable about the existence of an earlier casebook. Nor is it inherently out of the question that it survives somewhere unnoted. Not everybody will recognize the name as that of

Shakespeare's son-in-law, or have the requisite Latin, or be skilled in deciphering a seventeenth-century hand. Maybe an earlier Hall case-book is in some medical library. It would be wonderful to recover it, but it is only fair for me to confess that I wouldn't be surprised if the manuscript contained no mention of William Shakespeare's last days, for Dr. Hall tends to give accounts of successful treatments, not for the patients who perished. Still, one lives in hope. I can assure you that if one day I come upon something, the fact will not go unreported.

I am dreaming of the shape of things to come. Now, a backward glance over traveled paths, although I venture to think that not all of what I have to report is excessively familiar. In November 1582 the young Shakespeare was given a special dispensation to marry a local girl from Shottery, a hamlet three miles from Stratford. Pilgrims still find their way to the Elizabethan farmhouse now known as Anne Hathaway's cottage, even though the path leading to it has been overgrown by that peculiarly modern blight, creeping suburbia. The facts about the marriage are well known, although their significance has been much debated, and I shall be returning to this question.

But let me now regale you with an item which, although it has been available for a century and a half, may not have previously come your way. In 1811 a Richard Fenton—attorney, poet, topographer, and historian of the Welsh counties—reported how he had picked up at an auction in Carmarthen, Wales, a manuscript quarto volume containing, among numerous curiosities, verses addressed by Anne Hathaway to her spouse. One goes like this:

> From my throne in Willy's love,
> Whilst more than royall state I prove,
> Circled round with myrtle crown
> I on England's queen look down.
> And proud thy Anna well may be,
> For queens themselves might envy me,
> Who scarce in palaces can find
> My Willy's form, with Willy's mind.

These sentiments, no doubt true, are expressed in a poem entitled "To her own Loving Willie Shakespere," and signed, "Anna Hathaway. By Avon's Side." From another source we learn that Willy was not behindhand in reciprocating his Anna's ardent effusion. Verses he addressed to her include this stanza:

> Is there in heaven aught more rare
> Than thou sweet nymph of Avon fair?
> Is there on earth a man more true
> Than Willy Shakespeare is to you?

With this tribute Willy thoughtfully included a lock of his hair, which has been preserved to this day, and is in a splendid private collection. But the lock is, as you will have guessed, fake, just as Willy's verses are. They belong with the various exhibits that have been from time to time offered to a public avid for the intimate revelations which the authentic documents, being mostly dusty legal instruments, cannot pretend to offer.

If forgers have sought to re-create a life for Shakespeare, so too have legitimate artists in their plays and novels. The West End in London not long ago saw a revival of Edward Bond's play *Bingo*, dealing with Shakespeare's life after his retirement from the stage. Bond is an English playwright of some originality and power, so his *Bingo* merits a word. The play centers on a crisis in the town of Stratford, where Shakespeare was born and where he passed his last years. During this latter phase several powerful local landowners moved to reorganize the agricultural life of the neighborhood by converting small farms, run by tenants, into large expanses of pasturage, used for sheep-grazing, and surrounded by ditches and hedges—a development known in agricultural history as the enclosure movement. It affected people's pocketbooks by dispossessing the poorer farmers and adding to the wealth of the already rich landholders; and so, naturally, it aroused fierce emotions. Shakespeare, as one of the men of property and influence in the affected fields, was drawn into the controversy. His cousin, the Town Clerk Thomas Greene, whose property was also involved, sought Shakespeare's advice; we know this from Greene's diary, which is preserved to this day in the Stratford Records Office. Bond's play *Bingo* dramatized Shakespeare's response to this challenge in the ordinary daily life of the town in which he lived. Bond depicts the dramatist who had sympathized with the poor naked wretches in *King Lear* as siding with the ruthless landholder William Combe for the sake of increased profits, even though (as a result) the poor rolls would be swelled with the names of the dispossessed. In a crucial scene in *Bingo* Shakespeare, after driving a strict bargain, signs the document that signifies his acquiescence in the scheme of the rich property-owners. "Pity you didn't go into business before," Combe the landholder says admiringly. "You can bargain."

Mostly, however, in this play about his life, Shakespeare sits in his garden and broods. His wife, we hear, keeps to her bed and hides from him. "She doesn't know who she is, or what she's supposed to do, or who she married," his daughter Judith upbraids him. Later, in a Stratford tavern Shakespeare has a reunion with his friend and arch professional rival, Ben Jonson. They drink together, and Shakespeare slumps over the table, spilling his wine. The great poet and playwright of the English stage moves through *Bingo* like a sleepwalker, depressed and dissatisfied with his achievement, which, however great as art, did nothing to alleviate the poverty, cruelty, and injustice of his world. At the end of the play Shakespeare ends his life by swallowing poisoned tablets. The last despairing words of the author of *Hamlet, Othello*, and *Macbeth* are, "Was anything done?" They have a resonance that would not be present if spoken by any other dramatized historical character.

When the performance was over, and the well-heeled and well-educated middle class audience was leaving the theater to stroll into the mild London night, I eavesdropped shamelessly on the comments of the spectators. Several said they had not been aware that Shakespeare's last years were so sad. Evidently these theatergoers had come to the playhouse to satisfy some craving to know more about who the greatest playwright in the English language was. If so, that was a pity, for Bond's play certainly would not have reliably informed them.

In his own life Shakespeare no doubt knew disappointment, but there is no evidence that, like his creation Hamlet, he ever contemplated suicide. The earliest report we have of Shakespeare's mood during his last years comes from his first biographer, Nicholas Rowe, in 1709. Rowe says:

> The latter part of his life was spent, as all men of good sense will wish theirs may be, in ease, retirement, and the conversation of his friends. He had the good fortune to gather an estate equal to his occasion, and, in that, to his wish; and is said to have spent some years before his death at his native Stratford.

No hint of despair here; rather, at twilight, the afterglow of a life well spent. Nor is the evidence clear that Shakespeare sided with the landowners, of whom he was one, during the dispute over the enclosure of the fields near Stratford. Bond, however, is not a biographer but an artist. In *Bingo*, which he subtitles "Scenes of Money and Death," he wants to give expression to some passionately held convictions about the role of a writer in society.

Nevertheless, whatever Bond's conception of his task, some people go to see *Bingo* for biographical enlightenment; mistakenly, as it turns out, but curiosity about the lives of great men and women is neither unnatural nor ignoble. To what extent may curiosity be legitimately satisfied? How much do we really know about that monumental figure carved in the Mount Rushmore of bardolatry? Little, according to popular wisdom. We are told that all the facts can be written on a postcard and still leave plenty of room for the address. Or, to state it another way, "Everything we know about Shakespeare can be put into a half-hour sketch." So George Bernard Shaw said. Of course Shaw was very concise. George Steevens was even more concise—he summed up Shake-speare's life in a single memorable sentence:

> All that is known with any degree of certainty concerning Shakspeare is—that he was born at Stratford upon Avon—married and had children there,—went to London, where he commenced actor, and wrote poems and plays,—returned to Stratford, made his will, died, and was buried.

All that is known concerning Shakespeare. . . .

But Steevens wrote these words in the eighteenth century. He exaggerated then, and we have learned much since. Anyway, the facts of most lives, unless they are of public figures, can be boiled down to an irreducible minimum. Actually, as a result of the indefatigable researches of scholars over more than two centuries, we know more about Shakespeare than we do about any other playwright of his age, except Ben Jonson, whose aggressively assertive personality ensured the powerful imprint he left on contemporary records. For Shakespeare it is the nature of the record that mainly leaves us dissatisfied: no letters or diaries, no verses from Anna Hathaway, by Avon's side, to her beloved Willy. Yet what we can glean raises, for the biographer, fascinating historical questions. We learn something about how, in a vanished age, people had their births recorded and went to school and got married, how they acquired property and bequeathed it, and how, in general, they ordered their personal and professional lives. As we all—or most of us—do these things ourselves, temporal variations hold their own interest.

The circumstances surrounding Shakespeare's marriage furnish an ideal illustration of the problems faced by his biographer. In those times a marriage license was not normally required to certify a legally binding union. All that was needed was the proclamation of the banns in church on three successive Sundays or holy days. But with Shakespeare's marriage there were special considerations. He was only 18, and therefore subject to the laws affecting minors; and his bride, some 8 years older than he, was pregnant. I have heard learned Shakespeare specialists refer to Shakespeare's marriage license; but in fact no such document now exists, although in this special case a license would have been required. Instead, we have a marriage-licence *bond*, dated 28 November 1582, in which two farmers from the bride's neighborhood swore to indemnify the Bishop of Worcester or his ecclesiastical officers in the event that any legal action arose from the granting of the license. These sureties were friends of the bride's family. Her name is given as "Anne Hathwey of Stratford," although she came from the village of Shottery, which was in Stratford parish. This bond granted a special dispensation for the couple to marry with only one, instead of the usual three, readings of the banns.

Now, the day before this marriage-license bond was furnished, the clerk of the ecclesiastical court recorded in the Bishops' register the granting of a marriage license to William Shakespeare and Anne Whateley—not Hathaway—of Temple Grafton. We know from other sources that Shakespeare married Anne Hathaway. These curious circumstances have given rise to a good deal of confusion and misunderstanding. Biographers, in the first instance, have noted that only the bride's interests were represented by the two bondsmen. What of the young groom, a mere youth of 18? Was this, then, as many have concluded, a shotgun marriage, with the unwilling boy, helpless before irate parents and their brawny yeoman supporters, sacrificed for a passionate indiscretion one summer night in the fields near Stratford? And what of the mysterious Anne Whateley who appears in this one record and nowhere else? Was she Shakespeare's true, chaste sweetheart, the maiden he yearned to marry, and was indeed about to marry when the Hathaways made their move?

But William Shakespeare could not have married Anne Hathaway without his father's consent; so the law, protective of minors, decreed. And it was customary for the guarantors of such marriage bonds to be friends of the bride's, not the groom's family; for unmarried heiresses rather than their prospective husbands stood most in need of legal safeguards against unscrupulous fortune-hunters. As for Anne Whateley, about whom so much ink has been spilt, it is my unromantic view that she probably never existed but was merely created by an erring clerk's careless substitution of a name. He had been seeing Whateleys earlier that day, and they were much on his mind; by a process of unconscious association with which we are all familiar, he carelessly exchanged one name for another. The bride's pregnancy indeed presented a problem; her condition called for matrimony as early as possible, yet the Church prohibited the reading of the banns during certain seasons, and the couple had missed the last opportunity for proceeding with their marriage in the customary way. Hence the necessity for a special dispensation.

To sum up: there is no evidence that Shakespeare at this stage of his life had any sweetheart besides Anne Hathaway. Later, in his *Sonnets* he would express in impassioned lyric verse his entanglement with a Dark Lady, but she had not yet made her appearance when Shakespeare was courting Anne. Nor is there any evidence that he married his Anne unwillingly. In 1583—just six months after the wedding—she gave birth to a daughter, Susanna. Less than two years afterward, she bore her husband twins, Hamnet and Judith. Thus Anne had given William a male heir.

But was the marriage happy? The proverb holds, *marry in haste, repent at leisure*. Did he repent his "o'erhasty marriage"? Biographers, conscious of the discrepancy in years between this husband and wife, have combed Shakespeare's works for passages that might give some clue to his feelings. Their searches have not gone unrewarded. In *Twelfth Night*, the Duke speaks thus to the disguised Viola:

> Let still the woman take
> An elder than herself; so wears she to him,
> So sways she level in her husband's heart. . . .

But the difficulty, of course, is that such passages occur in plays, not in autobiographical memoirs, and the writer does not speak with his own voice, but with the lips of the figments of his dramatic imagination. The theater is, after all, a public forum; a playwright always creates with his audience in his mind's eye, and the opinions that his characters express cater to that audience and also to the necessities of the dramatic context. Shakespeare's *Sonnets* are more intimate, and perhaps we may there feel on safer ground in discerning reflections of his personal predicament; "With this key," Wordsworth said of the *Sonnets*, "Shakespeare unlocked his heart." As they deal in part with an intense liaison with a woman herself married, they suggest that for Shakespeare the marital bed was not always a contented one. The identity of the other woman, the so-called Dark Lady, has stirred up fierce academic passions. But we do well to remember that in the *Sonnets*, too, experience is shaped by the poet's transfiguring imagination, and it is at our peril that we read these wonderfully wrought poems as straightforward autobiographical testimony.

I have mentioned the bed, and here Shakespeare's will, drawn up shortly before his death, provides a clue. The will contains only one reference to the woman Shakespeare had married thirty-odd years previously. "Item [the will reads]. I give unto my wife my second best bed with the furniture," that is, with the hangings, bed linen, and the like, that make up this elaborate item of Jacobean domestic furnishing. That is it; not a word more. What are we to make of this bequest, probably the most notorious in literary history? Some biographers see it as derisive, a husband's scornful dismissal of his wife. As far back as the eighteenth century, Edmond Malone, arguably the greatest of Shakespeare scholars, interpreted this provision of Shakespeare's will thus:

> His wife had not wholly escaped his memory; he had forgot her,—he had recollected her,—but so recollected her, as more strongly to mark

how little he esteemed her; he had already (as is vulgarly expressed) cut her off, not indeed with a shilling, but with an old bed.

Well, that is one way to look at it, and this view has had supporters up until the present day.

But another interpretation is possible. May not the best bed have been kept in a special room, and there reserved, out of gracious hospitality, for overnight visitors to the splendid house Shakespeare had bought in Stratford? If so, the best bed would have been regarded as an heirloom, and would have naturally formed part of the estate he wished to keep together for his legal heir. The second-best bed, according to this interpretation, would then have been the matrimonial bed, with a special, intimate significance. Other wills of this period refer to such beds with tender associations. In fact we do not know what Shakespeare was thinking when he made his wife this bequest; but we can be sure that he did not have to provide otherwise for her in order for her to be looked after properly when he died. By English common law, enforced by local custom, a widow was entitled to a life interest of one-third of her husband's estate.

We really can't say with any confidence whether Shakespeare's marital life was contented or miserable, or any of the innumerable gradations between those polarities. We can say that he married only once and that his wife bore him three children early in the marriage. His professional obligations as the leading playwright for his acting company required his presence in London, the hub of the theatrical life of the nation, through most of the year. In London he had lodgings. We do not know who, if anyone, shared his bed there, but it was probably not his wife, for she had the house and children to look after in Stratford, almost one hundred miles away. As a rule, long separations do not encourage marital harmony. Yet it is true that Shakespeare, according to a reliable tradition, returned regularly to Stratford each year. So the domestic ties were maintained; in what fashion we cannot, with any assurance, say.

The Shakespeare records, then, in the aggregate would require a very large postcard indeed. But what of their quality? Who was the Shakespeare that emerges from them? The mass of material is so prosaic: entries of baptisms, marriages, and deaths, conveyances of lands and tithes, minor litigation, theatrical records, entries of titles in the Stationers' Register, a last will and testament. Many of these documents could chronicle the life of any Elizabethan man of property who pursued a materially successful career in the metropolis and spent his last years in comfortable back-water retirement. How are we to reconcile the everyday nature of the records with the impassioned genius that finds expression in the *Sonnets*, and in the great tragedies which harrow us with pity and dread—*Hamlet, Othello,* and *King Lear?* Where in these records will we find traces of the laughter that bursts the sides of propriety in Falstaff? Nowhere.

Yet one document we have, his will, which, while anything but poetical, tells us a good deal about the position Shakespeare had achieved for himself in the world—not as an artist but as a Jacobean gentleman whose art had brought him financial and social prominence in his Warwickshire town that apparently mattered to him. The will also tells us about the family members and friends, mostly townsmen, he valued most, and teases us with its bequest of a second-best bed. Omissions can sometimes be as intriguing as what is included: Shakespeare unsurprisingly makes no reference to the Earl of Southampton, to whom he had dedicated his two early poems, *Venus and Adonis* and *The Rape of Lucrece,* or (for that matter) to any other high-born aristocrat; but nor does he mention any Hathaways from his wife's family, although they farmed in the neighborhood—Bartholomew Hathaway, for example, the brother-in-law, who came into possession of the picturesquely thatched cottage in which Shakespeare courted Anne.

The testament is a bourgeois document that records a success story. Shakespeare amassed a considerable estate that he was at pains to hold together for his heirs. The College of Arms granted his father a coat of arms, probably at the son's instigation; in later documents William Shakespeare does not fail to use the honorific title of gentleman, and his Stratford Church monument is emblazoned with the family arms. There is little in the will that accords with the romantic idea of the poet, but of course Shakespeare lived before the Romantic Age. The will and the other documents fail to convey the pain he must have experienced. So we can only guess what he felt when his only son Hamnet was buried in Stratford on 11 August 1596, at the age of eleven and a half. Shakespeare could not then have foreseen that his entire direct line would become extinct before the end of the seventeenth century; nor, if he still bedded his wife, could he be sure that she would fail to give him another son, although, as she was already past forty, he may have reckoned that as unlikely. Presumably, Shakespeare was present for the burial of Hamnet; but even that we can only infer, not truly know. Those facts we have do not help us in fathoming the deep inner well-springs of genius. Shakespeare could have had the sort of career I have been describing and been merely competent.

But if the documentary record fails in most particulars to express what was extraordinary about the life, it does in one respect do so; and this point I have reserved for the last. The documents reveal strikingly Shakespeare's professional commitment to the stage—first, to the Lord Chamberlain's Men when they played at the Theater in Shoreditch; then, to the same company when it became known as the King's Men and performed at the Globe on Bankside and the Blackfriars near St. Paul's. Shakespeare served his company as actor, playwright, and shareholder for almost two decades. He was, as a leading authority has observed, "the most complete man of the theatre of his time." Every now and then we encounter a playwright who also acts or directs; Harold Pinter, in the present, comes to mind. But to be involved as a principal voice of the management side in addition to the other commitments is extremely rare. One thinks of Molière, and then one thinks again for a long time.

That professional dedication reminds us, as we continually have to be reminded, of the special nature of Shakespeare's literary achievement. It also helps to explain why he presumably took no interest in giving his unpublished plays the permanence of print; for, when he died, fully half had never appeared on the bookstalls, including *Macbeth, Othello, Julius Caesar, As You Like It.* So we celebrate Shakespeare fittingly at a time when the comedies, histories, and tragedies which Shakespeare's old acting colleagues gathered together in a handsome Folio volume "to keep the memory of so worthy a friend and fellow alive, as was our Shakespeare"—when those plays are reaching greater numbers of spectators, by far, than ever before. An artist's personality, recorded to be sure in the dusty vellum of the muniment room, appears most expressively in his creations. These we watch, enthralled, as they unfold on stage.

# Subtext in Shakespeare

## Jay L. Halio

**P**art of an actor's job in developing a Shakespearean character on the stage is finding the "subtext." This term, since it has come into increasingly wide use, has become subject to loosening definition. It may be useful, therefore, to go back to its origin in the work of Constantin Stanislavski, the great actor, director, and producer of the Moscow Art Theater, whose influence has extended well beyond the Russian stage. The term first appeared in English in Elizabeth Hapgood's translation of *Building a Character* (New York, 1949), the sequel to Stanislavski's *An Actor Prepares* (New York, 1936), also translated by Hapgood.[1] But the essential concept is strongly implied in the earlier book, particularly where Stanislavski, in the persona of the director, Tortsov, speaks about the inner feelings and thoughts an actor must have to produce effective, honest representation. In the chapter on "Adaptation," Tortsov says to his students:

> Do you suppose that words can exhaust all the nicest shadings of the emotion you experience? No! When we are communing with one another words do not suffice. If we want to put life into them, we must produce feelings. They fill out the blanks left by words, they finish what has been left unsaid.[2]

If the text is the essential thing in a Shakespearean or any other play, it is not the only thing, and the actor must endeavor to find those unwritten, or unspoken, indications—those feelings, ideas, thoughts— that help make a character what he or she is, or make him or her behave in certain ways.

This is why subtext is important. It is directly related both to the script the actor is performing and to the actor's inner creative life—the ability to infuse life into a role, or rather breathe life from it. Subtext "lies behind and beneath the actual words of a part"; it is

> the manifest, the inwardly felt expression of a human being in a part, which flows uninterruptedly beneath the words of the text, giving them life and a basis for existing. The subtext is a web of innumerable,

31

varied patterns inside a play and a part, woven from "magic ifs," given circumstances, all sorts of figments of imagination, inner movements, objects of attention, smaller and greater truths and a belief in them, adaptations, adjustments and other similar elements. It is the subtext that makes us say the words we do in a play.[3]

Stanislavski goes on to say that "only when our feelings reach down into the subtextual stream that the 'through line of action' of a play or part comes into being." And it is this "through line of action" that to him is successful theatrical representation; without it a play exists only in fragments, broken bits and pieces that, however brilliantly contrived, fail to cohere into the unified whole without which no play or part can be called successful.

Important as the "through line of action" is, the focus here remains on subtext, the full development of character, and the interaction among characters. For Stanislavski, as for most actors and directors, the printed text is no more a finished product than is a musical score. Both require performance for full realization, and performance means interpretation, in actual stage performance or in the "theater of the mind." Words need to be spoken, to be heard; characters need to act, to move about; feelings must be aroused, questions raised, thinking stimulated. Only then does a play come alive, and finding the subtext is a very large part of each actor's task in bringing the play to life.

Although Stanislavski may have invented the term, the idea of subtext, the undercurrent of thought and feeling with which the text is charged, was familiar to actors before him. In *Shakespeare's Plays in Performance*[4] John Russell Brown cites Macready's definition of the art of acting, as recalled by another great nineteenth-century actor, Henry Irving:

> What is the art of acting? . . . It is the art of embodying the poet's creations, of giving them flesh and blood, of making the figures which appeal to your mind's eye in the printed drama live before you on the stage. "To fathom the depths of character, to trace its latent motives, to feel its finest quiverings of emotion, to comprehend the thoughts that are hidden under the words, and thus possess one's self of the actual mind of the individual man"—such was Macready's definition of the player's art.[5]

The actor's responsibility here is enormous: how indeed is he or she to trace the latent motives of a character, to comprehend thoughts hidden under the words, and in these ways to fathom the depths that dialogue only partly reveals? How can he or she know any representation is what the playwright originally conceived? Or course neither he nor she nor anyone can know this, for much of it lies beneath the conscious level both in its original creation and in its later embodiment. The only guide is, once more, the text and its various clues and suggestions.

That Shakespeare was aware of a reality underlying his dialogue is clear from a number of passages, such as those John Russell Brown quotes from *A Midsummer Night's Dream, Hamlet,* and other plays.[6] In his first speech to his mother, Hamlet refers pointedly to external trappings of mourning that belie the real feelings he has about his father's death (and indirectly hurls an accusation at Gertrude about her own behavior). Disguise is another means that Shakespeare uses to indicate a disparity between spoken words and their underlying reality, according to Brown. Puns and quibbles function in this way, too, as Hamlet's opening lines to Claudius reveal.

Often the imagery that a character uses offers an important clue to the subtextual reality that can provide a major motivation for attitude and behavior. Ambition has usually been cited as the main reason for Macbeth's murder of Duncan, but the subtextual reality shows that his situation is far more complex than that. Fear is an important part of his being, both the fear of retribution "here, upon this bank and shoal of time" (1.7.6) and the fear of seeming unmanly to his wife. His essential humanity is revealed not only by Lady Macbeth's concern that he is "too full of the milk of human kindness," but by the imagery Macbeth uses of the "naked new-born babe, / Striding the blast" or the vision of heaven's cherubin blowing his "horrid deed" in every eye, "That tears shall drown the wind" (1.7.21–24). Like Lady Macbeth, he too must somehow eradicate all sense of feeling and remorse, the "great bond" that unites him to his fellow human beings, if he is to go forward in his plan to seize the crown and hold on to it. The extreme effort it takes to do this is a vital part of his nature, and the actor playing the role must derive from subtextual reality the energy, thought, and feeling to realize the character fully. If he is successful, Macbeth's later despair and his feeling of being utterly worn out by the end can become overwhelmingly effective. Apparently, this is how Nicol Williamson conceived the role in the BBC-TV production of *Macbeth.*

Derek Jacobi's performance of Prospero in the Royal Shakespeare Company's production of *The Tempest* (1982) was informed by a refreshing interpretation. Averse to playing Prospero as an old man, Jacobi saw him as someone in his forties (the actor's own age), plausible enough from the text. As a basic part of his subtext, Jacobi found Prospero not only younger but angrier than he is usually played. Still smoldering with resentment after many years of exile on his enchanted island, Prospero awaits his opportunity, finally at hand, to take revenge on the malefactors who forced him from his dukedom and set him adrift in a "rotten carcass of a butt" with his only child, Miranda. This subtext was suggested by the last act's opening dialogue with Ariel. By this time, Prospero's plot has worked exceedingly well. He has all his enemies completely in his power—Alonzo, Sebastian, Antonio—and Caliban and his motley crew have also been taken care of. Ariel has carried out his instructions perfectly, and the magician's project "gathers to a head." Ariel informs his master that Alonzo and his followers are all prisoners confined together

> In the line-grove which weather-fends your cell;
> They cannot boudge till your release. The King,
> His brother, and yours, abide all three distracted,
> And the remainder mourning over them,
> Brimful of sorrow and dismay; but chiefly
> Him that you term'd, sir, "The good old Lord Gonzalo,"
> His tears run down his beard like winter's drops
> From eaves of reeds. Your charm so strongly works 'em
> That if you now beheld them, your affections
> Would become tender.
>
> (5.1.10–19)

Prospero—surprised at Ariel's reaction to their plight (he is not human and Prospero is)—takes Ariel's point and resolves to be compassionate:

> Hast thou, which art but air, a touch, a feeling
> Of their afflictions, and shall not myself,
> One of their kind, that relish all as sharply
> Passion as they, be kindlier mov'd than thou art?
> Though with their high wrongs I am strook to th' quick,
> Yet, with my nobler reason, 'gainst my fury
> Do I take part. The rarer action is
> In virtue than in vengeance. They being penitent,
> The sole drift of my purpose doth extend
> Not a frown further.
>
> (5.1.21–30)

Prospero's compassion works, and the malefactors are penitent; certainly Alonzo is; accordingly, he is reunited with his son, now betrothed to Miranda, discovered with him chastely playing chess. About Antonio and Sebastian we are less sure; the text suggests that they may be recalcitrant, everything they have experienced notwithstanding. The subtexts for these roles welcome investigation, too.[7]

Without doubt Falstaff is one of the greatest dramatic characters ever created—and one of the most difficult to perform. The complexities inherent in the character are profound, as Anthony Quayle, who has created the role on both stage and television, has commented. One of the most fully alive personages in all Shakespearean drama, Falstaff is aware of his own shortcomings and failings as well as those of others on whom, parasite that he is, he preys. Genuinely fond of Prince Hal, he uses him shamelessly, but he also feels hurt, Quayle insists, in their wit-combats when Hal scores against him by calling him a "Manningtree ox" or a ton of lard, because the points Hal makes are accurate. Falstaff has tremendous wit and skill, which he demonstrates superbly, for instance, in the Boar's Head Tavern scenes; he can be outrageous and funny and extremely good company. But somewhere inside him, according to Quayle, "there's a terrible grief . . . an immense hurt.[8] Perhaps that accounts for the dark side of Falstaff that Quayle and others have recognized.[9] Witty, warm, and full of life, he is also worldly-wise and cynical. His behavior at Shrewsbury Field brings out some of the worst in his character, particularly his treatment of the slain Hotspur. "That's the crucial point where the relationship between Falstaff and Henry falls apart," Quayle says. "It's horrible. You mustn't pull your punches if you're playing Falstaff at all. In that sequence he's a rat, a great fat rat."[10]

Sometimes a subtext will be found not to work and must be discarded, as Sir Laurence Olivier discovered when playing the role of Coriolanus for the second time after a period of eighteen years. In this production, directed by Peter Hall, he tried to find some new secrets about the character, whom he had considered basically "a very straightforward, reactionary son of a so-and-so . . . a patrician first and foremost" whose pride is so great that he is "too proud even to accept praise."[11] In rehearsal Olivier and Hall experimented with the idea that his inability to accept praise had something to do with the fact that Coriolanus was not really a good soldier, that he was a "phoney." But the idea did not work and could not, for if Coriolanus is not an exceptional warrior, who would follow him into battle?

Tyrone Guthrie's conception of Coriolanus is more subtle and psychologically more complex—and perhaps more convincing. He believed the role of Aufidius is crucial and shows how Shakespeare carefully builds that character through the first three acts to the culminating scene in act 4 where Coriolanus, exiled from Rome, meets his former enemy in the Volscian city, Antium. For Guthrie, the scene is nothing less than a love scene, expressing powerfully the positive aspect of the love-hate relationship that has grown between the two antagonists. After a long pause during which the audience cannot tell what effect Coriolanus's speech has had on Aufidius, the Volscian general starts speaking gently and emotionally. At line 106, when Aufidius expresses his absolute belief in him, Coriolanus at last breaks down in tears, and Aufidius embraces him, like a father embracing his wayward son.[12]

In this interpretation, the subtext is Coriolanus's lack of a father or an older brother whose love would be a counterforce to the influence of his dominating mother. It helps explain in more profound psychological terms Coriolanus's betrayal of Rome—not a spoiled child's pique (as in Shakespeare's source, Plutarch), but compensation for rejection by his mother, both his real mother and Rome, his mother country. In Guthrie's view, Coriolanus feels deeply his mother's rejection insofar as it was she, against his better judgment, who compelled him to stand for the consulship and confront both the tribunes and the plebeians, actions that led directly to his expulsion from Rome. Wounded and homeless, he at last finds shelter in Aufidius, who warmly takes him in. "The image of the career-rival now presents itself as a possible father or elder brother, something which has always been missing from his life."[13]

While examining the text—what it reveals and what it conceals—helps one to discover possible subtexts for representing Shakespeare's characters, how can an audience, sitting in the theater, find the subtext that an actor is using for the character he or she is presenting? And how can that subtext be verified? Moreover, how can the intelligent spectator judge whether the subtext, once ascertained, is an appropriate or useful one? The best indication of the working subtext is the emphasis, or slant, the actor has adopted. For example, several subtexts are possible for Isabella in *Measure for Measure*. Although the actress in the role will usually indicate which she has chosen very early, its fullest expression may not become manifest until the final scene. There she must react to the Duke's repeated proposal of marriage, and how she responds is the clearest indication of the kind of person the actress conceives Isabella to be. Is she a young woman deeply committed to the religious life, as she appears to be in 1.4.1–5, wishing that the sisters of Saint Clare, strict as they are, had even stricter regulations to observe? Or is she a woman sexually repressed, whose devotion to religion attempts to sublimate feelings she cannot otherwise express? What exactly does she mean by those terrible words, "More than our brother is our chastity" (2.4.185)? In 3.1 she seems genuinely devoted to her brother and is at first unable to tell him about Angelo's despicable propositon. Tender and considerate, she unleashes a furious tirade only after Claudio's resolve falters and then breaks, as he begs her to save his life.

Doubtless, Isabella has a great deal to learn about herself and about the world's ways. What she learns, guided mainly by the Duke's interventions from act 3 onward, is partly revealed by her willingness to beg for Angelo's life at the end, believing all the while that her brother is dead at the Duke's command. Here she demonstrates that she has learned much about Christian mercy, especially within the context (which the Duke appears to provide) of unmitigated justice, although her mercy is directed as much to the wronged Mariana as to Angelo. But the situation is more complicated, and her learning does not stop there.

When Claudio enters, alive after all, and the Duke's schemes are revealed for what they are, Isabella must sort out conflicting thoughts and emotions. How shall she regard Vincentio now? As a manipulating intruder into other people's lives? As a beneficent ruler guided chiefly by his subjects' welfare? As a meddling old busybody who takes pleasure in his own contrivances?

The answers to these questions depend in part on how the Duke is played—what subtext he manifests (again, several are possible)—and Jane Williamson has discussed both his role and Isabella's in an interesting essay.[14] But regardless of how benevolent the Duke is or intends himself to be, Isabella has several choices, which a number of recent stage productions have shown. Up until John Barton's Royal Shakespeare Company production of 1970, Isabella typically joined hands with Vincentio at the end, accepting his proposal of marriage (this is a comedy, after all[15]), and went merrily off with the other happy couples. In point of fact, however, Shakespeare's text does not—either through dialogue or stage direction—give an explicit cue for such an ending. It is left, as John Barton viewed the situation, entirely open, and many other directors have since adopted that view. Hence, Estelle Kohler as Isabella in Barton's production could reasonably choose at the end to remain bewildered and dismayed at the Duke's proposal, even angry and defiant at his presumption.[16] Isabella in Keith Hack's RSC production four years later, according to Ralph Berry, was "tense and resistant, appeared at the end as an animal trapped in the clutches of demoniac Duke. Given the pantomime villain confronting her, she could scarcely appear otherwise, and one reviewer saw her progress as a 'slow withdrawal into complete horror and implied madness.'"[17] Directing at Stratford, Ontario, in 1975, Robin Phillips emphasized the ending's inherent ambiguity. Martha Henry's Isabella, "at one moment almost vomiting sexual disgust, the next caressing Claudio in a manner that suggests the nunnery is her refuge from an incestuous passion,"[18] was left alone at the end, circling the stage, "plainly in an agony of doubt."[19] But by far the most extreme reaction was Penelope Wilton's as Isabella in Jonathan Miller's production the same year. There was no sex or gentleness in this Isabella, played as "a flat chested, flat footed nun in black rubber soled shoes, clutching with purple hands a nasty handbag, into which she claws for a handkerchief to scarify her raw nose."[20] Her rejection of the Duke was absolute, and there was no question of her intention to return forever to the convent from which Lucio had anxiously coaxed her in 1.4. For this Isabella, "More than our brother is our chastity" was the key to her character, and we can imagine the fury with which she attacked Claudio in 3.1 for so much as suggesting she might still save him.[21]

Still more complex is Hamlet, unquestionably the most difficult character in all Shakespearean drama to grasp. Any number of subtexts are available to the actor, though he probably will have to alter the subtext as he perceives the character of Hamlet itself altering. At the outset, Hamlet is alienated, grief-stricken, and alone in the court of King Claudius, the man who has married his mother within a month of Hamlet's father's death. Hostile and unhappy, he sounds his disposition's keynote in his opening lines, "A little more than kin and less than kind"; "I am too much in the sun"; "I know not seems." His subtext may be inferred from his first soliloquy's last lines: "It is not, nor it cannot come to good, / But break my heart, for I must hold my tongue" (1.2.158–59). Thus Gordon Craig conceived Hamlet for his famous 1912 Moscow Art Theater production, in which Vasili Ivanovich Kachalov played the prince: "All the tragedy of Hamlet is his isolation. And the background of this isolation is the court, a world of pretence. . . ."[22] Hamlet, like his father, is the best of men, the only good man in an evil environment which it becomes his duty, after hearing the Ghost's story, to purge of wickedness ("The time is out of joint—O cursed spite, / That ever I was born to set it right" [1.5.188–89]).

Hamlet's reluctance to take immediate action has been many times examined, and many explanations for his delay have been offered. Perhaps the most notorious explanation is that offered by Freud's disciple, Ernest Jones. As Francis Fergusson has observed, the Oedipus complex Jones saw as the main inhibiting force is definitely in the play. Shakespeare did not require Freud's theorizing to observe the phenomenon upon which the theory was based, or rather to sense and feel deeply the kind of problem a young, sensitive young man in Hamlet's position confronts. When during the "Mousetrap" play-within-the-play Hamlet identifies Lucianus as "nephew to the king" (3.2.244), he identifies himself indirectly but still very closely with the murderer of the Player King, his father's surrogate[23]—proof positive that Oedipal feelings are at work. But as Fergusson shows, they are only a small part of what Hamlet feels and what the play presents; they do not govern the entire structure of the tragedy, which is involved as well with moral issues of murder and usurpation, vengeance, and loyalty, to say nothing of other emotional or psychological involvements, such as Hamlet's with Ophelia or with schoolfellows Rosencrantz, Guildenstern, and especially Horatio.

Freudian overemphasis was what most of all marred Laurence Olivier's film version of the play. As Guthrie remarks, the film's motto, "This is the story of a man who could not make up his mind," was not only a gross simplification, it was in actual fact contradicted at nearly every point by Olivier's portrayal of the Prince:

How could Hamlet be irresolute or incapable of action in view of the determined and efficient way in which he was seen to carry through the intrigue with the Players, the ruthless break with Ophelia, the forcible interview with his mother, the stabbing (albeit mistaken as to the victim's identity) of Polonius, the hoisting of Rosencrantz and Guildenstern with their own petard, the grapple with the pirates, the struggle with Laertes in Ophelia's grave?[24]

So much for the man who could not make up his mind. But the film also erred in focusing insistently on Hamlet's attitude toward his mother, wrestling with her on a bed in the Closet Scene, for example, where no bed belongs (this is the Queen's dressing chamber, not her bedroom). This is the bed that in the final shots of the film, as Hamlet's body is being carried to the ramparts, the camera pauses before in a manner both reminiscent and highly suggestive. Thus Olivier chose two subtexts for his interpretation of Hamlet, one not so much wrong as exaggerated, the other belied by his own vigorous rendition of the role.

In choosing a subtext, therefore, an actor must be careful not to choose one that oversimplifies or exaggerates, whether in tragedy or in comedy. Shakespeare's major characters in both genres (and the history plays tend to one or the other or are a mixture of both) are highly complex individuals, motivated by conflicting ideas and attitudes that reductive interpretation falsifies, whether in dramatic representation or in critical analysis. The actor's search for subtext will help penetrate to the character's inner core, the deeper psychological truth, as Stanislavski argued. At the same time the actor—and the audience—must realize that a subtext is not the whole character, that interactions with other characters are also of utmost importance, as are interactions of a character with other aspects of his or her being. A subtext's final test may well be its resistance to easy formulation in a phrase or quotation, unless that phrase or quote is itself richly ambiguous or complex.

## Notes

1. Constantin Stanislavski, *Building a Character*, trans. Elizabeth Hapgood (New York, 1949) and Stanislavski, *An Actor Prepares*, trans. Elizabeth Hapgood (New York, 1939).

2. Stanislavski, *An Actor Prepares*, 212.

3. Stanislavski, *Building a Character*, 107–8.

4. London: Edward Arnold, 1966; rpt. Penguin Shakespeare Library, 1969. References are to the reprint.

5. Ibid., 65.

6. See ibid., 69.

7. See 5.1.126–29 and note Philip McGuire's analysis of the situation in *Speechless Dialect: Shakespeare's Open Silences* (Berkeley: University of California Press, 1985), 38–44.

8. Quoted by Judith Cook, *Shakespeare's Players* (London: Harrap, 1983), 71.

9. Cf. Hugh Griffith's conception of the part, as Michael Greenwald describes it in *Directions by Indirections: John Barton of the Royal Shakespeare Company* (Newark: University of Delaware Press, 1985), 59. Citing a program note, Greenwald says that Griffith's nonromantic Falstaff showed what the good life in Eastcheap really implied: "deceit, murder, swindling, chaos, vanity, viciousness—an attack on the basic and precious laws which bind men together."

10. *Shakespeare's Players*, 72.

11. Ibid., 94.

12. Tyrone Guthrie, *In Various Directions: A View of Theatre* (New York: Macmillan, 1965), 90–91.

13. Guthrie, 92. Although he does not specifically use the term *subtext*, Guthrie's comments suggest that it is this which he has in mind: ". . . it is apparent that the text alone is only a limited guide. 'Over and above,' and 'between the lines,' not in them, lies the real meaning" (91).

14. "The Duke and Isabella on the Modern Stage," *The Triple Bond*, ed. Joseph G. Price (University Park: Pennsylvania State University Press, 1975), 149–69.

15. See Nevill Coghill, "Comic Form in *Measure for Measure*," *Shakespeare Survey*, 8 (1955): 14–27.

16. Williamson (168) cites Anne Barton's program note for the production: "We do not know how Isabella reacts to her sovereign's extraordinarily abrupt offer of marriage in the final moments of the play, because she says nothing to him in reply. It is at least possible that this silence is one of dismay." She also cites the reviewer in *The Listener* who saw an even stronger response from this "feminist" Isabella, who had "silent rage written all over her high forehead and stubborn chin" and stood alone downstage at the end "glaring at the audience." Cf. Greenwald (103) who comments on the ambiguous aspects of Barton's ending.

17. *Changing Styles in Shakespeare* (London: George Allen & Unwin, 1981), 44.

18. Williamson, 169; cited also by Berry, 44.

19. Berry, 45.

20. Craig Raine, *The New Statesman*, 22 August 1975; cited by Berry, 45.

21. See also McGuire (63–96) who discusses not only Isabella's "open silence," but those of several other characters in the final scene, including Claudio and Juliet, Barnardine, and Angelo. He analyzes implications of the staging, particularly the blocking, of the scene to show how the relationships of erotic and filial love are concluded.

22. Laurence Senelik, *Gordon Craig's Moscow "Hamlet"* (Westport, Conn.: 1982), 64; quoted by Joyce Vining Morgan, *Stanislavski's Encounter with Shakespeare* (Ann Arbor: UMI Research Press, 1984), 91.

23. See Francis Fergusson, *The Idea of a Theater* (Princeton: Princeton University Press, 1949; rpt. Anchor Books, 1953), 135 (references are to the reprint). Fergusson's discussion of Jones's interpretation (122–23) is important, but so is his entire chapter devoted to the play.

24. Guthrie, 78. Guthrie regards Hamlet as "not only highly intelligent, but also a resolute and capable man, rendered irresolute and incapable by self-conflict, by qualms of conscience, only in the single matter of avenging his

father's death by the murder of his uncle." He believes Jones's interpretation is convincing but offers little that can be expressed theatrically. Using analogies from two episodes in Queen Elizabeth's experience, Guthrie concludes with Salvador de Madariaga that Hamlet did not so much fail to act as to postpone action, until the moment for action had clearly been revealed, as it was in the final scene. See 79–82.

# Seeing and Believing: Eavesdropping and Stage Groupings in *Twelfth Night* and *Troilus and Cressida*

## Michael W. Shurgot

J. L. Styan observes correctly that the convention of eavesdropping, which illustrates clearly the freedom of Elizabethan stage groupings, requires a "special pattern of movement."[1] The spatial relationship between observer and observed must ensure an audience's simultaneous grasp of the characters' discrepant awareness and the dramatic significance of the scene. The complexity and staging of an eavesdropping scene are determined primarily by whether or not the observer speaks. In *Hamlet* 3.1, for example, Polonius and Claudius remain silent, so this scene requires only that they and Hamlet be visibly separate on the stage, since the convention itself, as accepted by the Elizabethan audience, dictates that Hamlet does not see his adversaries. If the observers do speak, however, the blocking and direction are, as Styan remarks, far more demanding.[2]

Speaking eavesdroppers are dramatically more complex because their comments necessarily concern what they see, automatically complicating the theater audience's response to stage action. For the duration of most plays, an audience observes one stratum of action that it can judge as it wishes; however, in the presence of a speaking eavesdropper, the theater audience must balance its own reactions against internal comments on the same action emanating from the play. Such internal comments function severally: they may challenge the audience's reaction; reinforce its prevalent impression of a character or charactrers; or reveal characters' own idiosyncratic reactions that may not necessarily agree with the theater audience's view.

Since a speaking observer is overheard by the theater audience but not by the observed stage character(s), the characters' relative proximity and their position on the stage must be carefully designed for particular dramatic effect. On the Elizabethan thrust stage, an observer's position would determine simultaneously and immediately his relationship with the observed and with different segments of the theater audience, and the spaciousness and fluidity of the stage would have permitted several different stagings of most eavesdropping scenes in Shakespeare's plays. While this last assertion is simple enough, what are not so simple are the different interpretations of an eavesdropping scene that the Globe stage would have permitted Shakespeare and his actors, and we can learn much about Shakespeare's art and how he adapted it to Elizabethan stage conditions by examining different possible stagings of some of his eavesdropping scenes and the equally different reactions to such scenes that these stagings would have created in an Elizabethan playhouse.

I examine here two eavesdropping scenes in two very different plays probably written within two years of each other, possibly sequentially:[3] *Twelfth Night* 2.5, in which Toby Belch, Fabian, and Andrew Aguecheek watch Malvolio respond to Maria's forged letter; and *Troilus and Cressida* 5.2, in which Ulysses, Troilus, and Thersites watch the assignation between Cressida and Diomedes. Although these two scenes' dramatic situations are quite different, they are strikingly similar in one important respect: blocking significantly affects how the theater audience reacts to the observed character(s).

*Twelfth Night* 2.5 opens with the three characters who will play "audience" in the scene's minidrama, and where they stand during Malvolio's reading of Maria's letter is crucial to an audience's reaction. Let me begin with two basic choices that the Globe stage would have provided Shakespeare's company: (A) to position Toby, Andrew, and Fabian downstage left or right, perhaps behind the posts, between Malvolio and the audience; or (B) to position the trio upstage behind Malvolio and away from the audience in the yard. Since the text does not indicate how (or even if) a "box-tree" was brought on stage,[4] we can assume substantial freedom in placing these three characters. While they might have used one of the stage posts as their "tree," they might just as easily have used a small, portable prop thrust on stage from behind the central curtain of the tiring house or from a corner of the stage. They might have used simply the curtain or one of the tiring house doors as their shield. Eavesdropping conventions demand only some physical space between observer and observed. Regardless of whether or not a separate "tree" were used, where the conspirators stand in relation to Malvolio will affect a theater audience's perception of them and Malvolio.

Consider option A (see fig. 1). If Toby, Fabian, and Andrew are downstage left or right as Malvolio speaks, between him and the audience in the yard and in the central sections of the tiers (termed hereafter the "central audience"),[5] then this trio becomes the intermedi-

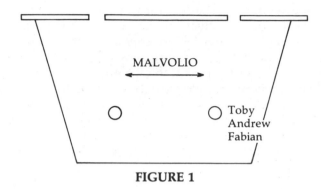

**FIGURE 1**

ary through whose eyes the central audience watches Malvolio and through whose comments it judges him. The trio interprets Malvolio's words and actions for the central audience, and as they are physically closest to this portion of the audience, the conspirators' evaluations influence these spectators' view and make them apt to agree with Toby that "Here's an overweening rogue!"[6] As Malvolio becomes increasingly pompous and conceited, so the conspirators become increasingly impatient and irritated. As their impatience and irritation increase, so does the desperation of Fabian's pleas for silence among them: "O, peace, peace!"; "O peace, peace, peace! Now, now"; "Though our silence be drawn from us with cars, yet peace"; "Nay, patience, or we break the sinews of our plot" (51, 57, 63–64, 75–76). If Fabian speaks these lines facing upstage with his back (more or less) to the central audience, his "our" includes this audience: it shares in the chicanery it watches, enjoying and approving the robust hilarity Toby et al. provide. The trio's downstage position, most effective because in full view of the central audience (Styan, 105), physically symbolizes the dominance of Malvolio's tormentors at this point in the play. Toby and company's downstage position justifies and endears their revenge for most of the theater audience; as Styan remarks, characters' positions on stage add a dimension of meaning to their performance (82).

And what of Malvolio in option A? Shakespeare frames this scene with Maria's entrance and exit; at line 15 she says Malvolio is coming and orders her companions to hide, and after Malvolio has performed, she reemerges at line 186 to ask how well her plot has worked. Maria is then the "director" of this minidrama, the creator of Malvolio's role in his little scene, for which she is heartily praised by her "audience," Toby and company, and us. Option A reinforces visually for the central audience what Maria's carefully placed entrance and exit, the trio's obvious glee at Malvolio's gulling, and their involving us in their plot suggest: that Malvolio is an egocentric, vain fool, a puppet of his own "self-love," as

Olivia says (line 5), whose string can be pulled by others to make him play the role they want him to play. The central audience watches Malvolio dance as Maria, offstage, pulls the strings according to "the sinews of [her] plot," and shares so thoroughly with Maria's allies this plot's exuberance and success that it accepts uncritically Maria's proclamation that Malvolio is nothing but a "time-pleaser, an affection'd ass" (2.3.148).

Consider option B. Styan writes that if the box-tree were used on stage, then "the freedom to eavesdrop suggests that it could be planted anywhere." In the same paragraph, nonetheless, he asserts that the conspirators must have played their comedy from downstage, for only then "could the spectator completely share in the joke" (105). Such directional dogmatism ignores the Elizabethan stage's plasticity and the elasticity of the Shakespearean scene. Option B (fig. 2) places the conspirators upstage right or left, perhaps behind the movable tree, and Malvolio downstage center. The trio would enter from one of the doors, and then, after being instructed by Maria, would scramble upstage near the door from which they entered as Malvolio struts in from the opposite door and parades downstage center. This arrangement alters the central audience/conspirators relation; whereas in option A the conspirators stand between Malvolio and this audience, and interpret and judge him for it, in B this audience judges Malvolio for itself without their mediation. In option B the central audience is not made co-conspirators with Toby and company: their upstage position distances them from this audience, concentrating now on Malvolio at the dominating downstage center location. Because this blocking denies the central audience an intimate partnership in Maria's plot, it neither immediately condones the conspirators' plot nor uncritically accepts their assumed dominance. Whereas in option A the central audience, like the conspirators, secretly spies on Malvolio, and readily accepts and enjoys its privileged position, in B this audience watches *both* Malvolio and his tormentors from the same aesthetically distanced position. Option B does not draw this audience directly into the play world as does A, and thus in B the central audience judges Malvolio and the conspirators for itself, and independently of each other.

From this independent judging follows, potentially, a different reaction to the entire scene, especially to Malvolio's gulling. While I do not claim that a sensible audience pities Malvolio here (he certainly gets what he deserves), nonetheless the central audience's view of him is not skewed by option B as it is in A. The central audience can judge Malvolio as it wishes, without the intermediary guidance provided by the conspirators in option A. The central audience watching B is just as likely as one watching A to judge Malvolio a fop, but one watching B is more

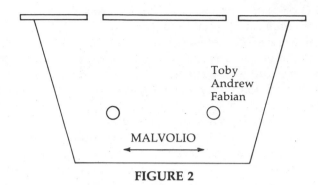

Toby
Andrew
Fabian

MALVOLIO

**FIGURE 2**

likely to judge Toby et al. as a pack of rogues little wiser than their pathetic victim. Certainly both blockings are potentially hilarious, and only a director as dense as Andrew Aguecheek could ruin this scene; to quote Iago, "Fie, there is no such man; it is impossible" (*Othello*, 4.2.134). But what is possible is an audience's deciding that the tricksters here are just as egocentric, just as much "time-pleasers," potentially just as malicious as the man they assume they can humiliate with impunity. The central audience watching option B is more likely to judge Malvolio, Toby, Fabian, and Andrew equally, rather than assuming as in A, because the staging invites it, that Malvolio is far more reprehensible than his tormentors. Later in the play, of course, Toby and his cronies learn the limits of this holiday misrule—the everyday of 7 January haunts Toby's revels—and by 4.1 the audience, like Feste, would not be in any of this trio's coats for "twopence," or anything else: Sebastian is utterly fearless! But a director who wants to allow the central audience to judge Malvolio's gulling for itself, and to suspend its estimation of the participants' roles, can promote this independent judging by adopting option B.

Styan's assertion—that only by placing the conspirators downstage can the audience share completely in the joke of Malvolio's gulling—presumes that the director of *Twelfth Night* can play the scene with only one intention and, more seriously, with only one view of Malvolio, his antagonists, and their relationships. If the director wants to prepare his audience for the conspirators' nearly disastrous clash with Sebastian in 4.1, in which they simply carry their nonsense too far, he can suggest by adopting option B in 2.5 that Toby and his crew are not as superior as they pretend and that they are as fit subjects for ridicule as poor Malvolio. Simply stated, the Elizabethan stage granted Shakespeare and his actors the freedom to have their theater audience either laugh with or at the stage audience of Maria's merry plot.[7]

So far I have spoken of the "central audience," implying a distinction among the Globe's spectators. The Globe's thrust stage was surrounded on three sides by audience, and there were two "side audiences" whose sight lines were considerably different from those of the central audience. Thus, the (right or left) side audience's experience of either of the above stagings of 2.5 would have been different from that of the central audience's. So, regardless of blocking, no audience of this scene in *Twelfth Night* could have had a completely uniform experience. In option A, the side audiences would have "seen" Malvolio without the three conspirators as mediators, for they would be downstage and (from the side audience's perspective) behind Malvolio, and the trio's remarks would be less influential in the side audience's view of him. In option B, however, the side audience's perspectives would be more complex and less unified. If the three conspirators were grouped on one side behind a movable tree, the audience on that side would watch Malvolio through the conspirators' eyes and be drawn into the conspiracy, as the central audience is in option A. But the audience on the opposite side would view Malvolio unassisted by the conspirators, much as the central audience would. If the conspirators were divided between two "trees" or other props on either side of the stage (a possible though less likely blocking because of Fabian's urgent pleas for silence), then the two side audiences would have similar experiences of the scene, whereas the central audience would, as indicated, view and judge Malvolio without mediation.

These numerous possible blockings indicate how complex the total audience response to an apparently simple scene could be. Most scholars agree with Styan (105) that the downstage central position was dominant at the Globe and that this scene's critical "interpretations" should proceed from this assumption. Even if we do agree that downstage center dominated the Elizabethan stage, and that most major scenes were played thereabouts, such agreement does not eliminate the fact of multiple perspectives on an eavesdropping scene in a thrust-stage theater. This fact leads inevitably to the next: within an Elizabethan theater different members of the same audience had different reactions to such an eavesdropping scene. In even as simple an eavesdropping scene as *Twelfth Night* 2.5, where one character is observed by speaking eavesdroppers sharing similar attitudes toward their victim, the audience's experience approximates the scene's dramaturgy: no one "view" of Malvolio and his adversaries is complete, either "in the play" or "in the theater." Regardless of how Shakespeare's company blocked this scene, it communicated this central idea visually. A spectator seated anywhere in Shakespeare's Globe could watch not only the eavesdropping scene but also other spectators watching that same scene. The entire theatrical event—acting, observing, and observing of observing—became a visual analogue of the scene itself, where Malvolio acts a role, is observed, the observers are observed, and no one in the theater is certain whose "view" of the proceedings is correct. This aspect becomes even more pronounced, more phenomenal, in *Troilus & Cressida* 5.2.

Whereas in the theater Maria's ingenious plot inevitably pleases, *Troilus & Cressida* 5.2 inevitably chafes. Regardless of how one judges, or has prejudged, Troilus and Cressida in or before this scene, by its end one is deeply disturbed by Cressida's words to Diomedes and by Troilus's profound despair. The terrible conflicts inherent in this scene— Cressida's halfspoken, anguished fears; Troilus's sense of betrayal and his inability to comprehend Cressida's actions; Ulysses's ambiguous motives in accompanying Troilus; and Thersites's roguish, cynical remarks—assault an audience almost too rapidly, and the flood of remarks from the five characters creates a dizzying sense of multiple realities analogous to the experiences of the stage characters themselves.

This aspect of the scene warrants scrutiny. The most extensive treatment of its dramaturgy heretofore is by Douglas Sprigg.[8] Sprigg's suggested blocking, integral to his analysis of its theatrical impact, places Cressida and Diomedes upstage right and left respectively, Ulysses and Troilus downstage right, and Thersites downstage left (fig. 3, option A). Brilliantly, this blocking allows Cressida's physical movements between Diomedes and Troilus to image her ambivalent motives, shifting loyalties, and moral uncertainties; it also juxtaposes the choric comments of Ulysses and Thersites against Troilus's growing incredulity, making the stage "a physical manifestation of a moral tug-of-war":

> From the audience's vantage point, every movement toward Diomedes sends her away visually from the observing Troilus, and every movement away from Diomedes brings her back visually toward Troilus. Equally important, a movement toward Diomedes is not only away from Troilus; it is also a movement in the direction of Thersites. On both a literal and symbolic level, the nature of her inner psychological struggle is given an external physical manifestation. Cressida's movement, in relation to the positioning of the other characters onstage, enacts her dilemma and creates a visual emblem of the forces warring within.[9]

Sprigg's analysis of this scene's multiple perspectives demonstrates convincingly Shakespeare's creative use of his flexible stage. However, Sprigg's blocking assumes, as he says, that Thersites's perspective is the broadest in the scene: Cressida and Diomedes are aware only of each other; Troilus registers his reactions to them as filtered through his own emotions; and Thersites "views the upstage interaction in juxtaposition to the reactions of Troilus." Sprigg envisions an emotional chain reaction

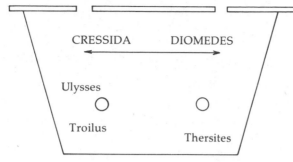

**FIGURE 3; BASED ON SPRIGG**

originating between Diomedes and Cressida, darting zig-zag across the stage from Troilus and Ulysses to Thersites, and terminating in the central theater audience:

> By creating such a system of observed observers, Shakespeare insures that the slightest response from the upstage couple will be magnified by a chain reaction of responses from the series of eavesdroppers. In a sense, Shakespeare has created a series of mutually informing plays within plays, each with its own frame of reference, receding in depth away from the audience toward Cressida. (152)

Sprigg's assumption, that the reference point of these multiple perspectives is the downstage, or central, audience, seriously weakens his argument. For all of its cogency, Sprigg's perspective on the scene is too narrow; the "series of mutually informing plays within plays" is more complex than he suggests, for the side audiences in his blocking have contrasting perspectives. The right side audience sees/hears all from Cressida's perspective, while the left side audience is influenced more by Diomedes. The "zig-zag" pattern Sprigg mentions (emotions from Diomedes/Cressida to Ulysses to Troilus to Thersites to central audience) is actually a web of criss-crossing lines: the right-side audience observes Cressida directly, and sees/hears Thersites's remarks through Ulysses and/or Troilus; the left side observes Diomedes most directly, but may be more influenced by Thersites, depending on how far up stage he is positioned. As Cressida and Diomedes move, even these perspectives change; the entire scene becomes a kaleidoscope of changing audience and character perspectives. Shakespeare thus creates here, for and within the entire audience, an even more faithful analogue to the stage action than he does in *Twelfth Night* 2.5. Theater spectators observe stage characters being observed from at least two perspectives, and the discrepancy among the observers' remarks, unlike the singular attitude of Toby and company toward Malvolio, is mirrored in conflicting views of the stage action. The central audience watches Cressida being observed by people near Ulysses and Troilus, and Diomedes being observed by other people nearer to Diomedes and (possibly) Thersites. Similar complications abound from the two side audiences watching the central audience closer (on one side) to Ulysses and Troilus, and (on the other) to Thersites. Different positions of the theater audience relative to the several speaking eavesdroppers (and to Diomedes and Cressida) create different angles of vision on, degrees of involvement with, and judgments about the stage action. The "meaning" of this scene, like its dramaturgy and the stage characters' emotions, is changing constantly.

Sprigg's blocking raises a second question. Doesn't he presume that Shakespeare intended Thersites to be the scene's final arbiter for the entire audience, determining where Sprigg positions Thersites on stage? Doesn't this blocking prejudice the majority of the spectators' reaction to Cressida's meeting with Diomedes, assuring them that what they see/ hear is only what Thersites says it is: "Lechery, lechery, still wars and lechery, nothing else holds fashion" (194–95)? What might different blockings of this scene yield?

Consider figure 4, option B: Cressida and Diomedes, like Malvolio in *Twelfth Night* 2.5, are downstage center; Ulysses and Troilus are upstage right; and Thersites, whose position is now radically different from Sprigg's placement, is upstage left and is no longer positioned to suggest that his comments on the action are definitive. If Cressida and Diomedes interact downstage center, without either Troilus's or Thersites's exclamations interposed between them and the central audience, then this audience can judge the couples' words for itself, much as it can judge Malvolio independently of his molesters' jibes in option B of *Twelfth Night* 2.5. Furthermore, now one small portion of the total audience—the left side—views the scene through Thersites's eyes, and his "authority" on this spectacle is considerably diminished. Also changed radically are Troilus's and Ulysses's positions relative to Diomedes and Cressida;

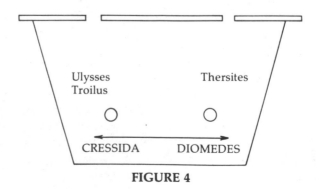

**FIGURE 4**

whereas in option A Troilus and Ulysses were, like Thersites, relatively close to the central audience, in option B they, like Thersites, are close to only a small portion of the total audience—the right side. Without Troilus's or Thersites's reactions to "guide" the central audience's interpretation of this scene, these spectators can weigh more objectively the frightening emotions that Cressida, perilous and anguished, can only allude to. Yes, Cressida betrays Troilus; but hasn't Troilus also betrayed Cressida by his inability to understand her and his selfishness when he learns that she is to be given to the Greeks? And has not Calchas brutally betrayed his own daughter?

Before pursuing a third possible blocking—using the upper stage—let me consider what happens to standard critical notions of "character"—especially Cressida's—in these two blockings, especially option B: first from the perspective of the central audience and then from that of the two side audiences.

The assignation of 5.2 is far more than Cressida's "betrayal" of Troilus. We err if we assume that only one blocking, and thus one "meaning," is possible. Option A presumes that the principal points of the scene *for the entire audience* are Troilus's reaction to Cressida's "betrayal" and Thersites's reaction to and comments on Troilus's dismay.[10] Sprigg says that Thersites "functions as a Greek Pandarus, an emblem of the potentially repulsive aspects of human sexuality," while Troilus suggests ideal sexual relations (153). Cressida moves between these poles, either toward Diomedes, and thus Thersites, or toward Troilus. The audience is tugged between these poles as it juxtaposes these diametrically opposed character reactions. Thus, for Sprigg, Cressida's emotions are judged for the central audience by Troilus and Thersites; she becomes whatever one of them says she is at the moment he is talking: a betrayer of a sensitive, if naive, lover; or an emblem of omnipresent lechery. But if, as in option B, Cressida and Diomedes are downstage center, with Troilus/Ulysses and Thersites upstage right and left, then the majority of the audience judges for itself what Cressida is, what she is doing, and why. Most of the audience in option B hears from equidistant parts of the stage disparate choric comments, the truth of which it can also judge for itself. The distance of Thersites and Troilus from the action's center and from the central audience minimizes their authority as commentators: their knowledge of what the central audience witnesses is incomplete and limited. Furthermore, because the central audience watches Diomedes and Cressida being observed by Thersites on one side and by Ulysses/Troilus on the other, this audience also observes one half of the side audience being more influenced by Thersites and the other more by Ulysses/Troilus. As the central audience juggles the "validity" of these two sets of choruses, it is simultaneously juggling its own theatrical experience and that of the characters onstage: one portion of the total audience sees/hears the stage action primarily through Thersites; the other, through Ulysses/Troilus. Which set of commentators is right about Cressida's "assignation"? Which set of the theater's side observers is more "correct" in its view? Is either portion of the side audiences seeing/ hearing *all* correctly, and thus "right" about what Cressida/Diomedes are doing/saying? The very uncertainty of this brutal scene, especially of Cressida's motives, is mirrored in the central audience's own discordant view of the *total* theatrical experience it sees/hears (i.e., stage + audience). Option B, then, clearly places Thersites and Troilus in positions suggesting a seminal point of this scene: that Cressida is not necessarily what any man here says she is. Throughout the play, Cressida is far more complex and enigmatic than most of the men she meets, including Troilus. Positioning Troilus and Thersites in this scene to suggest that Cressida is either or only what one says she is limits her dramatic role and minimizes her character.

For the two side audiences, this scene is equally elusive and enigmatic. The right-side audience sees/hears the stage action from Ulysses and Troilus's perspective, while the left side sees/hears from Thersites's. But each side audience observes the other experiencing the scene from an equally limited perspective; each is influenced by one set of commentators. Whereas for the central audience the sets of commentators are (more or less) equally distant from it, for the side audiences even this equanimity is shattered. For the right side audience, Ulysses/Troilus, being closer, assume more prominence as commentators, and Thersites's remarks, which Sprigg assumed dominated this scene, are minimized; while, for the left side audience, Thersites dominates and Ulysses's/ Troilus's views are minimized. Which set of commentators is "right?" No certainty is possible; and, I contend, none should be—the major point of this scene *for the entire audience*. Further, the side audiences see the central audience observing this spectacle from a perspective that is irreconcilable with their own. Thus, Cressida may be what either Ulysses/Troilus or Thersites says she is, but each side audience's view is as limited as that of the observers closest to them. Perhaps, as the side audiences watch the central audience observing Cressida/Diomedes and balance the eavesdroppers' comments, they realize how limited their own perspectives are, for they mirror what they see/hear: three men judging a complex woman trapped in horrendous circumstances, making her be, or become, what they want her to be or become. Regardless of the sight-line of the Globe's spectators, this scene became a perfect analogue of the stage action and thus an image of its most difficult element: judging characters' motives, especially Cressida's.

Like the entire play, 5.2 of *Troilus and Cressida* is unpleasant. We usually agree with Thersites's closing evaluation: "Lechery, lechery, still wars and lechery, nothing else holds fashion. A burning devil take them!" (2.194–96). However, Thersites is but one character, and his view is often narrow: throughout the play he is "lost in the labyrinth of [his] fury." We err if we assume that his view of 5.2 is the correct one or that Shakespeare intended his to determine a theater audience's reaction. Rather, Thersites's is but one judgment of a compelling, frightening scene in which love and sexuality are simply pawns and anyone failing to protect his or her best interests is a fool. Cressida, rather than being simply what Troilus or Thersites alternatively labels her, symbolizes, in the very movements that Sprigg so brilliantly analyzes, the essence of this scene; and blocking so as to limit, rather than expand, this symbolism can narrow and prejudice an audience's experience of it.

Finally, I want to consider briefly a third alternative for this scene in the Globe theater; using the upper stage. I doubt the upper stage would have been used for *Twelfth Night* 2.5,[11] but it could have been used readily in *Troilus and Cressida* 5.2. If, for example, Shakespeare had wanted to suggest the superior vision of either Ulysses/Troilus or Thersites, he could have placed them or him on the upper stage. Such an arrangement might convey moral superiority or judgment on the ensuing scene and might convey visually what Sprigg tries to assign to Thersites in his blocking, were Thersites to be placed above. Obviously, placing either Thersites or Ulysses/Troilus above would eliminate much of the complexity I have analyzed and that I find intrinsic to the entire scene, for the characters as well as for the total audience. However, this blocking would certainly have been an option for Shakespeare's company and would have created a distinct visual impression in the theater. But such an option, as with some features of Sprigg's blocking, would have diminished the analogous nature of the audience's theatrical experience. Many of the multiple perspectives I have examined would disappear, and Cressida might more readily seem for the entire audience what either Ulysses/Troilus or Thersites says she is. Similarly, Cressida's emotional complexity might be diminished, were the audience to see eavesdroppers above her clearly judging her every word and movement from a privileged, physically superior position.

The different approaches to the two scenes I have discussed demonstrate a seminal fact: that Shakespeare's theater granted him a marvelously fluid medium for his revels. None of the blockings I have examined, mine or Sprigg's or Styan's, is "right"; each is different, and each can be used by a director to suit his view of the play and its characters and to determine what an audience sees and believes in these complex scenes. Such decisions affirm the simple truth that a scene's "meaning" cannot be isolated from performance, and remind us that all Shakespearean scenes are dramatic scripts written for a unique theater.[12]

## Notes

1. J. L. Styan, *Shakespeare's Stagecraft* (Cambridge: Cambridge University Press, 1967), 103.

2. Ibid. Styan remarks that "A player's position on the stage add[s] a dimension of meaning to his performance even when he remain[s] silent" (82).

3. G. Blakemore Evans, ed., *The Riverside Shakespeare* (Boston: Houghton Mifflin, 1974), lists 1601–2 as the proposed date for both *Twelfth Night* and *Troilus and Cressida* (54).

4. Bernard Beckerman, *Shakespeare at the Globe* (New York: MacMillan, 1962), writes, "Although property trees were regularly employed on the Elizabethan stage, no tree definitely appears on the Globe stage" (81).

5. Throughout my essay I divide the Globe audience into "central" and "side." C. Walter Hodges's drawing of the second Globe in Craig and Bevington's *The Complete Works of Shakespeare*, rev. ed. (Glenview, Ill.: Scott Foresman, 1973), between 68 and 69, perfectly illustrates this difference and shows clearly that one cannot speak accurately of a unified theatrical experience for an audience in a thrust-stage theater. For a review of some of the practical and aesthetic aspects of playing before a thrust-stage audience, see Derek Peat's fascinating and challenging essay "Looking Up and Looking Down: Shakespeare's Vertical Audience," *Shakespeare Quarterly* 35 (Special issue, 1985): 563–70, esp. 564.

6. *Twelfth Night*, 2.2.29. All textual references are from *The Riverside Shakespeare*.

7. The importance of the director's choices in 2.5 is emphasized by Toby's brief appearance in 4.2. Here Toby and Maria overhear and enjoy Feste's badgering of Malvolio, yet midway through the scene Toby wishes they were all "well rid of this knavery" (67–68). Toby's position on stage when he says this line could (should?) remind the audience of his position during the earlier gulling of Malvolio, and may thus reinforce *visually* Toby's fear that the revelry begun by Maria's letter may be getting dangerous for everybody.

8. Douglas Sprigg, "Shakespeare's Visual Stagecraft: The Seduction of Cressida," in *Shakespeare: The Theatrical Dimension*, Philip C. McGuire and David A. Samuelson, eds. (New York: AMS Press, 1979), 149–64.

9. Sprigg, 154. Styan observes that this "three dimensional scene of double perspective could only have been conceived for the Elizabethan platform" (130).

10. Sprigg writes: "All the touching becomes an excitement to trembling rage and despair from Troilus on one side of the stage and an excitement to lecherous imaginings from Thersites on the other" (157).

11. I argue thus for two reasons. First, Maria says to the conspirators: "Get ye all three into the boxtree; Malvolio's coming down this walk" (2.5.15–16), and four lines later: "Close, in the name of jesting" (20). Malvolio enters just two lines later; and only six lines later Toby speaks: "Here's an overweening rogue" (29). I do not believe the trio would have time to get to the upper stage before Toby speaks, especially since his line implies one already set in his position and acutely aware of Malvolio's actions. Secondly, at 136–38, Fabian says, "Ay, and you had any eye behind you, you might see more detraction at your heels than

fortunes before you." These lines would make little sense if the conspirators were *above* Malvolio.

12. Research on this article was initially supported by an NEH Summer Fellowship to the University of Iowa in 1981. I wish to acknowledge especially the assistance and encouragement of Miriam Gilbert, seminar director, and Bruce Wheaton.

# The Recovery of the Elizabethan and Jacobean Playhouses

## C. Walter Hodges

### I

Fifty years after the death of Shakespeare, the last of all the old playhouses that he had known and worked for, which by their method of operation had helped to form his dramatic style, had been demolished. They were quite lost. Nothing remained to indicate what they had looked like or how they had worked. A new sort of theater— not a playhouse any longer but a theater: even the designation was different—had emerged, and the new style had obliterated and washed away the old. The purpose of this essay is to review briefly the long process by which the form and features of the lost Shakespearean playhouses have been recovered. This recovery is still not complete. Room must still be left for some adjustment; but the form that now stands (as it were) excavated from the limbo of history by means of a sort of intellectual archaeology, may at last, I think, be accepted with some confidence.

To begin this account, let us in imagination take up a historical position in the middle of the eighteenth century. The theaters in London, and in the provinces also, are now all designed, in the physical sense, as machines for the showing off of changeable painted scenery, such as had first been introduced into England by Inigo Jones as an ingenious and enchanting toy for the pleasure of King James I and his court, but which had eventually taken over the whole physical business of the stage. Playwrights in those days, being learned and literary people dedicated to classical traditions in the morality and structure of plays, had found no difficulty in accommodating their classical standards to these new scenic stages. What they and their audiences, actors, and stage managers found difficult to accommodate in that way, however, were the plays of Shakespeare as Shakespeare had left them.

And since it was of course impossible to deny either the genius or the continuing popularity of Shakespeare, it was a source of some irritation for his classically educated admirers in the eighteenth century continually to be coming up against the irregularities and technical obscurities that were scattered so liberally throughout his printed texts. It had been thought beneficial by such as Davenant and Dryden actually to rewrite Shakespeare into a more fashionable, a more tasteful, a more cultivated style. It had been thought useful by Nicholas Rowe to edit his apparently floundering stagecraft into a form of regular acts and scenes, which readers of plays could better appreciate—to pat the plays gently into a shape their author would surely have intended, had he only known better or had more time for thought.

For Dr. Johnson, the friend of David Garrick, familiar with Garrick's Theatre Royal in Drury Lane (which was as fine an example of a "proper" theater as any to be found in Europe), it certainly seems to have been a matter for regret that Shakespeare had not been born in better times. In the preface to his 1765 edition of Shakespeare's plays, Dr. Johnson finds himself ruefully obliged to acknowledge certain shortcomings in his hero. There was a laxity of moral tone as well as of proper dramatic construction and characterization to be found in many important parts of Shakespeare's work: faults that, says Johnson, "the barbarity of his age cannot extenuate." However, Johnson does try to use this earlier age for extenuation, if only a little, by observing that the theater-going public for which Shakespeare wrote was for the most part "gross and dark." Thus, we may safely assume that Johnson in 1765 would certainly have found nothing to admire in the physical conditions of Shakespeare's play-houses, which had been designed for the gross and dark entertainment of a barbarous age, and no reason therefore to bewail the loss of such places: certainly no reason to consider restoring them.

But even had Johnson wished to do so, there was little or no material available at that time that could have helped him form the sketchiest of pictures in his mind. Pictures of Elizabethan theaters from their own time are few even today, after a century of research. In Dr. Johnson's time they were almost entirely unknown. Antiquarian friends might have shown Johnson those little details seen as circular features in old maps of London, labeled as the Globe, the Bear Garden, or the Swan. He might possibly have seen somewhere a copy of J. C. Visscher's panorama of London, made in 1616, with a Globe playhouse shown as an improbable-looking building in the foreground; but it is doubtful. He may also perhaps have seen in some private collection a copy of Hollar's London panorama of 1647, but it is not certain. In any case, as far as the Globe playhouse was concerned, neither representation of it in these pictures was consistent with the other; and both, as buildings, appeared unattractive and certainly hard to associate either with Shakespeare or with plays. And there, so far as any visual evidence was concerned, the matter of Shakespeare's theater had to be left.

Nevertheless, the old Globe theater must have been an occasional topic of discussion in Dr. Johnson's circle, for it is interestingly referred to as an object of antiquarian curiosity by his friend Mrs. Thrale. Johnson had first met her and her husband in 1765, the same year he published his edition of Shakespeare. It will be remembered that Mr. Thrale was a brewer and that his brewery was built over the very site where the Globe had once stood. In 1767, two years after his first meeting with Johnson, Henry Thrale was having some old houses demolished on his property, and many years later Mrs. Thrale recalled the event in her memoirs. She described the wreckage as having been "the curious remains of the old Globe playhouse, which, though hexagonal in form without, was round within." This account has sometimes been taken as the evidence of a last eyewitness as to the form and structure of the Globe. But that is not so. The demolition she had seen was not that of the Globe, and her memory was not that of an eyewitness but of a book she had read, as I shall show.

What Mrs. Thrale's remark does reveal, however, is that in her time educated people were beginning to take an inquiring interest in the matter. The attitude of Dr. Johnson had already become old-fashioned. Only one year after Mrs. Thrale had observed the demolition of what she mistook for the Globe, we find a direct reference to that vanished theater as an object worthy of study in its own right. In those days new editions of Shakespeare were following each other from the press with an enthusiasm that had hardly been seen before (and has hardly stopped since). In 1768 Edward Capell published a preface to his edition of the plays in which he remarked, with reference to the sources of Shakespeare's technique as a dramatist, that "even the stage he appeared upon, its forms, dressings, actors should be inquired into, as every one of these circumstances had some considerable effect upon what he composed for it." We may note here that this, 152 years after the death of Shakespeare, was the first time it had been publicly suggested by anyone that the conditions of the theater Shakespeare had worked in might be a matter of interest for educated people.

It was to be another ten years before this idea was to be taken up, not by Capell himself, but by a scholar of genius who followed him: Edmond Malone. Malone had come to London from Dublin in about 1774 and, after joining company with Dr. Johnson and his circle, was collaborating (with George Steevens) in the preparation of yet another edition of Shakespeare; and with this he undertook a new sort of work, which he called *An Historical Account of the Rise and Progress of the English Stage*, that was published as an appendix to Steevens's third edition in 1780. Malone's *Historical Account* began with a description of the English medieval drama and followed through to "the period of its maturity and greatest splendour"—that is, the age of Shakespeare, whereupon Malone said he would "endeavour to exhibit as accurate a delineation of the internal form and economy of our ancient theatres, as the distance at which we stand and the obscurity of the subject will permit." At that point he published a single picture of his obscure subject, a primitive woodcut derived from a sketch made for him by a clergyman friend in Cambridge, from a copy in the Pepys Library in Magdelene College, of what he called the "Antwerp View of London"—namely, the now very familiar panorama of London by J. C. Visscher, of 1616.

As for the obscurity of the subject itself in Malone's day, one is surprised to be reminded how deep it was, and yet how much Malone managed to make of it. Nothing was known about the first old Theatre, its demolition, and its re-erection on Bankside as the Globe in 1599. "I am unable to ascertain at what time the Globe was built," writes Malone. "I believe it was built not long before 1596"—which was of course a good conjecture. And later he says: "I formerly conjectured that the Globe, though hexagonal at the outside was perhaps a rotunda within." (Here, of course, practically word for word, is the source of Mrs. Thrale's recollections, quoted earlier.) Malone states that he conjectured his rotunda idea from Shakespeare's "Wooden O" reference in *Henry V*. He then goes on to lay down a sort of grammar of the Globe and its practices, which has retained its general use almost down to our own time and which we may call the "Malone tradition." It was he who originally conjectured the architectural derivation of the Elizabethan playhouses from the form of the galleried inn-yards used by the strolling players; the identification of scene changes by the display of written boards ("Rome: the Capitol" or "The Forest of Arden"); the rudimentary "inner stage" with its hand-operated curtains ("not drawn by lines and pullies. . . . an apparatus to which the simple mechanism of our ancient theatres had not arrived") and so on.

Such was the state of things in 1780. But then, with his history of the English stage still mint-new in the bookshops, Malone came upon an unexpected treasure. "Just as this work was issuing from the Press," he wrote in a later edition, "some curious manuscripts relative to the stage, were found at Dulwich College, and obligingly transmitted to me from thence." Thus was announced the discovery of the famous Alleyn-Henslowe collection of papers, and thus, with the happy-go-lucky liberality of late eighteenth-century scholarship, did the Master and Fellows of Dulwich College allow Malone to carry the whole lot off with him, back to his den. "I am unwilling," he then wrote, "that the publick should be deprived of the information and entertainment these very curious materials may afford, and therefore shall extract from them all such notices as appear to me worthy of preservation." He published his

The Globe playhouse, Bankside. (A woodcut made from a copy-sketch of the detail in J. C. Visscher's panorama of London, 1616.) From Malone's *Historical Account of the Rise and Progress of the English Stage.*

Bankside, with the Bear Garden and the Globe. Detail from J. C. Visscher's panorama, 1616.

selection in the 1790 edition of his history under the heading of "Emendations and Additions." Among them was the now-famous contract between Philip Henslowe and Peter Street for the building of the Fortune playhouse. Among them also was another much-quoted document, the inventory of the properties of My Lord Admiral's men, of 10 March 1598, beginning with "i rock, i cage, i tomb, i Hell Mouth. for the Jew." Malone's transcription of this document is in fact its only source, for the original is, since then, unfortunately lost.

When Malone died in 1812, his editorial work was continued by his amanuensis and executor, the younger James Boswell. Possibly for a time the Henslowe documents remained in Boswell's keeping, and if so it is likely he showed them to a distinguished German visitor who came to London in 1817 to collect material for a work on Shakespeare that he had in mind. This was Johann Ludwig Tieck, poet and theatrical impresario, and it is with him that the history of the rediscovery of the Elizabethan theaters really continues. When Tieck returned from England to his home in Dresden, he evidently took with him a set of Malone's 1790 Shakespeare, with its historical appendix containing the transcript of the Fortune contract. He did not immediately make use of it, for he was busy during the next few years collaborating with A. W. Schlegel in their great translation of Shakespeare that has made a German classic of the English dramatist.

But then in 1834 an architect, Gottfried Semper, came to Dresden to build an opera house there. Semper, of the full-blown nineteenth-century German historical-romantic school (who later burnt his fingers at that fire, working with Richard Wagner), was an artist after Tieck's own heart. They worked together on a reconstruction of the Fortune playhouse, using Malone's transcription, apparently with some idea of rebuilding it at full scale on the banks of the Elbe. Whatever else might have been behind this idea besides Tieck's enthusiasm and Semper's skill, or how likely it ever was that the Fortune might actually have been rebuilt in Dresden, we cannot know. What we do know is what it would have looked like, for we have Semper's drawings of it. These were published in 1836 in a book about Ben Jonson and his followers written by a younger colleague of Tieck's. What we see here is the first systematic reconstruction of an Elizabethan playhouse. It is described in its caption as "an old English summer theater," which is in fact the description Malone had used.

It is clear that one of the things Tieck and Semper could not understand in reading the Fortune contract was the strange and seemingly illogical condition in it about the arrangement of the stage. According to the contract, taken literally, the stage would seem to have stood out like a peninsula into the yard, with a space for "groundling" spectators around it on three sides. How could Tieck and Semper have believed or imagined such an arrangement? Where was there any sense in it or any precedent for it? Semper therefore abandoned it, without more ado, for the much better arrangement he shows here. There was until the Second World War (when it was destroyed in the devastation of Dresden) a perspective watercolor drawing of Semper's Fortune, made from his plans; but there still remains a photograph of it (unfortunately not very good) from which we can see the general effect. Except for his filling-in at the sides of the stage, Semper has kept strictly to the conditions and dimensions of the contract. In many ways his stage is remarkably modern in style—or nearly modern. One is reminded of Reinhardt or Jessner or Norman Bel Geddes in the 1920s. It would still serve very well for modern productions and is a close cousin to Tanya Moisevitch's original stage at the Festival Theatre in Stratford, Ontario, of 1953. It would itself have been a delightful and practical Shakespearean theater, and it is a pity it was never built.

In the same book on Ben Jonson that contained Semper's drawings was a reconstruction picture of an Elizabethan indoor, or "private," theater, such as the Blackfriars. We can see that as a concept this, too, was much ahead of its time. Indeed, it is not unlike a reconstruction of the Blackfriars made by the American Irwin Smith, with all the results of modern theory and research at his command, only twenty years ago. In the nineteenth century nothing else like it, not even as an imaginative drawing, seems to have been attempted anywhere until at least twenty years later.

By the 1860s the stream of Victorian historical romanticism was in full flood, fed by the tributary novels of Walter Scott, Bulwer Lytton, and others; and each year at the Royal Academy by countless elaborate paintings of historical subjects. A study of the correct details of ancient costume and armor was a standard requirement for every student of art. In the theater the productions of Shakespeare mounted by Charles Kean would keep his audiences repeatedly watching the lowered front curtain, while a series of scene-painted visions of the people, castles, and battlefields of, say, the time of Henry V—all warranted for their historical accuracy—were prepared and then magically revealed from behind it. Even Shakespeare himself, in his doublet and hose, with his rather bohemian private life and his quaint old-world sense of humor, had become part and parcel of the romantic historical scene.

Nor were those prodigious Victorian literary scholars and bibliophiles who had followed in the footsteps of Malone—J. O. Halliwell-Phillips, F. J. Furnivall, and the rest—by any means immune from the romantic spell. In a world of archival bundles tied with ancient string, the relics of the Elizabethan stage were a very rich soil for the breeding of romantic

The Fortune playhouse. From the watercolor of Gottfried Semper's projected reconstruction in Dresden, ca. 1835.

"An Old English Indoor Theatre," from Wolf von Baudissin's *Ben Jonson und seine Schule,* 1836.

sensations. For example, in the mid-century the Dulwich Collection of Henslowe papers had come into the hands of another very famous scholar, John Payne Collier, who was so inspired by them and who entered so thoroughly into the spirit of old Henslowe's career that, when Collier at last returned the papers to the Dulwich library, they contained rather more exciting material than they had had when he first saw them. Scholars since his time have had much ado de-Collierizing the record. It is not my purpose here simply to wag the finger at wicked Collier, whose forgeries in any case are mostly by now well enough known, but to ask why he did it. To some extent, of course, it was to increase his reputation as a scholar, by creating scholarly items for himself to discover; but that does not follow through to the Dulwich papers, which had been discovered, anyway, before his time; and there seems no particular reason to be adding little tidbits into Henslowe's bound diary wherever a conveniently unwritten space presented itself. There may indeed have been some sport of simple scholarly mischief in it, but I think there was more than that. I suggest there was in all these fabrications an element of romantic creativity, a pleasure in historical reconstruction for its own sake—which can, if one is not careful, turn into the creation of a history that never really existed. In a study of the reconstruction of Elizabethan theaters, it is an element that perhaps one ought not to forget.

So far, except for Semper's drawings of the Fortune, we have been concerned chiefly with researches in the literary field. That has the limitation that it rarely leaves the printed page. Now, however, we have to consider a contribution from quite another quarter—from the profession of acting. As early as 1844 the actor-manager Benjamin Webster put on in London a production of Shakespeare based on an idea that had consequences far beyond anything he could have foreseen. Webster's idea was that, in order to be historically accurate within its own terms, *The Taming of the Shrew* should be set up and enacted in the bedchamber where the drunken tinker Christopher Sly is awakened and where the joke is played on him that he is a great lord now recovered from a bout of madness. So the play within a play is then presented for the entertainment of this supposed lord while he eats and drinks, all in the bedchamber, with the help of some portable screens and a few other available props. Webster was thus able to have it both ways, combining a single set of painted scenery representing a lordly bedchamber with the free-moving unlocalized adaptability of the original Elizabethan staging. One must suppose that it was not seen at the time as anything more than a piece of interesting—even economical—quaintness; but it was nevertheless a potent idea, and it was remembered.

It was a long time before anything more was done in that direction, however: but then what was done was done with very great effect. A movement was started by the students of University College, London, called the Shakespeare Reading Society. Its method was to have actors seated together on a platform, simply reading the plays, uncut and without scene divisions. The instructor appointed to direct these readings was William Poel, and it is to him more than anyone else that the whole modern revival of the understanding of Elizabethan (and therefore Shakespeare's) stagecraft owes its being. It was Poel who pioneered the producing of Shakespeare upon open stages without the use of front curtains and, of course, without conventional scenery. In 1894 he founded The Elizabethan Stage Society, from which emerged a school of actors and directors, such as Harley Granville-Barker and, later, Sir Tyrone Guthrie, who carried forward into modern times the ideas planted by Poel. Thus the Elizabethan stage revival, far from being an exercise in antiquarianism, as some might think, has played a central part in the stylistic revolution that has transformed the theater of our own day.

But that is anticipation. Let us return to the evangelist Poel spreading the gospel of the true and undivided text of Shakespeare in the late nineteenth century. Usually when he worked in conventional theaters, to provide a neutral background without scenery Poel draped his acting area all round with fixed curtains. Curtains, in any case, once they have been accepted in their own right by an audience, have an impressive theatrical presence of their own, like a kind of soft architecture. On one occasion, however, in 1893 at the Royalty Theatre in London for an Elizabethan-style production of *Measure for Measure*, Poel converted his stage into a picturesque semblance of a reconstructed Elizabethan play-house. The "reconstruction" was, of course, in this case only a stage setting, like Webster's Elizabethan bedchamber for the *Shrew* nearly fifty years before. As the critic C. E. Montague said at the time, it was "a picture of an Elizabethan stage seen through the frame of a modern proscenium." But it has a particular point of interest for us here. What was it, we may ask, that had suddenly caused the puritanical Poel to go lusting after the false gods of painted scenery, to bow himself down thus in the house of Rimmon? What had tempted him?

In general terms Poel's reconstructional stage picture derived from the pioneering deductions of Malone and his successors, notably in this instance from Collier, who, in spite of his misguided hobbies noted above, was nevertheless a very considerable authority. The derivation is seen chiefly in the curtaining of the upper and lower levels of what was

**William Poel's "Fortune playhouse" setting for *Measure for Measure*, Royalty Theatre, London, 1893.**

known to have been called the tiring-house, at the back of the open stage. The use of curtains somehow or somewhere upon the Elizabethan stage was and is an established fact. Curtains in theaters, as Malone and Collier understood theaters, were, in any case, almost a fact of nature. Thus, quite naturally, the idea of a curtained recess that could be used as a constant ancillary to the open space in front of it, a recess that had come to be called the "inner stage" and that could be supposed to have developed by logical degrees into the form of the "proper" proscenium-and-curtains stages of the eighteenth and nineteenth centuries, had established itself into the idea of the reconstructed Shakespearean scene without any question. There was, after all, some evidence for the idea, and we must remember that there was no organized history of theatrical *production* methods at all at that time, whereby this supposed development might be disputed. So there, in Poel's picture, we see the curtains of *two* "inner stages," above and below, set across the frontage of the tiring-house. But, as well as these, we may notice on each side between two tall posts on the stage two additional curtains, here drawn aside but clearly intended for closing together as a "traverse." For the rest, the general arrangement is based upon evidence already fairly well known: the satyr-heads on the capitals of the stage pillars, for example, derive from the Fortune contract; and the gentlemen spectators seated on the stage come from a well-known chapter in Dekker's "Gull's Hornbook"; and so on. But what had really given rise to this whole stage-picture of Poel's and tempted him so untypically into the hands of the scene-painters was a newly discovered document, first published only five years before this adventure of Poel's, a document that was surely the most important single "find" for Elizabethan theater history since the Henslowe papers and that at last allowed the whole process of reconstructing its playhouses to move forward under the control of a validating pictorial image.

Once again, as so often, it was the enthusiasm of German scholarship in Shakespeare that found this key. A librarian from Berlin, Karl Theodor Gaedertz, discovered in the library of the University of Utrecht in Holland a commonplace book once kept by a certain Arend Van Buchel, who had copied into it a letter and a drawing sent to him by a friend, one Johannes de Witt, who was in London in 1596 and who had visited the then newly built Swan playhouse on Bankside. The drawing is of the interior of that playhouse, showing the stage. It is the only contemporary picture of the inside of an Elizabethan playhouse that exists, even now. It is not very good as a drawing but neither is it very bad, and it is very explicit. Also, it is supplemented further by explicit detail in its accompanying letter. When it was published by Gaedertz in 1888, it was received with astonishment and some reserve, if not actual hostility.

Certainly its imperfections of draftsmanship allowed room for doubt about what it had to say, but that doubt was chiefly caused because what it said did not fit at all well with ideas that had previously been formed without it. Where, for example, was that indispensible item, the "inner stage"? As was known from other evidence, there had to be such a curtained area somewhere about the stage, and it was (and usually still is) supposed to lie somewhere central in the wall of the tiring-house at the back of the stage; but in this sketch of de Witt's no such thing is shown. The usual explanation, apart from the possibility that de Witt simply forgot about it, is that during his visit that opening was never used but was covered by an arras, and so he never knew it was there.

The absence of curtains from the Swan sketch was for all the earlier theorists its most disturbing feature. A stage without scenery was imaginable, but a stage without curtains was not. Curtains and theaters were almost synonymous. We have seen that, in his scenic reconstruction, Poel had furnished it with tall traverse curtains between the posts that supported the stage roof. Such an idea was firmly incorporated into the reconstruction of another scholar, the German Cecil Brodmeier—who proposed in 1904 that, when he visited the Swan in 1596, de Witt had been unable to observe from his position in the auditorium that there were actually two walls stretching back from those two forward stage-posts to connect with the rear wall and that two curtains hanging behind the pillars could be drawn together at will, thus dividing the stage into a sort of inner box and an outer area, so that the playing of different scenes could be alternated between these two areas. Such are the devices we employ to protect our favorite preconceived notions in the face of upsetting evidence to the contrary.

## II

Let us now survey the state of affairs at the beginning of the present century. Most of the essential information needed for the rediscovery of the lost Elizabethan and Jacobean playhouses had by then been put together in some sort of order: the Henslowe papers, with the two building contracts for the Fortune and Hope playhouses; a huge collection of early play texts with all their wealth of technical references (puzzling though much of it was); and the collection of documents relating to the Royal Revels at the Courts of Elizabeth and James, with which the professional players were to some degree associated. There were even a few contemporary or near-contemporary pictures of playhouses, notably J. C. Visscher's and Wenzel Hollar's exterior views of the Globe; and finally there was the picture by Johannes de Witt of the interior of the Swan. The task now was to interpret all this; but here was a difficulty.

The (second) Globe playhouse on Bankside. Pencil sketch on the site by Wenzel Hollar, ca. 1636.

There was still no context of organized theater history into which all the disparate parts of this puzzle could be fitted. Even the history of art itself was by modern standards still only in its infancy, regarded more or less as a comparative study and admiration of the greater masters of painting and sculpture than as a history of styles and cultural modes in society, with all their many different degrees of context and excellence. The history of the theater, in spite of Malone's early attempt to explain primitive English stage conditions, was really still only a history of dramatic *literature*, with a few biographical recollections of the actors who delivered it. So the phenomenon of the Elizabethan theater remained an enigma without a proper home. Nevertheless, it was an enigma crowned with the genius of Shakespeare, and the time had surely come to give it, if not a proper home, at least a proper picture of one.

The obvious example to select for the purpose was the one that Ludwig Tieck had selected years before—Henslowe's Fortune playhouse—and for the same reason, that its building contract existed. It was a pity the contract was not complete in all its details, but still it seemed to have details enough. It was also a pity that it was not Shakespeare's Globe, since that, of course, was the theater most especially desired; and

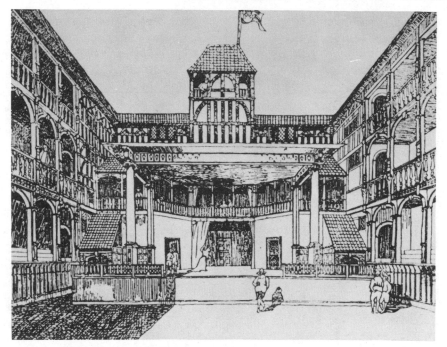

**Interior of the Fortune playhouse. Reconstructional drawing from the original contract, by Walter H. Godfrey, 1908.**

it was a pity again that it was a square playhouse, not a round one, the familiar "Wooden O" of Shakespeare's famous reference; but at least the Fortune contract does mention the Globe by name, which gives a kind of blessing to it and to the use of it for Global purposes.

So in 1908, encouraged by the dramatic critic William Archer, the architect Walter H. Godfrey—a specialist in the history and restoration of ancient buildings—created a set of reconstructional drawings of the Fortune made, like Gottfried Semper's earlier ones, directly from the contract; but now, of course, with a greater knowledge than Semper had had of Elizabethan stage conditions—for, on top of all the rest, the Swan drawing had been brought into the evidence.

Godfrey's reconstruction is excellent for its day and was widely published. Where there had previously been conventional ideas based on timber-framed cottages, it threw on the subject a light of new perception about the degree of architectural sophistication available to Elizabethan builders. But the stage conditions Godfrey gives, especially as to the curtained inner stage, are according to the conventional opinion of the time, which was still lacking in the comparative history of theatrical structures. We may also note one very interesting error. In all the old views of the Bankside playhouses, without exception, they are shown as having a small house or hut standing up out of the open circle formed by the main body of the amphitheater itself. De Witt's drawing of the Swan from the interior shows this as well and even shows more or less how it was done. Because the drawing is crude and because the old exterior views such as Visscher's are crude also and because he had little knowledge of comparative theater history and stage mechanics, Godfrey, as a practicing architect, felt obliged to dismiss the evidence given in these old pictures. Since a sort of tower seemed to be indicated, he put one where an architect would naturally put one, firmly based on the body of its house; and very nice and picturesque it looked. But looking picturesque was evidently all it had to do, in Godfrey's understanding at that time, unless it was to provide a suitable station for hoisting the playhouse flag and sounding the playhouse trumpet.

Evidence existed, therefore, for the Fortune and the Swan; still, naturally, it was the Globe that was most desired; and of the Globe, in the early years of this century, not even the site where it had stood was known for certain. Much work went into the search for its location, and in 1913 the then still-existing Shakespeare Reading Society, believing they had finally tracked down its site, erected a commemorative bronze plaque to the Globe upon the wall of Barclay Perkins's brewery in Park Street, Bankside. But still the dispute continued, generating so much scholarly contention that in the end the London County Council set their own archivist, W. W. Braines, to go into the whole thing and settle it: which in fact he did very satisfactorily. The plaque on the brewery wall, though not exactly in the right place, is not so far wrong as seriously to require being moved, and it is still today where the Shakespeare Reading Society placed it. The London City Council published Braines's findings in a little booklet in 1921, and for good measure they included a set of reconstruction drawings of the Globe made by their architect, G. Topham Forrest, drawings that excellently represent the prevailing state of opinion at that time.

Looking at Topham Forrest's reconstruction, the first thing that strikes one is how very *small* a building he has made. Why did he make it so? He had no sort of warrant for it. We have just seen that the Fortune, of which we know the dimensions exactly, was a fairly large building, eighty feet across, and square. Yet Forrest here, with a round building, makes a diameter of only sixty-four. To make a round building approximate the measure of a square one, the diameter of the circle must be wider, not smaller than the square; and we know from the contract that the Fortune was supposed to be comparable with the Globe. Moreover, in his *vertical* dimensions Forrest has kept strictly to the specifications for the Fortune; that is, an overall height of thirty-two feet above the founda-

**Interior of the Globe playhouse. Reconstructional drawing by G. Topham Forrest for the London County Council, 1921.**

tions. So why has he done these things? It is because he is attempting to imitate the upright, barrel-like appearance of our familiar, picturesque old example from Visscher's panorama of London—an appearance that is in fact more picturesque than probable. The appearance of the Globe in that other, far better panorama by Wenzel Hollar, which by contrast is more probable than picturesque, he disregards except for one thing. He borrows from it, though in a very modified way, the picturesque double-gabled effect of the tiring-house superstructure with its picturesque cupola. Yet note once again how this superstructure is set back squarely on the body of the house, not overhanging the stage in the yard.

Here then, in 1921 is the picture of the official or "school solution" of what Shakespeare's Globe looked like: small, quaint, picturesque, respectably primitive, and, with its thatched roof, "cottagey"—all of which was only to be expected from the romantic offspring of an inn-yard in Merrie England. It was the Malone tradition still in full bloom.

So far I have been able to pursue a fairly simple narrative in a fairly straightforward way; but now, unless I am careful, I am going to run into difficulties. I have to recognize, in the first thirty years of this century, the existence of an enormous body of research devoted to this subject, increasingly in the United States as well as in Great Britain, headed by such great scholars as Sir Edmund Chambers and Sir Walter Greg. The collection of Elizabethan theater studies has become close and deep and rich with detail, and this might be a place to pay tribute by name to the many scholars who have made it so. Yet, with all respect to them, I wish here to avoid their path, which still wanders in the forest of literature, in favor of the different landscape opened up by the new study of theater history as a whole subject, not seen only as play literature but also from the technical, architectural, and presentational point of view as an integral part of the history of international artistic culture.

As an example of this, we know how, since the coming of radio and recorded music, there has been a rapid increase in the knowledge and understanding of music of all kinds. Since the Second World War, there has developed a particular love and understanding of baroque music, with its accompanying revival of the works of composers such as Monteverdi and Cavalli, who had lain dead as doornails in the dictionaries for hundreds of years. Monteverdi was Shakespeare's contemporary. It is now possible to see a common ground of style between an opera by Monteverdi and Shakespeare's masque in *The Tempest*, as between the Italian designers who set and dressed the *intermedii* at the ducal courts of Florence and Mantua and Inigo Jones who brought these forms back to the London of Ben Jonson and King James. Such associations of stylistic ideas were not easily available to students of the Elizabethan theater until Allardyce Nicoll published his *The Development of the Theatre* in 1927.

What is at once apparent to anyone looking through Nicoll's book is the comparative poverty of contemporary pictorial references in his section dealing with the Elizabethan theater, compared with any other period of theater history and compared also, of course, with the richness of its literary remains. It is this that has so urgently stimulated the processes of reconstruction by one conjecture or another. Among the conjectures that Nicoll allowed and published was one by (yet again) a German scholar, Wilhelm Creiznach. In 1916 he had published a book in Germany called *The English Drama in the Age of Shakespeare*, in which he suggested the possibility of a stylistic connection between the Shakespearean playhouses and certain traditional forms of theater typical of the Renaissance in the Netherlands, just across the sea. He published pictures of some of these Dutch theaters, showing their general conformity with Shakespearean stage requirements and, though they were more ornate in appearance, to the layout given in the now-famous old sketch by Johannes de Witt. Of course, in 1916 the English were not listening very sympathetically to the Germans in cultural affairs, and so the idea had to wait out the eleven years until Nicoll's English publication of it in 1927. Some years after this it was followed up and developed further by the American George Kernodle, in a book called *From Art to Theatre*, with considerable effect.

Americans had been joining in the hunt for the missing Globe since early in the century, with all the resources of their formidable and enthusiastic scholarship; and it was an American book first published in 1942 that made the next most stimulating contribution toward the discovery of the lost playhouse.

The book in question is *The Globe Playhouse: Its Design and Equipment* by John Cranford Adams. It is possibly one of the most influential books on the subject ever written; certainly, rightly or wrongly, it has generated more creative enthusiasm than any other single volume I can think of. It has also generated an equal amount of dissent. Unfortunately, because it is the purpose of this paper only to trace the pathway leading to the playhouses and because time must be limited to that generality alone, there is no space to detail the arguments for and against the case that Adams has proposed but only to describe it briefly. Adams's reconstruction of the Globe is a composition made by bringing together all the action of all the plays in the whole range of Elizabethan and Jacobean drama and postulating from this a system of stage architecture and management that can accommodate them all. Thus, it achieves its effect by a creative synthesis of the plays it digests, and of most of the reconstructive theories that had preceded it. In its way, it is the last end product of the long line of scholarship descended from Malone. It presents the "inner-stage" theory in its ultimate and most comprehensive form, since it operates not one but several interior places of action within the tiring-house structure at the rear of the stage, each identified with a specific purpose. Beyond this there is only time to say that Adams's *Globe Playhouse* is a watershed book: it stands at a peak between all the old Elizabethan theater scholarship, which it gathers into itself, and a new school, which to a large extent has sprung out of it or been impelled by it.

This new school takes a quite opposite view: that the different decades of Elizabethan and Jacobean drama developed different dramatic attitudes and techniques, and that over the period the dozen or more different playhouses were differently built with differing individual characteristics at different times. A seminal book for this style of thinking actually preceded Adams's by four years: G. F. Reynolds's *The Staging of Elizabethan Plays at the Red Bull Playhouse*, of 1940.

### III

In all investigations so far there has been one controlling feature that has seemed unassailable and that has dominated most reconstructions: the dimensions given in the Fortune contract. Even where they are not used exactly—and since they are for a square theater they cannot apply exactly to a round one—they are nevertheless always glanced at for guidance. They are something firm, which we have. However, it is the trend of modern research (and I am sure a correct one) to remember that all the London theaters were in themselves individual, different from each other. Therefore, the dimensions of the Fortune should not be taken as applying necessarily to any other theater. They are a controlling point of reference and no more.

The time has now come to take up another point of reference that for almost all two hundred years of the search for the Globe playhouse has been virtually ignored; that is, the picture of the Globe itself as left to us by the reliable Bohemian topographical illustrator Wenceslas Hollar, dating from the middle of the seventeenth century, shortly before the old playhouse was pulled down. Certainly the fault in this neglect is partly Hollar's own: because in his engraving showing the Globe and its neighbor the Hope, he reversed their names (as is now well known). Now that that difficulty has been satisfactorily solved, we are left with two good pictures: Hollar's engraving of the exterior and the original drawing from which the engraving was done. The drawing first came to light in Sotheby's saleroom in 1931 but did not appear in the Shakespeare arena until 1949, when Professor Shapiro published it with his comments in *Shakespeare Survey 2*.

It has been pointed out by Professor Richard Hosley of the University of Arizona that the many Elizabethan playhouses, all different in one way or another, were also very different in their relative sizes. Some were larger than others. The Globe was a large one. So was the Swan. Of both those theaters there is contemporary reference to their having had a capacity for an audience of three thousand people. Students of the subjects have been apt to doubt such reports. Hosley, on the other hand, points out that they are consistent with the large playhouse frame Hollar shows us. It must also be remembered that Hollar shows not the first Globe in 1599, which burned down, but the second, which was built to replace it. The rebuilding, however, was on the same foundations that supported the first Globe; and the first Globe was built with the same framing timbers, in the same positions, with which the first playhouse of all, the Theatre, was built. Therefore the Theatre, the first Globe, and the second Globe were all of the same basic size.

In 1979 at Wayne State University a symposium was convened to study the whole idea of taking the second Globe as a model for an actual rebuilding of it by that university on the waterfront in the city of Detroit. Richard Hosley was a member of the symposium, where he put his case for the large Globe. He was supported by Professor John Orrell of the University of Alberta, arguing from a thesis that Hollar, a most skilful draftsman in any circumstances, was in this case aided by the use of an optical device equivalent to an early form of *camera obscura*. From this Orrell argued that the drawing could be analyzed so as to extrapolate the actual dimensions of the building which, he estimated in agreement with Hosley, must have had an external diameter of about 100 feet.

The study continues. In due course it is hoped that the great timber frame of the Globe, containing its characteristic stage and stage devices, will be reerected on the banks of the Detroit River. Another scheme, now very prominent, proposes to rebuild it where it certainly should be—on the banks of the Thames in London. Within these reconstructions the details of Shakespeare's stagecraft will at last be able to be analyzed in circumstances similar to those of their original presentation. We will then be able to claim that the long-lost features of the Elizabethan and Jacobean playhouses, or at any rate of this one, the Globe, have been rediscovered at last.

# Shakespeare's Tragic Homeopathy

## Maurice Hunt

$S$ *imilia similibus curantur.* The Classical homeopathic idea that "likes are cured by likes"—that diseases are purged by doses of compounds resembling the diseases themselves—gained new life during the sixteenth century in the writings of Paracelsus. Believing that "each sphere of the universe is in sympathy with all other parts and 'that nothing is in heaven or earth that is not in men,' " Paracelsus asserted that each feature of the human body is "signed" in the zodiac, which indicates the metal, stone, or herb in sympathy with a disease.[1] For example, in the words of one of Paracelsus's interpreters, "Blood is 'signed' by Mars. So also is a limb of the universe—iron. Iron is the metal of Mars. There is an affinity of blood and iron. Hence prescribe iron."[2] In the case of a supposed disease of the blood, one nail thus drives out another.

The doctrine of homeopathy attracted not only Renaissance physicians but prominent aestheticians and imaginative writers as well. For example, the august Elizabethan George Puttenham in *The Arte of English Poesie* (1589) accounts thus for the emotional effect of a literary complaint:

> Therefore of death and burials, and of th' adversities by warres, and of true love lost or ill bestowed, are th' onely sorrows that the noble Poets sought by their arte to remove or appease, not with any medicament of a contrary temper, as the Galenistes use to cure *(contraria contrariis)* but as the Paracelsians, who cure *(similia similibus)* making one dolour to expell another, and in this case, one short sorrowing the remedie of a long and grievous sorrow.[3]

By contradicting the Galenic teaching that *contraria contrariis curantur*, Paracelsus created for Europe not only a medical but also a philosophical conflict, one that certainly reached Shakespeare. In a recent essay, Richard K. Stensgaard has revealed the Galenico-Paracelsian controversy's presence in *All's Well That Ends Well*, in addition to Shakespeare's preference for homeopathy both in Helena's language and in her cure of the king's fistula.[4] Moreover, by describing homeopathy's importance

for Shakespeare's dramatic method in *Measure for Measure*, Robert
Grudin has shown that the playwright's interest in the subject is not
limited to a single play.[5] In fact, homeopathy to some degree informs the
dramaturgy of such different plays as *The Taming of the Shrew, As You Like
It, Cymbeline,* and *The Winter's Tale.*[6]

With the exception of the inaccurately classified *Cymbeline,* the drama
previously cited appears in the section of the First Folio reserved for
comedies. Critics have yet to demonstrate that homeopathy plays more
than an incidental part in Shakespearean tragedy, especially as that
dramatic genre creates distinct emotional effects. It is true that Shakespeare occasionally employed homeopathy in his tragedies as a means
for further defining character. When Benvolio, for example, advises
Romeo of a remedy for the misery of love, he states:

> Tut, man, one fire burns out another's burning,
> One pain is less'ned by another's anguish;
> Turn giddy, and be holp by backward turning;
> One desperate grief cures with another's languish:
> Take thou some new infection to thy eye,
> And the rank poison of the old will die.[7]
>
> (*Romeo and Juliet,* 1.2.45–50)

The utterance—"Take thou some new infection to thy eye"—has an
ironic ring in *Romeo and Juliet,* ironic not only in Benvolio's skeptical
attitude toward romantic love but ironic also in Romeo's self-destruction,
which indirectly results from Juliet's displacing a prior love (Rosalind) in
Romeo's eye—from, that is, a like purportedly curing a like. Interpreting
the quotation from this early tragedy suggests that casual homeopathy
can be ruinous rather than curative. Still, Benvolio's homeopathy mainly
defines his nonromantic character; the dynamism of displacement never
acquires the status of a fatal force driving Romeo to his doom. His
tragedy results mainly from fatal accidents, such as Capulet's man select-
ing Romeo to read the invitations to his festivities, combined with
character flaws, such as Romeo's penchant for defining love through
death. Among these tragic elements, homeopathy holds a minor place.

For Shakespeare's contemporaries, the principle of homeopathy per-
tained mainly to tragic catharsis. During the sixteenth century, Italian
neoclassicists, especially Castelvetro and Minturno, applied Paracelsian
homeopathy to their understanding of Aristotelian poetics. In his *Arte
Poetica* (1564), Minturno claimed that "as a physician eradicates, by
means of poisonous medicine, the perfervid poison of disease which
affects the body, so tragedy purges the mind of its impetuous perturbations by force of these emotions beautifully expressed in verse."[8] The
Preface to *Samson Agonistes* reveals how thoroughly Milton absorbed the

homeopathic doctrine. "Tragedy, as it is anciently composed," Milton asserts,

> hath been ever the gravest, moralest, and most profitable of all other Poems: therefore said by *Aristotle* to be of power by raising pity and fear, or terror, to purge the mind of these and such like passions, that is to temper and reduce them to just measure with a kind of delight, stirr'd up by reading or seeing those passions well imitated. Nor is Nature wanting in her own effects to make good this assertion: for so in Physic things of melancholic hue and quality are us'd against melancholy, sour against sour, salt to remove salt humors.[9]

Nevertheless, it is a far cry from *Samson Agonistes* to a play like *King Lear* or *Coriolanus*. Critics have generally agreed that Shakespearean tragedy relies more upon the techniques of native medieval drama and the conventions of popular plays of the 1570s and 1580s than upon the strict neoclassicism of a Jonson or a Milton.[10] Consequently, Roy Battenhouse and Virgil Whitaker both argue that the catharsis of Shakespearean tragedy cannot be understood in the homeopathic terms established by neoclassical critics and writers.[11] Still, any commentator, regardless of his or her critical persuasion, who attempts to define Shakespearean tragedy's emotional effects confronts a basic interpretative obstacle. Catharsis is designed for the theatrical audience, whose members stand outside the realm of the written text; accounts of contemporary audiences' reactions to Shakespeare's tragedies are so virtually nonexistent that we are left without the obvious key for identifying the specific nature of any emotional purging at his plays' ends.

Moreover, with one exception, J. V. Cunningham's catalogue of the emotional reactions of Shakespeare's characters to the catastrophes enacted before them is not sufficiently detailed to allow comfortable generalizations about the playwright's notion of tragic catharsis.[12] Horatio, for example, implies simply that he has been struck by woe and wonder (5.2.363). This one exception in Cunningham's listing involves the character of Edgar. Cunningham remarks that

> Edgar is the ideal spectator. He has attained the moral effect of that excitation of feeling; he has been "made tame" by participating in "fortune's blows," which are the material of tragedy; he has penetrated into that experience consciously and has attained the habit of, the capacity for exercising, the virtue of pity.[13]

Confronted on the heath by the spectacle of ruined Lear, Edgar (disguised as Tom O'Bedlam) provides a clear account of the cathartic working of Shakespearean tragedy:

When we our betters see bearing our woes,
We scarcely think our miseries our foes.
Who alone suffers, suffers most i' th' mind,
Leaving free things and happy shows behind,
But then the mind much sufferance doth o'erskip,
When grief hath mates, and bearing fellowship.
How light and portable my pain seems now,
When that which makes me bend makes the King bow:
He childed as I fathered!

(3.6.102–10)

Commentators on this speech sometimes remark that Edgar seems emotionally detached from Lear's suffering; they claim that his moralizing reflects a certain aloof, intellectual attitude toward the king's disaster. Yet such a judgment must ignore Edgar's general reaction to the spectacle of human wretchedness. Late in act 4, Edgar tells Gloucester that he is

A most poor man, made tame to fortune's blows,
Who, by the art of known and feeling sorrows,
Am pregnant to good pity.

(4.6.221–23)

Edgar's empathy, in fact, has been apparent throughout the play. Concerning Lear on the heath, Edgar exclaims, "My tears begin to take his part so much, / They mar my counterfeiting" (3.6.60–61). As witness to Lear's and Gloucester's pathetic dialogue on lechery and the nature of authority, he confesses, "I would not take this from report; it is, / And my heart breaks at it" (4.6.141–42). In light of this empathetic consistency of character, the audience has every reason to believe that Edgar's emotions are fully involved in the spectacle of the bowed Lear.

In the primary speech quoted at length above, Edgar implies that his grief and Lear's are potentially equal in intensity since they have a common cause—the absolute loss of a relative's love and the disillusionment attending it ("He childed as I fathered"). Extreme grief, however, only bends Edgar while it bows the king himself. In comparison to the tragic Lear, Edgar discovers that he bears his sorrow in a royal fashion. The line "How light and portable my pain seems now" indicates that the image of tragedy has worked an emotional catharsis within Edgar, a purgation homeopathic in nature. Quite simply, one worse—to adopt the play's language—for the most part has driven out another, lesser evil. More precisely, the tragic image of Lear (the man and the incidents of the play itself) has displaced Edgar's idea of his own calamity, tempering and reducing in the process the latter character's passions "to a just measure." In this respect, Shakespeare's view of homeopathic catharsis anticipates Milton's. Potentially self-destructive passions have not been completely purged from Edgar; rather, homeopathic catharsis has re- fined fear and pity (especially self-pity), making them tolerable and nonlethal. In fact, the intellectual clarity of Edgar's soliloquy testifies to the refining effect of one version of homeopathic catharsis—the notion of dross in an oven sublimated to gold or silver by fire (the heat of the tragic experience).

What place does Edgar's homeopathic catharsis have within the play as a whole? Shakespeare clearly qualifies the homeopathic displacement of one worse by a greater evil when Edgar, convinced (as homeless Tom O'Bedlam) that he has experienced the worst, is suddenly confronted by the brutal image of his blinded father:

> O gods! Who is't can say, "I am at the worst"?
> I am worse that e'er I was . . . . . . .
> And worse I may be yet: the worst is not
> So long as we can say, "This is the worst."
>
> (4.1.25 28)

Rather than constituting a refining catharsis, the effect of one worse following another here resembles a sledgehammer's numbing blow. Clearly, Edgar's painful reeducation in act 4 prepares us for the end of the play. Struck by the horrific vision of dead Cordelia and mad Lear, the audience realizes that Edgar's mid-play catharsis is the exception rather than the rule in *King Lear.* In act 5, scene 3, the terror of learning of Regan's and Goneril's deaths does not displace the previous passion over hearing Gloucester's death reported; rather, it increases the general effect of terror. Likewise, the vision of strangled Cordelia and the mad, despairing Lear provokes a greater horror, one that somehow gathers the previous emotions of terror within itself. The composite passion repre- sents an unbearable pain of several parts. At no point in the play's catastrophe is the refined emotion resulting from homeopathic catharsis evident. In summary, Shakespeare apparently introduced homeopathic catharsis into act 3 of *King Lear* so that the savage emotional effect of the play's ending would be intensified even more by the presence of an earlier foil.

Does the primary catastrophe of Shakespearean tragedy ever reveal homeopathic catharsis? While Shakespeare's use of homeopathy in *King Lear* generally resembles Milton's prescription in the Preface to *Samson Agonistes,* his staging of the doctrine during the catastrophe of *Coriolanus* more nearly fulfills Minturno's definition. For Minturno, homeopathic catharsis in dramatic tragedy is a complete purgation of feeling—the cleansing of "the mind of its impetuous perturbations." A definite in- stance of this complete purgation occurs in *Coriolanus* when the antag-

onist Aufidius's suddenly expressed rage attending his final accusation
and killing of Coriolanus drives out his previous wrathful jealousy
concerning the Roman's military prowess. Challenged by Aufidius's
calculated phrase "boy of tears," Coriolanus predictably and impru-
dently rages, again setting his former enemies' hearts against him. "O
that I had him," Coriolanus angrily exclaims, "With six Aufidiuses, or
more, his tribe, / To use my lawful sword!" (5.6.127–29). The outburst
ignites Aufidius's rage; "Insolent villain!" the Volscian replies. It is this
envious wrath that the angry act of killing Coriolanus specifically drives
from Aufidius's heart. In the final speech of this late tragedy, Aufidius
states, "My rage is gone, / And I am struck with sorrow":

> Take him up.
> Help three a' th' chiefest soldiers; I'll be one.
> Beat thou the drum, that it speak mournfully;
> Trail your steel pikes. Though in this city he
> Hath widowed and unchilded many a one,
> Which to this hour bewail the injury,
> Yet he shall have a noble memory.
>
> (5.6.146–53)

As regards Aufidius's great wrath, one nail has driven out another spike,
leaving his mind dispossessed before an empathetic sorrow suitable to
the tragic fact can fill his purged consciousness.

The homeopathy apparent in the catastrophe of *Coriolanus* is first
articulated as a principle in act 4, scene 7, of the play. There, assessing
Coriolanus's flawed character, Aufidius exclaims:

> And power, unto itself most commendable,
> Hath not a tomb so evident as a chair
> T'extol what it hath done.
> One fire drives out one fire; one nail, one nail;
> Rights by rights falter, strengths by strengths do fail.
> Come, let's away. When, Caius, Rome is thine,
> Thou art poor'st of all; then shortly art thou mine.[14]
>
> (4.7.51–57)

Invoking homeopathic proverbs concerning fire and nails,[15] Aufidius
implies that one power dislocates another, even as one man of authority
displaces a previous chairholder, whose empty seat testifies both to his
personal loss and to the inevitably transitory nature of force in general.
In the context of his criticism of Coriolanus's character, Aufidius's homeopathic idea provides a way of understanding the tragic destruction
of Coriolanus's being.

For example, Aufidius has suggested earlier in the same scene that Coriolanus's inability to moderate his austerity, a strength on the battlefield, may be the root of his failure as citizen during peacetime:

> First he was
> A noble servant to them, but he could not
> Carry his honors even. Whether 'twas pride,
> Which out of daily fortune ever taints
> The happy man; whether defect of judgment,
> To fail in the disposing of those chances
> Which he was lord of; or whether nature,
> Not to be other than one thing, not moving
> From th' casque to th' cushion, but commanding peace
> Even with the same austerity and garb
> As he controll'd the war; but one of these
> (As he hath pieces of them all, not all,
> For I dare so far free him) made him fear'd,
> So hated, and so banish'd. . . .
>
> (4.7.35–48)

Aufidius's assessment of Coriolanus's flaws reads like an authoritative summary. When the context for evaluation shifts from the battlefield (the "casque") to the senate house (the "cushion"), Coriolanus's uncompromising fierceness (his "austerity") drives out the honor and respect that the same ferocity won in war. In other words, the violent energy that wreaked havoc on the battlefield eventually issues as savage words, language that destroys Coriolanus's heroic reputation when the citizens' contempt upon hearing them displaces their adoration of him. Clearly, Coriolanus's demise depends primarily upon a character flaw rendered intelligible by the homeopathic principle informing the play's catharsis. Furthermore, Coriolanus, regarded allegorically, is often depicted in the play as a poison in the body politic of Rome (e.g., 3.1.80–88); his expulsion from one aperture of that body—the city gates—occurs homeopathically when the choler of Brutus and Sicinius—to say nothing of the citizens' wrath—is applied to Coriolanus, condensing his toxic choler and operating to cast him out in the process.

In conclusion, Shakespeare's use of homeopathy in dramatic tragedy is not negligible. An analysis of certain speeches in *King Lear* and *Coriolanus* suggests that Shakespeare on occasion employed versions of homeopathic catharsis associated with Minturno and Milton. That Shakespeare should have resorted to homeopathy is not surprising in light of his close contact with a neoclassicist such as Ben Jonson. Most certainly, the statement that Shakespeare never meaningfully employs homeopathy in his tragedies would be mistaken.

## Notes

1. Henry M. Pachter, *Paracelsus: Magic into Science* (New York: Henry Schuman, 1951), 85–86. For another explanation of Paracelsian homeopathy, see Robert Grudin, *Mighty Opposites: Shakespeare and Renaissance Contrariety* (Berkeley: University of California Press, 1979), 26–27.

2. Pachter, *Paracelsus*, 86–87.

3. Quoted by Grudin, *Mighty Opposites*, 28–29.

4. *"All's Well That Ends Well* and the Galenico-Paracelsian Controversy," *Renaissance Quarterly* 25 (1972): 173–88.

5. Grudin, *Mighty Opposites*, 88–93, 104–5.

6. See Maurice Hunt, "Homeopathy in Shakespearean Comedy and Romance," forthcoming in *Ball State University Forum*.

7. All quotations from Shakespeare's plays are taken from *The Riverside Shakespeare*, ed. G. Blakemore Evans (Boston: Houghton Mifflin, 1974).

8. Quoted by Joel E. Spingarn in *A History of Literary Criticism in the Renaissance* (1899; reprint, New York: Harcourt, Brace and World, 1963), 50. Also see Bernard Weinberg, *A History of Literary Criticism in the Italian Renaissance* (Chicago: University of Chicago Press, 1961), 2:739–40. For the origins of Minturno's homeopathy, see Baxter Hathaway, *The Age of Criticism: The Late Renaissance in Italy* (Ithaca: Cornell University Press, 1962), 210–11, 253–54.

9. Quoted from *John Milton: Complete Poems and Major Prose*, ed. Merritt Y. Hughes (New York: Odyssey Press, 1957), 549. For Miltonic homeopathy, see Georgia Christopher, "Homeopathic Physic and Natural Renovation in *Samson Agonistes,"* *ELH*, 37 (1970): 361–73.

10. See, for example, Willard Farnham, *The Medieval Heritage of Elizabethan Tragedy* (Oxford: Basil Blackwell, 1936), 340–452 passim; and S. L. Bethell, *Shakespeare and the Popular Dramatic Tradition* (Durham, N.C.: Duke University Press, 1944).

11. *Shakespearean Tragedy: Its Art and Its Christian Premises* (Bloomington: Indiana University Press, 1969), 183–203; *The Mirror up to Nature: The Technique of Shakespeare's Tragedies* (San Marino, Calif.: Huntington Library, 1965), 64.

12. The catalogue appears in *Woe or Wonder: The Emotional Effect of Shakespearean Tragedy* (1951; reprint, Denver: Alan Swallow, 1960). Cunningham suggests that the pity, fear, and wonder raised in spectators of tragic events remain within them, a burden, as the play ends; he thus implies that emotional purgation is not a feature of Shakespearean tragedy.

13. Cunningham, *Woe or Wonder*, 20.

14. The homeopathic idea of one fire driving out another blaze is explored in Shakespearean history by Roy Battenhouse, "King John and Henry VIII," *Shakespeare and English History: Interdisciplinary Perspectives*, ed. Ronald G. Shafer (Indiana: Indiana University of Pennsylvania Press, 1976), 126–28.

15. For the homeopathic proverb, see Morris Tilley, *A Dictionary of The Proverbs in England in the Sixteenth and Seventeenth Centuries* (Ann Arbor: University of Michigan Press, 1950), 147, 215–16, 275, 398–99, 489, 548, 715.

# Shakespeare's Dramaturgical Foresight in *King Lear*

## Norman A. Brittin

**D**ramaturgy is the art with which playwrights use the means at their disposal: language, a group of actors, and, usually, a theater. The scenes a playwright creates are, we might say, imitations of selected pictures from the ceaseless succession of actions that constitute life's flowing continuum, its unreeling movie. As playwrights make economical and efficient use of human resources, controlling the entrances, groupings, and exits of characters, they more or less successfully, according to their dramaturgic expertness, fabricate works of dramatic art.

For Shakespeare and his contemporaries, as we are well aware, this fabrication generally meant dealing with characters of narratives already in existence—that is, translating the events of historical or fictional narrative into effective drama. To develop a narrative, in verse or prose, is one thing; to transmute it into a vehicle for actors trained in traditions of theater is, of course, another. Studying how Shakespeare effects such transformations leads one to a better understanding of the craftsmanship of the great dramatic poet whose art Ben Jonson praised: "For though the poet's matter nature be, / His art doth give the fashion." In this essay I discuss some of Shakespeare's dramaturgical decisions and procedures in *King Lear*.

We know that the source of the Gloucester subplot in Shakespeare's *King Lear* is the story of the blind Paphlagonian prince and his two sons in Sidney's *Arcadia*. In fact, as long ago as 1948 Fitzroy Pyle demonstrated links between the main plot also and the *Arcadia* material.[1] To go one step further, I believe it is likely that the inception of Shakespeare's plan for his play—for his unique dramatic version of the *Leir-Arcadia* sources—lay in Edmund's character and motives as set forth by Sidney. Leonatus, the good son of the blind Paphlagonian prince, explains that

> this old man . . . was . . ., by the *hard-hearted ungratefulness* of a sonne of his, deprived, not onely of his kingdome . . . but of his sight. . . . Whereby, and by other his *unnatural dealings,* he hath bin driven to

such griefes, as even now he would have had me to have led him to the toppe of this rocke, thence to cast himself headlong to death. . . .[2]

The blind old father then explains:

> . . . I was caried by a bastarde sonne of mine (if at least I be bounde to beleeve the words of that base woman my concubine, his mother) first to mislike, then to hate, lastly to destroy, to doo my best to destroy, this sonne . . . undeserving destruction. What waies he used to bring me to it, if I should tell you, I should tediously trouble you with as much *poysonous hypocrisie, desperate fraude, smoothe malice, hidden ambition,* and *smiling envie,* as in any living person could be harbored.[3]

Here we have delineated not only the qualities of a wicked son but the comprehensive motive of ambition and the theme of ingratitude paralleling the same theme in the story of Leir.

This statement provides the blueprint, so to speak, for a character; in comparison with a stage-character that seems to have real life, it is a thin, shadowy figure—or, rather, a mere prefiguring of Edmund. To develop so thin a source figure entails definite decisions that will affect the dramaturgy throughout the play. (For parallels we might think of how Shakespeare had already developed Polonius from his shadowy prototype in Saxo and Belleforest, and Iago from Giraldi Cinthio's "Ensign of handsome presence but the most scoundrelly nature in the world."[4]) Shakespeare decided to open his tragedy with an Edmund "so proper" as to elicit a compliment from Kent; to have Edmund reveal his hypocrisy in soliloquy at the beginning of the second scene and then exemplify his deception of a "credulous father and a brother noble" in the rest of the scene; and further to dramatize his "desperate fraude" and "smoothe malice" in 2.1, where the favor shown him by Cornwall begins to fan the fire of his "hidden ambition."

Much the same procedure takes place regarding other characters. Credulous Gloucester is of course conceived as a parallel to Lear in several ways. He is a grosser man, most suitably contrasted to the kingly Lear through his physical sufferings imposed on him from outside.[5] Gloucester's role in the play's first three acts is largely shaped by his relation to Lear. But Gloucester is also a foil to the Earl of Kent, and Shakespeare's handling of the two earls who remain loyal to Lear reveals much about his dramaturgical skill.

One of Shakespeare's problems in managing this vast double-plot tragedy is to keep from getting over-involved in the source material, or, we might say, to avoid a sticky entrapment in dramatically unprofitable details. Thus, he must not only knit together the Lear and Gloucester stories but also keep the lines of each one clear. So if Kent is to function as the bold, blunt, tactless spirit who is punished for his rude, honest behavior, Shakespeare must keep Gloucester free from involvement with Kent, keep Gloucester clear of the situation that entraps Kent and leads to his banishment. To this end, Shakespeare composes Lear's first speech, "Attend the lords of France and Burgundy, Gloucester" (1.1.36), eight words beautifully efficient in the economy of Shakespeare's dramatic craft, which smoothly remove Gloucester from the scene. Thus, while the elder daughters flatter their father and Cordelia resolves to be painfully truthful, while the old king explodes into wrath and disinherits his youngest, while Kent speaks up for her and is banished by the aged tyrant, Gloucester is offstage. If he had not been removed, what should have been done with him? What part could be written for him? Should he remain silent when Kent spoke out? Then the audience would be obliged to draw invidious comparisons. If he took sides with Kent and Cordelia, he too would have to be banished. Shakespeare foresaw these problems, and by a stroke so light it is almost unnoticeable,[6] he eliminated them. When Gloucester reenters at line 190—"Here's France and Burgundy, my noble lord"—the inciting action has taken place. Gloucester has not been obliged to witness it or to display any responses to it. Shakespeare has not been obliged to grapple with extra complications. He has cleverly avoided anything that would embarrass the clarity of the action.

Having Lear go mad is one of Shakespeare's greatest changes in the Lear story—and one of his greatest theatrical achievements. In terms of dramaturgy, Shakespeare had to translate into scenes of increasingly violent confrontation the few lines of his sources that tell how Lear's daughters proposed to reduce his retinue. According to Geoffrey of Monmouth, whose *History of the Kings of Britain* is a possible source, Lear's two sons-in-law in Britain rose up against him and deprived him of power. The Duke of Albania, however, allowed him "sixty Soldiers, who were to be kept for State"; two years later Gonorilla ordered the number reduced to thirty.[7] In Holinshed's Chronicles the two Dukes took over the power and laid down the condition that Lear was "to live after a rate assigned to him for the maintenance of his estate, which in process of time was diminished. . . ."[8] The poetical account of the Lear story by John Higgins in *The Mirror for Magistrates* (1574) says they agreed that Lear "threescore knightes & squires / Should alwayes have . . ."; but later Gonerell and her husband took away "halfe his garde."[9] Shakespeare's Lear, however, tells his daughters that he will keep "an hundred knights" (1.1.135), and Goneril protests, "Here do you keep a hundred knights and squires" (1.4.262). Why, we may wonder, is the figure one hundred rather than sixty?

It seems likely that O.B. Hardison, Jr., has discovered why the number is one hundred. The reason is Shakespeare's use of mythic Ixion, once king of Thessaly, who was punished for sin by being "bound on a wheel and rolled eternally through hell. Lear explicitly compares his experience with that of Ixion when he exclaims, 'I am bound / Upon a wheel of fire, that mine own tears / Do scald like molten lead' (4.7.46–48)."[10] Ixion tried to seduce Hera (Juno), who formed a cloud in her own shape on which Ixion begot centaurs. Ixion had one hundred retainers, the original centaurs, who were "violent, unruly, and lustful."[11] Centaurs are interpreted as representing the animal part of man's nature. Thus, Shakespeare has Lear say of women that "Down from the waist they are centaurs" (4.6.126). It seems probable, too, that the centaurs in the Ixion myth are the basis of Goneril's complaint that Lear's knights are unruly and deboshed.

But as Hardison tells us, "The earliest and most persistent interpretation of the Ixion myth is that it symbolizes the desire for pomp (*dignitas*) without responsibilities."[12] After his abdication from power Lear insists upon retaining his one hundred knights and upon the ceremonial treatment—"all th'addition" (1.1.136)—belonging to a king. Geoffrey of Monmouth says that the Duke of Albania allowed Lear sixty soldiers *"ne secum inglorius maneret"*—so that he would not remain without glory—and I suspect that this idea of keeping up his glory or pomp lies behind Lear's "O, reason not the need" speech at 2.4.267, which is his climactic outburst presaging the madness he begins to fear—madness stemming from the indignities he suffers at the hands of his daughters. Holinshed says that "scarslie they would allow him one servant to wait upon him" (Bullough, 7, 318), and Shakespeare carries the affront to his royal dignity even further with Regan's "What need one?" (2.4.266). Thinking ahead about Lear's madness in acts 3 and 4, Shakespeare develops Lear's increasing perturbation in these scenes of confrontation in order to make the later scenes of madness seem plausible and to give them body.

For the interactions of his characters Shakespeare uses two chief points of assembly in *King Lear*: Gloucester's castle and Dover. We first hear of Dover in 3.1, when Kent sends a gentleman there to report to Cordelia on how Lear has been treated. Probably Shakespeare chose Dover because it is so near to France and thus a natural port for the landing of the invading French power. Gloucester, who knows of the French plans, sends Lear to Dover for the king's protection, and other Britons are obliged to go there to repel the invasion. Shakespeare has Gloucester elect to go to the Dover cliffs in order to commit suicide there—though Bradley wondered "why in the world should Gloucester . . . wander painfully all the way to Dover simply to destroy himself?"[13] The answer, of course, is so that the two old men, Gloucester and his king, can be brought together in 4.6, and so that Edgar can participate in that part of the action that leads to Edmund's destruction. For the working out of the tragic denouement, Edmund must defeat the French and capture Lear and Cordelia. But in this final part of the action, what to do with the King of France becomes an important matter.

Kenneth Muir rightly says that Shakespeare's reconciliation scene between Lear and Cordelia is greatly superior to the reconciliation scene in *The True Chronicle History of King Leir* because "the earlier dramatist was hampered by the presence of the King of France,"[14] whom Shakespeare removed. Bullough, after mentioning Bradley's enumeration of what he considered improbabilities in the tragedy, remarks: "Similarly, how casually the Fool and Cordelia's husband are dismissed when no longer wanted!"[15] The reconciliation scene of the *Chronicle History* took place in France. The situation is different when the French have come to Britain. There is, to be sure, the touchy point of handling a foreign invasion. Greg thought Cordelia had persuaded her husband not to try to gain territory in Britain;[16] but perhaps Britishers like Greg and Muir are overconscious of this matter. Though he uses blunt or transparent means, Shakespeare does take pains to give a reason for the return of France to his own land: "Something he left imperfect in the state, which since his coming forth is thought of; . . . his personal return was most requir'd and necessary" (4.3.4–6). Shakespeare has Kent say this to obviate difficulties foreseen by the dramatist should the king remain.

There are excellent dramatic reasons for removing France. The consideration of greatest importance for Shakespeare is to focus attention on Cordelia and Lear *after the battle*. Having France leave Britain of course makes more plausible the British victory over the French. But the looming dramaturgical question is this: If the king of France does not leave, what is to be done with him? He might be killed in battle; but, if so, how would his death affect Cordelia's feelings? Her grief over the death of her loving husband could not be ignored; thus, her concern for her father could not receive full emphasis, and the dramatic effect of the isolation of father and daughter would be weakened. But if the French king survived the battle, he would be a British prisoner; then his presence could not be ignored, and it would be even more of a distraction from audience concentration on Cordelia. With the King of France alive, even if the play were constructed as it now is, with Cordelia and Lear dying as they do, the disposition of France would still be a problem at the end. Shakespeare foresaw these potential difficulties and was shrewd in his dramaturgy, eliminating France and not having to build a part for him that would surely have been an interference with his tragedy's main thrust and effect.

Shakespeare's handling of Edmund also shows careful dramaturgical planning. By 3.5, Edmund has displaced his father from title and power, and the Duke of Cornwall awards him the title of Gloucester. But in 3.7 Shakespeare has Cornwall send Edmund away to accompany Goneril home to her husband, the Duke of Albany, and urge him to resist the invading French. Cornwall tells Edmund: "The revenges we are bound to take upon your traitorous father are not fit for your beholding" (3.7.7–9). The *exit* of Edmund shortly thereafter has a twofold significance: (1) While Edmund and Goneril are traveling together, she falls in love with him (or at least comes to prefer his vigorous amorality to the moral steadfastness of her virtuous lord), and this illicit passion leads to rivalry over Edmund between her and her widowed sister Regan; (2) The absence of Edmund from his father's dreadful ordeal also makes it possible for Shakespeare to have Edmund, mortally wounded, arrive at a difficult repentance—as he says, "Despite of mine own nature"—and try to reprieve Lear and Cordelia from execution after he hears how his half-brother Edgar helped their father and held him in his arms as the old man died. If Edmund had beheld without protest the blinding of his father, we could not accept his repentance and his attempt to right matters toward the end. And if he *had* protested—then of course everything would have had to be different. Shakespeare's dramaturgy here shows his foresight in controlling his characterizations as well as in complicating his plot.

## Notes

1. "Twelfth Night, King Lear, and Arcadia," Modern Language Review 43 (1948): 452–55; cf. also Hardin Craig, ed., The Complete Works of Shakespeare (Chicago, 1951), 980–81.
2. Geoffrey Bullough, Narrative and Dramatic Sources of Shakespeare (New York, 1975), 7, 403 (my emphasis).
3. Bullough, 404 (my emphasis).
4. Ibid., 243.
5. Richard Levin, The Multiple Plot in English Renaissance Drama (Chicago, 1971), 12–13, 19.
6. Students quickly conclude from Gloucester's allusion to Edmund's mother in the opening lines of the play—"good sport at his making"—that Gloucester is a man of small moral stature, and sometimes they blame him for not standing up, as Kent does, to defy the old king in Cordelia's favor. They have to be reminded of Gloucester's *exit* at 1.1.36.
7. Bulllough, 313.
8. Ibid., 318.
9. Ibid., 326–27.
10. "Myth and History in King Lear," Shakespeare Quarterly 26 (1975): 236.
11. Hardison, 237.
12. Hardison, 232.
13. A. C. Bradley, Shakespearean Tragedy (London, 1952), 257.
14. Kenneth Muir, Shakespeare's Sources: Comedies and Tragedies (London, 1957), 163.
15. Bullough, 283n.
16. Kenneth Muir, ed., King Lear, The Arden Shakespeare (Cambridge, Mass., 1959), 4.3.3–4n.

# *Macbeth* and Its Audience

## Michael J. Collins

As Stephen Booth has pointed out, "with the possible exception of *King Lear*, *Macbeth* is more often discussed *as* tragedy than the other tragedies of Shakespeare are."[1] While such discussions often seem attempts to evade or reconcile unsettling responses to the play, they nonetheless help to illuminate the relationship between text and performance by suggesting how the play on the stage becomes, in the words of Ronald Hayman, a "series of theatrical impacts"[2] that evoke, shape, and modify the response of the audience to the action it witnesses. Although by the end of act 4 Macbeth is responsible for six murders on the stage and, as Macduff tells Malcolm, countless others throughout Scotland, the play, for many critics, remains a tragedy, for as they see it Macbeth evokes and retains an audience's sympathy until the end. No matter what else it may tell about the play itself, the criticism of *Macbeth* makes one thing clear: if audiences (or critics) can continue to feel sympathy for Macbeth even after the gruesome murder of Macduff's son on the stage, then knowing what happens in a play does not tell us very much about the impact it may have in production or the responses it may evoke in an audience. What happens on the stage is far less important than how and when it happens, than the way it is presented to us.

In a now-classic essay, "Shakespeare's Tragic Villain," Wayne Booth, by tracing the play's impact on an audience, attempts to explain how Shakespeare maintains Macbeth "as a tragic hero with full stature commanding our sympathy to the end."[3] As Booth sees it, Shakespeare first convinces us, at the beginning of the play, that Macbeth "is an admirable man, a man who matters" (181). Then, in the structure of the play, he seems to be "following a rule that Aristotle never dreamed of . . .: by your choice of what to represent from the materials provided in your story, insure that each step in your protagonist's degeneration will be counteracted by mounting pity" (187). As Booth describes the play, after Duncan's murder "we have only Macbeth's conscience-stricken lament" (185). After Banquo's death, Macbeth suffers "the torments of the banquet scene" (186). After Macduff weeps for his wife and children, we see

Lady Macbeth's sleepwalking. Finally, Macbeth engages our sympathy with his "poetic gift. . . . We naturally tend to feel with the character who speaks the best poetry of the play, no matter what his deeds" (187).

In discussing Macbeth as a tragic hero, Booth recognizes and implicitly seeks to reconcile the conflicting responses the play can evoke in its audiences. While they inevitably understand that Macbeth is evil, they may also feel sympathy for him and see him, as Aristotle would say, a man like themselves, frail and suffering. As Booth describes it, once the audience enters the theater and submits itself to a performance, it is drawn irresistibly to the side of evil and responds to the play in ways it would hope to resist in the world outside. For Booth, the series of impacts the play makes upon its audiences keeps them, for all his evil, sympathetic to Macbeth and leads them at the end to "feel great pity that a man with so much potentiality for greatness should have fallen so low and should be so thoroughly misjudged" by Malcolm and Macduff (190).

The implications of Booth's essay are, from one point of view, frightening, for they suggest, particularly in its observations on the impact of Macbeth's poetic gifts, how our responses to things—in or out of the theater—can be shaped and managed by rhetoric and performance. In *Macbeth*, although audiences and critics encounter six murders and witness a country destroyed by a cruel and violent regime, they do not always, with Dr. Johnson, rejoice at Macbeth's fall, for the impacts of the play evoke sympathy for Macbeth and obscure the horror of the evil he has done.[4]

Not everyone, of course, finds the play a tragedy. Kenneth Muir calls it, at one point, "the greatest of morality plays,"[5] and (to take a familiar example) in an essay that follows Booth's in a collection of criticism, L. C. Knights sees it as "a statement of evil."[6] While his contention that "*Macbeth* has greater affinity with *The Waste Land* than with *A Doll's House*" is mistaken, Knights's analysis of *Macbeth*'s themes and images leads him to conclude that "for the last hundred years or so the critics have not only sentimentalized Macbeth—ignoring the completeness with which Shakespeare shows his final identification with evil—but  they have slurred the passages in which positive good is presented by means of religious symbols" (201).

Knights's reading of the play as a poem, for all its illuminating attention to the text, still leaves a director who finds it persuasive to discover ways to evoke in performance not sympathy for Macbeth but horror at his evil. Goodness in the play offers very little help: embodied as it is in the scenes with Malcolm, Macduff, and their allies, it is no match for Macbeth's theatricality and too often remains dull, undramatic, and therefore unable in production to evoke much sympathy or enthusiasm. But if an audience is not easily engaged by the forces of good, it can be brought, at other points in the play, to feel the horror of Macbeth's evil. When Macbeth goes back to the Weird Sisters in act 4, scene 1, his poetic gifts can be turned against him and the stunning language of lines 50–61 made to suggest that, in his violent, destructive, untrammeled ego-mania, he has rejected any remaining fellowship with humanity and given himself entirely to evil. The lines (146–55) that close the scene ("From this moment, / The very firstlings of my heart . . .") confirm Macbeth's now maniacal commitment to tyranny and murder and can evoke in an audience horror at the evil it witnesses.[7] Although the scene between Malcolm and Macduff will almost always seem long and wordy, Macduff's response at its end to the murder of his wife and children may be the most moving moment in the play and—unlike the earlier, general reports of a "suffering country / Under a hand accurs'd" (3.6.48–49)— bring an audience to feel, as it witnesses the suffering and sorrow of a single man, the terrible impact on individual lives of Macbeth's tyranny. Finally, Lady Macbeth's sleepwalking scene can evoke horror instead of sympathy, and her madness can image in little the violence and chaos that has engulfed the kingdom.

But even if these scenes are played to evoke in the audience horror at Macbeth's evil, he may still regain its sympathy in the last act, in part through his courage to "try the last" and in part through the impact of his famous speeches ("my way of life," "I have almost forgot," and "She should have died hereafter"). As Wayne Booth puts it, "even the forces of virtue gathering about his castle to destroy him seem petty compared with his mammoth sensitivity, his rich despair" (187). Through the rhythms and images of these speeches, Macbeth affirms himself as another suffering human being and asks the audience to admit him once again to its fellowship. But while they can evoke sympathy for him, they seem also, in their dramatic context, to be a sequence of shrewdly evocative but finally empty words by which an embattled tyrant, facing his kingdom's inevitable destruction, seeks to obscure and deny the truth about his own life and to reaffirm his common humanity with those who hear him.

Coincidentally, the words of Macbeth at Dunsinane were echoed, some three hundred years after Shakespeare wrote them, in a bunker beneath the Reich Chancellery in Berlin. With Germany in chaos and the Russian army just outside the city gates, in a "scene . . . marked," as Alan Bullock puts it, "by the theatricality" of his behavior, Hitler re-sponded to what he construed as "Göring's treachery": "His head sagged, his face was deathly pallid, and the uncontrolled shaking of his hands made the message flutter wildly. . . . 'Now nothing remains. Nothing is spared to me. No allegiances are kept, no honor lived up to, no disappointments that I have not had, no betrayals that I have not experienced—and now this above all else. Nothing remains. Every wrong has already been done me.' "[8] While they may lack the compelling metaphors (although not entirely the compelling rhythms) of Macbeth's speech, these words, in themselves, outside the bunker, might also be heard as "the rich despair" of a suffering human being.

In the dramatic context, in the chaos of his castle (another insane bunker), with servants and messengers rushing in and out, armor going on and off, the "cry of women," the maniacal threats and bravado, Macbeth's great speeches may seem only the final linguistic performance of a mad tyrant who once again attempts "to mock the time with fairest show"—to rewrite history with rhetoric and evoke in the audience sympathy for himself. The splendid metaphors by which Macbeth seeks to link himself to the rest of humanity mask the violence, the cruelty, the tyranny, the evil that have brought him and his kingdom to the edge of destruction. Macbeth's longing for "honour, love, obedience, troops of friends," like Hitler's for loyalty and allegiance, is absurd in the context of the beseiged castle and the life we have watched him live. As the play itself suggests, Macbeth in Dunsinane is Hitler in his bunker, and in production Macbeth's language can become the splendid but futile rhetoric by which a half-mad tyrant seeks to conceal the destructive evil of his life and reign and win sympathy for himself. The response of an audience to the reduction of a kingdom to bunker or madhouse is "the horror, the horror."

As actors, directors, audiences, and critics all testify, Macbeth is a complex, ambiguous, unsettling play.[9] In some productions, it brings the audience not only to feel the horror of Macbeth's evil, but to recognize and resist the power of his empty words at the play's end. More often, however, since many would say the words are neither empty nor resistable, they draw an audience's sympathy to Macbeth by blunting the horror of the evil he does and by affirming his frail, suffering humanity. But in the second case, "fair is foul and foul is fair": the play, to some degree or another, obscures Macbeth's evil and evokes from its audiences responses they might never want to make, as individuals, in the world outside the theater.

Since it often seems a way to reconcile unsettling conflicts between dazzling evil and dull virtue, between aesthetic and moral responses to the play (and thus to end up on the side of goodness after all), the tendency of critics to talk about Macbeth as a tragedy suggests something about the nature and meaning of the play itself. In Macbeth, Shakespeare brings an audience to recognize the power of language and performance to create their own versions of reality, to manipulate and shape the ways we understand and respond to events. Outside the play, either as a private citizen or a head of state, Macbeth would be what Malcolm judges him: a butcher. But in it, for all the ways his evil is made clear and his poetry is undercut, he can still retain the sympathy of an audience even after his death. In the end, the play leaves audiences (and critics) trying to reconcile two contradictory impulses: the impulse to condemn Macbeth as evil and the impulse to mourn and celebrate his courage and perverse magnificence.[10]

These contradictory impulses, as I have tried to show, are deliberately evoked by the play, for with its focus on good and evil and on the relation of language and performance to events, *Macbeth* suggests, through our own experience of it, through the shape of our responses to it, how readily we can be deceived and manipulated by skillful words and dazzling performances. As Macbeth is dazzled and deceived by the performance of the Weird Sisters in act 4, scene 1, so the audience is dazzled and deceived by Macbeth's later performance in Dunsinane. *Macbeth* is a disturbing play because it can draw its audiences irresistibly to evil, because in our response to it we can be duped by and made complicit with something we know should be resisted and condemned. Each time we read or watch or reflect on the play, we confront, not just thematically but in our own responses to it, our dangerous vulnerability to the rhetorician, the performer, the demagogue who would "mock the time with fairest show."

In discussing the play as a tragedy, critics tend to make *Macbeth* seem less disturbing than it is, for it gives them a category in which to reconcile their contradictory and unsettling responses to the play, one which affirms that they are all the time safely in the realm of theater. But as the play itself makes clear (particularly through Macbeth's famous speeches in the last act), theater has been known to move out to the real world—in the cult and pageantry of the Virgin Queen, in the festivals of light and music at Nuremberg, in the dictator for whom "speech," as Bullock puts it, "was the essential medium of his power" (372), in the image-making and media management that characterize politics and presidential leadership today. By evoking in its audiences the disturbing impulse to mourn the tyrant whose evil they themselves have witnessed, *Macbeth* makes felt the danger of those who—like a director in the theater, Macbeth in his castle, or Hitler in his bunker—can evoke in us, through rhetoric and performance, responses we ought not make.

## Notes

1. *King Lear, Macbeth, Indefinition, and Tragedy* (New Haven: Yale University Press, 1983), 81.

2. *How to Read a Play* (New York: Grove Press, 1977), 15.

3. Laurence Lerner, ed., *Shakespeare's Tragedies: An Anthology of Modern Criticism* (Harmondsworth: Penguin, 1963), 180. The essay is a revision of "Macbeth

as Tragic Hero," which first appeared in the *Journal of General Education* 6 (October, 1951).

4. *The Plays of William Shakespeare*. Reprinted in *Macbeth*, The Signet Classic Shakespeare (New York: New American Library, 1963), 165.

5. *Macbeth*, The Arden Shakespeare (London: Methuen, 1951), lxv.

6. "*Macbeth* as a Dramatic Poem," *Shakespeare's Tragedies*, ed. Laurence Lerner, 201. It is drawn from Knights's famous essay "How Many Children Had Lady Macbeth?" (1933).

7. *Macbeth*, The Arden Shakespeare. Subsequent citations are of the Arden edition.

8. *Hitler: A Study in Tyranny*, rev. ed. (New York: Harper and Row, 1964), 788–89. Beginning with the words "his head sagged," Bullock is quoting Hanna Reitsch's interrogation by the U.S. Army on 8 October 1945.

9. Marvin Rosenberg's *The Masks of Macbeth* (Berkeley: University of California Press, 1978) makes clear the great range of interpretation the play has had on the stage. The various possibilities I suggest throughout have all worked successfully on the stage.

10. Critics generally find it difficult to make a single judgment on Macbeth. Samuel Johnson: "though the courage of Macbeth preserves some esteem, yet every reader rejoices at his fall." Kenneth Muir: "we may indeed call *Macbeth* the greatest of morality plays, at the same time we are aware that Shakespeare . . . shows us also indomitable energy *burning in the forests of the night* . . . and human life . . . in all its splendours and miseries" (65). R. S. Crane: "If we are normal human beings we must abhor his crimes; yet we cannot completely abhor but must rather pity the man himself" (Lerner, 211). E. A. J. Honigmann: "Hearing him described as *tyrant, usurper, butcher* and so on, an audience that has thrilled to a competent actor's rendering of the terrible soliloquies cannot but feel that a man's outer life is a tale told by an idiot, full of sound and fury, signifying very little, and that the inner life is all in all" (*Shakespeare: Seven Tragedies* [New York: Barnes and Noble, 1976]; rpt. Robert B. Heilman, ed., *Shakespeare: The Tragedies*, New Perspectives [Englewood Cliffs: Prentice-Hall, 1984], 148).

# The Critical Reception of Shakespeare's Tragedies in Twentieth-Century Germany

## Rüdiger Ahrens

### I. The Sources in the Eighteenth Century

The foundations for the Shakespeare-myth in Germany were laid over two hundred years ago. Around the mid-eighteenth century the spark of Shakespeare-mania was ignited, firing numerous spirits of classical German literature who became intensely interested in the Anglo-Saxon genius. First attempts at translation by Christoph Martin Wieland and Johann Eschenburg, as well as general recognition of Shakespeare's literary and aesthetic value, inspired widespread enthusiasm and led to the permanent popularity of Shakespeare's plays in German theaters.

The cult of genius in Edward Young's *Conjectures on Original Composition* (1759), which spontaneously found a wide public through numerous German translations, also strengthened the fervor for Shakespeare on the continent.[1] Christian Heinrich Schmid augmented this in his biography of the poet in 1770, when he declared: "Shakespeare ist das originellste Original."[2] In the same spirit Johann Gottfried Herder—three years earlier—had already seen in Shakespeare the prototype of the creative mind, "ein poetisches Genie," whose work defies all the classical rules of drama.[3] In his great panegyric "Zum Schäkespeare Tag" (1771), Johann Wolfgang von Goethe takes up this theme of the irregularities that contravene the three unities of action, place, and time insisted upon by the French theorists. He speaks with historical exaggeration of "Shäkespear, mein Freund," who gives light to the world in a godlike gesture.[4] Gotthold Ephraim Lessing, in his seventeenth letter on literature (1759), underlined this mania for Shakespeare, which in the Romantic period amounted to the glorification of the "supernatural." This element was first seen by Ludwig Tieck, inspiring him and August Wilhelm Schlegel to make translations that have since become German literary and cultural classics. These translations ushered in the last great phase of Shakespeare glorification, as a result of which Shakespeare was eventually integrated into the German literary tradition.

At the same time, however, a tendency to view Shakespeare more objectively crept in, for the aging Goethe complained in 1825: "Wie viel treffliche Deutsche sind nicht an ihm zu Grunde gegangen!"[5] Earlier, in his famous "Bildungsroman" *Wilhelm Meisters Lehrjahre* (1795–96, book 4, chapter 13), he had used his ideas on Shakespeare as a theme and given it epic detachment by making it a "play within a play" in his famous *Hamlet* interpretation. Since then Shakespeare's reception in Germany has suffered from ambivalence between emotional attachment and objective critique, a polarity that has not been resolved to this day. .

## II. Ambivalent Attitudes in the Nineteenth Century

Early in the nineteenth century Shakespeare enthusiasm took root in university teaching, so that he soon superseded other popular English authors such as Milton, Pope, and Byron. *Hamlet* and *Macbeth* attracted most attention, followed by *Romeo and Juliet, King Lear, Julius Caesar,* and *Othello.* The comedies and histories were much less prominent among courses offered by German universities. Two main aims were pursued in reading Shakespeare. First, Shakespeare's plays, and above all his tragedies, were appreciated as classical works and analyzed along with other great works from various classical traditions—works by Goethe and Schiller, Corneille and Racine, and Calderón. This approach was crowned by the idealization of Shakespeare's dramatic art, of which the book by Georg Gottfried Gervinus on Shakespeare (1849–50), with its ethical approach, is a very good example.[6]

The second aim was more profane: Shakespeare's plays were used or abused for language learning; that is, students were trained in translating his texts or in evaluating and adopting his language and style. An 1830–31 University of Göttingen course announcement read: "Herr Lektor Banfield wird einige Trauerspiele von Shakespeare erklären und damit Stil-Übungen verbinden."[7]

At the same time, a change in the popularity of the plays as set books for university and grammar school teaching can be noticed: *Hamlet,* now considered too difficult and too obscure, gave way to *Julius Caesar,* because the play about the Roman dictator established a bridge with humanistic goals concerning study of Latin and Greek texts.[8] Toward the end of the century, this tragedy was joined by *Macbeth* and, as testimony to an already emergent racism, *The Merchant of Venice.* About the turn of the century, one could find fifty-one study editions of Shakespeare's plays in Germany, with *Julius Caesar* leading the list (twelve editions), followed by *Macbeth* (nine), and *The Merchant of Venice* (six).

## III. 1880 to 1918

Between 1880 and 1918 other aims came more and more to the forefront. The linguistic reform movement, initiated by Wilhelm Viëtor's pamphlet "Der Sprachunterricht muss umkehren" (1882), brought about a decisive separation between the teaching of literature and the teaching of language, the latter to be based mainly on the new claims of phonetics and of the "direct method" as a teaching principle.[9] The teaching of literature began to become an aim in its own right, a fact documented by lively discussion about the classical canon of set books. In his enthusiastic plea for reading Shakespeare (1895), Friedrich Glauning endorsed *Julius Caesar* and *Coriolanus*, but at the same time he demanded an evaluation of histories such as *Richard II, Richard III*, or *Henry IV*, "weil gerade in der Darstellung nationaler Geschichte Shakespeares poetisches Schaffen eigenartig hervortritt, und weil die Lektüre eines solchen Dramas, ganz abgesehen von dem ästhetisch-literarischen Werte, die Kenntnis der Schüler von englischer Geschichte erweitert."[10]

So, two new ideas that placed increasing emphasis on the tragedies and histories emerged at this time: nationalism and historicism. A good example of the search for humanistic universality in Shakespeare's works is Johann Hengesbach's essay "Shakespeare im Unterricht der preussischen Gymnasien," which drew attention to the "universellen Bedeutung" and the "Schatz tiefster Lebensweisheit" possessed by this splendid "Lehrer seines Volkes."[11] This aspect became standard in the following decades. The same kind of metaphysical appreciation, focusing on the tragedies, found its apex in Friedrich Gundolf's well-received book *Shakespeare und der deutsche Geist* (1911), which blamed the English for their "entschiedene Weltlichkeit."[12]

Before World War I, then, a connection with the Shakespeare-mania of the Romantic age had been reestablished. Already in 1910, A. Lüder reminded the German reader, that August Wilhelm Schlegel—through his verse translations—had turned the English poet into a German playwright.[13] Thus, Shakespeare had become a national stereotype for the German character. To preserve the connection with classical language teaching, he was regarded as a means of character formation and was analyzed for his moral values. Students were expected to discover transcendental qualities by reading not only *Julius Caesar* and *Macbeth*, but also *The Merchant of Venice, King Lear, Coriolanus, Hamlet*, and *Othello*.[14]

## IV. Shakespeare in the Period of Cultural Studies (1918–1933)

During this period, the humanist / idealist goal of character formation remained dominant. Guidelines for grammar schools in Prussia (1925)—the cultural pacemaker of the German federation—aimed at education of young people toward a "pan-European culture." Yet the racist element became clearly noticeable when Shakespeare was declared to be an exponent of the "Nordic Renaissance."[15] At this time the idea arose that only one Shakespeare play should be read in English lessons; other plays should be left to German literature instruction. The myth of the "German Shakespeare" was to carry the day also in English lessons and to assist in the search for national identity. In 1922 Philip Aronstein gave the Shakespeare canon a new direction, placing *Richard II, Julius Caesar, Coriolanus,* and *Macbeth* ahead of histories such as *Henry IV, Henry V,* and other tragedies such as *Hamlet, King Lear,* or *The Merchant of Venice.* The comedies were banned from any reading list as "eine Erholung von ernsterer Arbeit, ein geniales Spiel," as were *Romeo and Juliet, Othello,* and *Antony and Cleopatra* for obvious moral and ethnic reasons.[16] A few years later, in 1928, Hans Körbel justified this move by asserting:

Ja, durch eine (reichbelohnte!) willige Hingabe an seine Schöpfung, durch bindende Wahlverwandschaft, durch die grössere seelische Freiheit und Unvoreingenommenheit des deutschen Menschen ist er fast mehr "unser," als er an der normalen seelischen Enge seiner konventionstreueren britischen Landsleute teil hat.[17]

After words such as these, it was easy to integrate Shakespeare into the state's totalitarian claim (post-1933) to nationalistic education.

## V. Shakespeare in Nazi Germany (1933–1945)

Hitler's seizure of power made it possible for Nazi pedagogues to see "ein einheitliches Erziehungsziel in dem volksgebundenen deutschen Menschen"—as Wilhelm Bolle put it in his 1933 essay on Shakespeare and higher education.[18] Among Shakespeare's works the tragedies clearly dominated this search for the tragic and heroic mind, in part because of an affirmative reception of Carlyle's *On Heroes, Hero-Worship, and the Heroic in History* (1841). *Julius Caesar* and *Macbeth* still topped the lists, followed by *The Merchant of Venice, Hamlet,* and *King Lear.* The histories had definitely lost ground.

Nazi commentators seldom failed to point out that, as an Englishman, Shakespeare was at least Germanic, if not in fact Nordic. Mythographers from all quarters praised the Nordic nobility revealed in his heroes' tragic experiences, while farmers were told to admire Shakespeare's closeness to the soil and his rural origin. G. Plessow's racial analysis confirmed that "the Nordic element in Shakespeare was in fact predominant, though not quite without alien admixtures: the virtues of his perfect Nordic forehead were somewhat marred by Mediterranean eyes and hair and a chin of doubtful origin."[19] In the great tragedies and histories Shakespeare's Nordic soul was supposed to shine brightly, epitomized in such characters as Percy Hotspur, who in *Henry IV* appears as "this Nordic youth" of "glorious deeds."[20]

Among academic Shakespeareans, a few university teachers of English did use Nazi jargon in the odd book or article. But on the whole, they preferred politically neutral, traditional areas of research. Work carried out during the period mainly dealt with problems of sources, influences, stage history, and style. One work, Wolfgang Clemen's book on Shakespeare's imagery, was innovative enough to make a lasting international impression.[21]

## VI. Shakespeare in Post-War Germany

The period after 1945, which tried to reestablish former standards of Shakespeare criticism, was primarily characterized by a complete retreat from the positions occupied by cultural studies and by the search for new starting-points for interpretative teaching models. Theorists of education and of literature searched for new approaches to literature in general and to Shakespeare in particular. This period of uncertainty, well analyzed by Ruth von Ledebur[22] and Reiner Küpper, was to last until the mid-1960s.

Then, the literary text became the focus of formalistic interpretation, a development that was assisted by American New Criticism and by its German counterpart—the school of intrinsic criticism represented by Wolfgang Kayser and Emil Staiger.[23] The literary work of art was now regarded as a formal entity without aspects that transcended the text. Critics spoke about texts as "organisms," as did Joachim Höppner in his essay on the interpretation of plays. The text, according to him, was an organic entity without relation to its historical and political backgrounds.[24] There was not, however, and has not been since, a change in the choice of Shakespeare's plays: *Julius Caesar* and *Macbeth* dominate the English-speaking classroom, a choice documented in recently published, elaborate teaching models of these two plays.[25] The two models are still best-selling books; reading at least one Shakespeare play in German secondary schools remains compulsory.[26]

Over a period of time this textually based trend caused a more and more scholarly approach to literature, and to Shakespeare in particular.

Research done by Wolfgang Clemen, especially his commentary on *Richard III*,[27] contributed a great deal to this state of affairs. He did not rely on one analytic mode—intrinsic, structuralist, historicist, or psychoanalytic—but rather applied a synoptic interpretative method and aimed at (in his own words): "die fortlaufende Interpretation eines Shakespeare-Dramas, die sich jedoch nicht *einer* bestimmten Methode verschreibt oder nur *einen* bestimmten Aspekt in den Vordergrund rückt."[28] His synoptic method integrated historical presuppositions about conventions in style, about structure, character portrayal, imagery, and political implications. This step forward resulted in two main advantages: intensive, close reading and enriched interpretation by extrinsic aspects and texts. Already in 1962, Hans Combecher bade farewell to "der nur-philologischen Methode" and demanded the inclusion of the "Epoche Shakespeares" in the reading of his plays.[29] One year later, in 1963, Rudolf Haas advocated the interpretative advantages of wider horizons—theatrical, biographical, even dramaturgical conditions of the time—that would all be fruitful for the classroom treatment of Shakespeare.[30]

Two problems, however, became evident. First, the binding force of a particular interpretative method was abolished, replaced by a variety of valid ways to comprehend Shakespeare's works. Second, the reader-oriented method of reception (Wolfgang Iser and the School of Constance[31]) has made it more difficult to find a common, coherent framework by which students comprehend Shakespeare's texts. Both problems can only be solved convincingly when teachers successfully combine scholarly approved methods with the interests of students, without claiming, however, to treat all possible aspects of the work.

These perspectives have been drastically restricted in the German Democratic Republic (GDR), for even in 1951 English had already been replaced by Russian as the first compulsory foreign language. With this change Shakespeare's name disappeared from GDR official reading lists. In 1965 he was eliminated from any optional list, too.

In West Germany, however, Shakespeare's name has appeared in the official curricula ever since. Generally speaking, in the period from 1945 to 1972, despite the federal structure of the republic and even under the authority of individual states, the school system guaranteed that any graduate from high school had been taught some of Shakespeare's works (mainly *Macbeth* and *Julius Caesar*) and that any graduate from a university with a degree in English had acquired a thorough knowledge of the author and his time. The general school reform in 1972, however, reserved the plays for students in specialized English courses.[32] Besides *Macbeth* and *Julius Caesar*, other plays such as *King Lear, Coriolanus, Hamlet, The Merchant of Venice, A Midsummer Night's Dream*, and *Twelfth*

*Night* remained alternate choices. Of the histories, *Richard III* and *Henry IV* appear, obviously not only for their character portrayals but also for their interpretation of historical background.[33] In the mid-1970s the need for teaching models of the plays was felt most urgently. The German Shakespeare Society (West) inaugurated a series of conferences within the framework of its annual meetings to foster school and university initiatives aimed at extending the scope of Shakespeare's reception.

The synoptic method of interpretation, as applied by Clemen, proved to do justice to the polyvalence of the literary text and the multifunctionality of the plays in performance. According to this method, one is justified in restricting oneself to an interpretative perspective founded on the semiotic character of the linguistic sign as a semantic level of the literary text—its semiotic validity, so to speak.[34] Different contexts rooted in different semantic levels of Shakespeare's plays can then be revealed from a sound perspective.

With this theoretical foundation in mind, a number of Shakespeareans published a handbook of teaching models edited by me and containing forty sections by thirty-seven scholars.[35] In this publication, again, emphasis clearly lay on the tragedies. The leading ideas reflected in the following roughly outlined contexts allow one to establish various perspectives for the plays:

1. *The historical background of the plays:* Elizabethan political history, the state of the English language, the Elizabethan stage, and preceding literary traditions—all these historical factors contribute to the plays' strangeness for the present-day reader. In the case of *Richard II*, reactions by Shakespeare's contemporaries to certain passages can be adduced parallel to the reading, so that contextual knowledge about particular historical relationships is introduced directly. To compare the plays with near-contemporary texts—for instance, *Hamlet* (1.5) with the morality play *Everyman*, or *King Lear* (1.1.36ff) with the entrance scene of *Gorboduc* (1.2), or *Richard II* with Marlowe's *Edward II*—can illustrate the historicity of the Shakespearean dramas.

2. *The plays in performance:* This critical dimension, so strongly propounded by Harley Granville-Barker, has recently been revived in Shakespeare criticism.[36] Textual signals (including stage directions) relevant for theatrical production are an emphasis, as are theatrical notations important for movements on stage, for gesture and mimicry. Lady Macbeth's words in the banquet scene: "Sit, worthy friends, my lord is often thus" (3.4.52)—illustrate a hectic atmosphere and tension between chaos and order. At the same time they direct the actors to sit down again.

3. *Analytical approaches to Shakespeare's works:* There are several starting points for particular analytical approaches: to stick to an in-depth read-

ing of certain passages or to that of a whole play; which translation to use to allow interlingual comparison between English and German and intralingual comparison within the English language itself. With structuralist or communicative approaches other clearly defined objectives occur,[37] including Shakespeare's concept of history in the history plays and in tragedies such as *Macbeth*, where a fateful combination of historical and mythological elements contributes to the tragic end of the protagonist.

4. *Contrastive methods of textual analysis:* Perspective reading allows comparisons with authors beyond national boundaries, as in *Antony and Cleopatra* compared with Corneille's *Horace* (1640). A great variety of interpretative possibilities appear whenever a Shakespeare play is compared with other texts, with its sources, theater reviews or critical texts, or with narrative or thematic variations. (I have contributed pieces on usury in *The Merchant of Venice* and in Francis Bacon's essay on the same theme and on Jan Kott's existentialist analysis of *Macbeth*.) Above all, the numerous dramatic adaptations of our time have proved successful in intensifying engagement with Shakespeare's plays, illustrated here by *Romeo and Juliet, Coriolanus,* and *Hamlet*.[38]

Critical reception of Shakespeare's tragedies in Germany, therefore, has taken a variety of forms based on scientific, political, and theatrical justifications. New concepts propounded in recent research sometimes demand a great deal of energy, but Lessing's statement from the eighteenth century has lost none of its validity today: "Shakespeare will studiert, nicht geplündert sein."[39]

## Notes

1. For a comprehensive record of Shakespeare reception in German aesthetic theory, theater, and translation, cf. G. Erben in I. Schabert, ed., *Shakespeare-Handbuch. Die Zeit, der Mensch, das Werk, die Nachwelt* (Stuttgart: Kröner 2d. ed., 1978), 717–45, 816–32, 893–915. A short, dense outline can be found in H. Oppel, *Von den Anfängen bis zum Ausgang des 18. Jahrhunderts,* Englisch-deutsche Literaturbeziehungen, 2 vols. (Berlin: Schmidt, 1971), 1:98–125.

2. H. Blinn, ed., *Shakespeare-Rezeption. Die Diskussion um Shakespeare in Deutschland. I: Ausgewählte Texte von 1741 bis 1788* (Berlin: Schmidt, 1982), 98. ("Shakespeare is the most original original." All subsequent translations are mine.)

3. Ibid., 96 (" . . . a poetic genius").

4. Ibid., 100 ("Shakespeare, my friend").

5. Cf. I. Schabert, 729 ("How many splendid Germans have not been ruined by him!")

6. Cf. W. Habicht, "Shakespeare in 19th Century Germany: The Making of a Myth," *Nineteenth-Century Germany, A Symposium,* eds. M. Eksteins and H. Hammerschmidt (Tübingen: Narr, 1983), 141–57, 146.

7. Cf. K. Schröder, "Die Shakespeare-Würdigung in der Tradition des Eng-

lischunterrichts," *Shakespeare, Didaktisches Handbuch*, 3 vols., ed. R. Ahrens (München: Fink, 1982), 1:13–42, 23 ("Mr. Banfield, lecturer, will explain some of Shakespeare's tragedies and combine the examination with stylistic exercises").

8. The misleading evaluation of Hamlet's character was again instigated by Goethe's view in his *Wilhelm Meisters Lehrjahre* and basically adopted by Coleridge in his famous phrase: "Hamlet's character is the prevalence of the abstracting and generalizing habit over the practical." (*The Table Talk and Omniana* [London, 1884], 47). Cf. W. Erzgräber, "Probleme der Hamlet-Interpretation im 20. Jahrhundert," in Erzgräber, ed. *Hamlet-Interpretationen* (Darmstadt: WBG, 1977), 1–46. The preference for *Julius Caesar* is justified in E. John, *Plutarch and Shakspere* (Wertheim: Bechstein, 1889).

9. Cf. W. Viëtor, "Der Sprachunterricht muss umkehren" ("New Directions in Language Teaching") repr. *Didaktik des Englisch-unterrichts*, ed. W. Hüllen (Darmstadt: WBG, 1979), 9–31.

10. Cf. K. Schröder, 32 (". . . because Shakespeare's poetic art can best be seen in his presentation of national history and because reading such a play, apart from its aesthetic value, enlarges the student's knowledge of English history").

11. J. Hengesbach, "Shakespeare im Unterricht der preussischen Gymnasien," *Die Neueren Sprachen* 9 (1896): 513–23, 514 ("Shakespeare-Teaching in Prussian Grammar Schools": . . . "universal relevance" . . . "treasure of wisdom" . . . "teacher of his people"). Cf. R. Ahrens, "Die Tradition der Shakespeare-Behandlung im Englischunterricht", in Ahrens, ed. *Shakespeare im Unterricht* (1977; Trier: WTV, 3d. ed., 1980), 12–38, 15.

12. F. Gundolf, *Shakespeare und der deutsche Geist*, 1911 (repr. Bad Godesberg, 1947), 10 ("determined worldliness").

13. A. Lüder, "Shakespeare in den oberen Klassen des Realgymnasiums," *DNS* 18 (1910): 129–44, 131.

14. As for the Shakespeare canon during the period, cf. R. Küpper, *Shakespeare im Unterricht. Geschichte, Konzeptionen, Tendenzen* (Würzburg: Königshausen und Neumann, 1982), 197–222. The emphasis on character analysis and character formation was due to a fashion in Shakespeare criticism mainly initiated by A. C. Bradley, *Shakespearean Tragedy*, 1904 (London: Macmillan, 1960).

15. Cf. K. Schröder, 35.

16. Ph. Aronstein, *Methodik des neusprachlichen Unterrichts*, 2 vols. (Leipzig, 1921–22), 2:105 ("a diversion from more serious work, an ingenious game").

17. H. Körbel, "Zur Shakespeare-Lektüre an den höheren Schulen," *DNS* 36 (1928): 106–9, 106 ("Yes, by a well-rewarded willing devotion to his creation, by binding affinity through choice, by the greater freedom of the soul and impartiality of the Germans he is almost more 'ours' than a part of the normal and conventional life of his British compatriots.")

18. W. Bolle, "Shakespeare im Rahmen der Bildungsarbeit der höheren Schulen," *Neuphilologische Monatsschrift* 4 (1933): 362–74, 362 ("a unifying educational aim in the patriotic German").

19. Cf. W. Habicht, "Shakespeare in the Third Reich," *Anglistentag 1984: Passau. Vorträge*, ed. M. Pfister (Giessen: Hoffman, 1985), 194–204, 196.

20. G. Plessow, *Um Shakespeares Nordentum* (Aachen, 1937), 19.

21. W. Clemen, *Shakespeares Bilder* (1936); English version: *The Development of Shakespeare's Imagery* (1951, rev. ed. London, 1977). Cf. W. Habicht, 199.

22. R. von Ledebur, *Deutsche Shakespeare-Rezeption seit 1945* (Frankfurt/M., 1974).

23. W. Kayser, *Das sprachliche Kunstwerk* (München, 1948); E. Staiger, *Grundbegriffe der Poetik* (Zürich, 1946).

24. J. Höppner, "Zur Interpretation von Dramen im Englischunterricht der Oberstufe," *DNS* 5 (1956): 30–34, 32.

25. K. Emunds, *Kursmodell Englisch: Shakespeare's Macbeth* (München: Langenscheidt-Longman, 1983). E. Häublein and E. Weinig, *Shakespeare's Julius Caesar: A Teacher's Guide* (Bielefeld: CVK, 1984).

26. Cf. R. von Ledebur, "Die Shakespeare-Lektüre in den Curricula der reformierten Oberstufe," in R. Ahrens, ed. (1977, 3d. ed., 1980), 63–76 and id., "Shakespeare in den gymnasialen Lehrplänen seit 1945 und in den Curricula der reformierten Oberstufe", in R. Ahrens, ed., (1982) 1:69–86.

27. W. Clemen, *Kommentar zu Shakespeares Richard III. Interpretation eines Dramas* (1957; Göttingen 2d. ed., 1969). For a more comprehensive assessment cf. R. Gocke, "Laurence Oliviers Richard III: Motivationsföderung durch den *soundtrack* eines Filmklassikers," in R. Ahrens, ed. (1982), 3:1015–33.

28. W. Clemen, "Zur Methodik der Shakespeare-Interpretation," *Sprache und Literatur Englands und Amerikas*, ed. C. A. Weber, 2 vols. (Tübingen, 1962), 2:83–101, 84 ("the close reading of a Shakespeare play not emphasizing one particular method or one special aspect"). Cf. also id., "How to Read a Shakespeare Play," *Shakespeare's Dramatic Art* (London: Methuen, 1972), 214–27.

29. H. Combecher, "Zur Verbindung von Werk und Epoche Shakespeares im Unterricht," *Mitteilungsblatt des ADNV* (1962), 157–62, 157 ("the merely philological method" . . . "the history of the age of Shakespeare").

30. R. Haas, *Anglistikstudium und Englischunterricht* (Heidelberg: Quelle & Meyer, 1963), 39–51: "Shakespeare in Wissenschaft and Unterricht" ("Shakespeare in scholarly criticism and in the classroom").

31. Cf. W. Iser, *Der implizite Leser* (München: Fink, 1972) and id., *Der Akt des Lesens* (1976; München: Fink, 2d. ed., 1984).

32. Cf. R. von Ledebur, (1974), 185–98.

33. R. Borgmeier, "Shakespeare als Landeskunde? Staat and Gesellschaft des elisabethanischen England im Spiegel von Shakespeare Historien (dargestellt am Beispiel von *Richard III*)," *NM* 4 (1983): 216–23.

34. Cf. R. Ahrens, "Die Relation von Text and Kontext als perspektivisches Lesen," *Literaturwissenschaft/Literaturdidaktik/Literaturunterricht: Englisch*, ed. H. Hunfeld (Königstein: Scriptor, 1982), 75–93. This approach is essentially based on Umberto Eco, *Einführung in die Semiotik* (München: Fink, 1972).

35. Ibid., 1982.

36. H. Granville-Barker, *Prefaces to Shakespeare*, 6 vols. (London: Batsford, 1971–74). For exemplary interpretations cf. also J. Hasler, *Shakespeare's Theatrical Notation: The Comedies*, The Cooper Monographs, 21 (Bern: Franke, 1974); W. Edens et al., eds., "Seeing and Hearing the Play," *Teaching Shakespeare* (Princeton: Princeton University Press, 1977); P. Thomson, *Shakespeare's Theatre* (London: Routledge and Kegan Paul, 1983).

37. For a distinct plea for a structural approach cf. L. Marder, "Teaching Shakespeare: Is There a Method?," *College English* 7 (1964): 479–87.

38. Numerous interpretations of modern adaptations can be found in H. Priessnitz, ed., *Anglo-amerikanische Shakespeare-Bearbeitungen des 20. Jahrhunderts* (Darmstadt: WBG, 1980). For interpretations of *Julius Caesar* transcending the text cf. K. Busacker, *Shakespeares Julius Caesar* (Würzburg: Königshausen & Neumann, 1982). J. Kott, *Shakespeare, Our Contemporary* (London: Methuen, 1965).

39. G. Erben in I. Schabert, ed., 727 ("Shakespeare is to be studied, not plundered").

# Revising a Map Misread: Hamlet, Romantic Self-Consciousness, and the Roots of Modern Tragedy

## Daniel W. Ross

### I

In "A Disturbance of Memory on the Acropolis," Sigmund Freud captured modern man's sense of inadequacy in the face of his most important precursor, the father:

> It seems as though the essence of success were to have gotten farther than one's father, and as though to excel one's father were forbidden.[1]

This is the late Freud speaking (in 1936, at age eighty). Freud, a major intellectual influence on his age, had certainly "gotten farther" than his father, yet he maintained an irrefutable sense of guilt for his achievement. Indeed, the notion of going far, both literally (Freud's father had never traveled so far as to Athens), and metaphorically, underlies Freud's guilt: he senses that his success implies a criticism of his father, an act that "from the earliest times [has] been forbidden."[2]

This sense of committing a primal crime attends creative achievements since they implicitly judge the efforts of the past as incomplete or insufficient. Harold Bloom has made the poet's guilt for sins against his poetic fathers a recent critical focal point. Bloom even believes that we can trace the evolution of Romantic self-consciousness on a direct and unbroken line to the Romantics' chief precursor or father: Milton. For Bloom, Romantic poetry is inaugurated by two of Satan's proclamations: "We know no time when we were not as now" and "To be weak is miserable, doing or suffering."[3] But a focus on self-consciousness does not originate with Milton; the Romantics themselves were the first to recognize and to comment extensively on Shakespeare's preoccupation with self-consciousness. Bloom wishes to evade Shakespeare's influence by branding him an antediluvian poet who wrote "before the anxiety of influence became central to poetic consciousness."[4] Shakespeare's plays,

I will try to show, do not validate this judgment. In fact, Bloom's repression of Shakespeare's influence is a curious contradiction, since the brunt of anxiety falls not on the precursor but on his successor. Shakespeare proved a greater influence on the Romantics than Milton, particularly in his anticipation of a modern obsession with self-consciousness.

One measure of Shakespeare's influence is the Romantics' failure to write successful dramatic tragedies in spite of their desires to do so. Recognizing this failure, George Steiner has called all English poetic dramas from Coleridge to Tennyson "feeble variations on Shakespearean themes." Steiner detects in Romantic drama a lack of confidence, a nervousness in the creation of stage characters; writing a decade before Bloom, Steiner notes that "the Greek and Elizabethan achievements seem to lie on the back of all later drama *with a wearying weight of precedent*" (my italics).[5] Steiner's emphasis on anxiety toward predecessors' achievements points to an important lacuna in Bloom's theory, for the Romantics' difficulty with dramatic tragedy is as important as their difficulty with epic. Furthermore, if Milton's achievement with epic overwhelmed the Romantics' desire to write in that form, surely Shakespeare's tragedies provided a similar impediment to their desires to be dramatists. In truth, Shakespeare was the more formidable precursor for, while Romantic epics are fragmented, they nonetheless are read as major texts. Romantic tragedies have been far less successful, and their tragic vision has thus been diverted to forms other than drama.

By their own testimony, the Romantics were awed by Shakespeare's achievement, particularly in his tragedies. And while they failed as tragic dramatists, the Romantics gained enough from Shakespeare to create a body of tragic literature all their own, though not in the dramatic form. The Romantics, indeed, adopted Shakespeare's focus on self-conscious characters like Macbeth and Hamlet and applied it to the genres they excelled in, first the lyric and, later, the novel.[6] Bloom's analysis of the importance of a precursor's greatness to a later poet is useful, but he underestimates the *opportunity* a precursor like Shakespeare bequeaths his successor; it is the opportunity that this essay will stress, for if the precursor takes away with one hand, surely he gives with the other. Shakespeare's perfection of dramatic tragedy may have thwarted the Romantics' desire to be dramatists, but his alteration of the tragic mode to a new emphasis on self-conscious protagonists offered new possibilities for tragedy that are still being explored in literature today, though in different genres: the dramatic lyric, lyrical drama, or lyric tragedy. In spite of this change in tragedy, however, there remains a perceptible link between ancient and modern tragedy that this essay will trace. The prototype of the new tragic hero is Hamlet, whom Steiner rightly calls the Romantics' "emblem and guardian presence."[7]

## II

Several of Shakespeare's plays, most notably *Macbeth* and *Hamlet*, provide models of his analysis of self-consciousness. My focus rests on *Hamlet* primarily because of its unique place in literary history; it bridges classical tragedy (characterized chiefly by emphasis on ritual, man's domination by fate, and an inflexible conception of universal order) and modern tragedy (characterized by more relative notions of order and freedom or, at least, the illusion that its heroes are freer to act). *Hamlet* is both the oldest and newest of tragedies. With its theme of a retributive cycle of justice demanding that a son avenge his father's death, *Hamlet* echoes *The Orestieia*. Freud and his successors have found numerous similarities between *Hamlet* and *Oedipus Rex*. On the other hand, *Hamlet* is in many respects more modern than classical. It is Shakespeare's most subjective tragedy. Its hero is less guided by fate than is Oedipus, who knew not what he did when he killed his father and married his mother. Hamlet understands much more; and after the performance of "The Mousetrap" he can no longer even claim that the ghost exhorting him to action might be a demonic one. Hamlet is in every respect the archetype of the modern, Prufrockian hero: aware at every turn of his actions' many conceivable results and thus paralyzed by his fears of those complications. Paradoxically, however, Hamlet, in being less manipulated by fate and freer to choose his course of action, is at the same time less the master of his own fate than Oedipus, who orchestrates a complete investigation that expeditiously solves the mystery of his identity. Hamlet cannot resolve his problems so swiftly; in the words of Jacques Lacan, Hamlet is always "at the hour of the Other." As I will demonstrate, for Hamlet and the Romantics the Other incorporates the past as well as the present, in the form of Hamlet's father or precursor poets such as Shakespeare.[8] Lacan regards this difference as significant to modern literature:

> This is the sense in which Hamlet's drama has the precise metaphysical resonance of the question of the modern hero. Indeed, something has changed since classical antiquity in the relationship of the hero to his fate.

What is that "something"? For Lacan, "the thing that distinguishes Hamlet from Oedipus is that Hamlet *knows*."[9] Just as the Romantics would have it, then, Lacan sees the modern hero's dilemma as a culmination of the Fall. Once Oedipus has gained knowledge, his life as an active man is finished. Hamlet, on the other hand, must kill the new king fully aware of the potential consequences of his actions. As with many a tragic hero to follow, Hamlet's knowledge renders him unable to act with the swiftness and decisiveness of an Oedipus.

Lacan makes another distinction about Hamlet that, if we use Bloom's appropriation of the family romance for literature, connects Hamlet closely to the Romantics. Whereas in *Oedipus*, the crime is at least committed "at the level of the hero's own generation," in *Hamlet* "it has already taken place at the level of the preceding generation."[10] Thus, Hamlet has a sense of belatedness unknown to Oedipus. Such belatedness encumbers freedom; Hamlet is more bound to the past than is Oedipus; he feels more keenly than any previous tragic hero, even Orestes, his bonds to the previous generations. Hamlet's dilemma closely resembles Bloom's descriptions of the Romantic poets' sense of belatedness.

For Bloom, this belatedness is the central feature of Romantic psychology, primarily because the Romantics, like Hamlet, are so conscious of their belatedness.[11] The Romantic poets, coming so late in the tradition of English literature, faced a struggle analogous to Hamlet's: a struggle to free themselves from the bonds of previous generations. Belatedness limits or circumscribes choices so, just as it exacerbates the problem of originality for the Romantics, it also leaves Hamlet in the position of having to act when no action can occur without dreadful consequences. To state the analogy another way, for the modern poet to confront his precursor is to risk sinning against his precursor, while to avoid such a confrontation is to risk sinning against his own generation by not becoming the poet he might have been.

Similarly, for Hamlet not to kill the king means to sin against his father, king of the previous generation, while to kill him means to sin against the new generation. Hamlet, then, is much like a Romantic poet and, indeed, in his musings, Hamlet often sounds like a Romantic poet, particularly a Coleridge, Byron, or Tennyson, all of whom were especially susceptible to morbidity and separation from the object world. When Coleridge, for example, in the depths of his dejection, says he can see but not feel the beauty of the world, he echoes Hamlet's description of the world as "a sterile promontory." The awareness of one's belatedness, then, seems likely to produce morbid introspection, a brooding on one's relative insignificance in the face of a vast tradition, which can lead to paralysis, an inability to act so as to fulfill one's destiny.

The focus on consciousness in *Hamlet* has had irrevocable effects on tragedy as a literary form. *Hamlet, Macbeth,* and *Othello* gradually remove tragedy from the stage. The word "drama," from Greek, means "to do";

these plays shift the emphasis from action, or doing, to thought.[12] In 1853 Matthew Arnold described this change:

> What those who are familiar only with the great monuments of early Greek genius suppose its exclusive characteristics, have disappeared; the calm, the disinterested objectivity have disappeared; the dialogue of the mind with itself has commenced; modern problems have presented themselves; we hear already the doubts, we witness the discouragement, of Hamlet and of Faust.[13]

Shakespeare, as Arnold indicated, takes us into the minds of his characters as no playwright before him ever had. The difficulty of translating Shakespeare's tragedies into successful stage presentations reflects this emphasis on thought. The trend of emphasizing the central character's consciousness has an ancillary effect of bringing the hero down from his Aristotelian pedestal, making him/her more like "one of us." John Bayley has aptly described both of these effects:

> Macbeth's ambition, the wish to become king, makes us enter into him not as murderer and usurper but as a man beset with an absolute problem, the problem not of what to do, but how to live with the consequences of doing it. We enter the consciousness of Hamlet on the same absolute terms, as if the problem that confronted him had released all of his mind into our keeping and understanding.[14]

Nowhere in Greek or Roman tragedy do we enter so fully into the consciousness of the hero.

In a very real sense, then, Hamlet's knowing is his problem and ours as audience, as his modern inheritors; for the play focuses on the results of his knowing. And Hamlet's problem is not to be underestimated, for knowledge is anathema to action. Once Oedipus gained knowledge, his life as an active man was finished. But the significance of knowledge and its increasingly problematical role in the evolution of tragic literature has led some critics to miss the important elements of continuity linking ancient and modern works. Nietzsche's is the most blatant case. Assigning knowledge (which, he says, leads to nausea) a principal role in the death of tragedy, he equated Hamlet with his Dionysian man:

> . . . both have once looked into the essence of things, they have *gained knowledge*, and nausea inhibits action; for their action could not change anything in the eternal nature of things; they feel it to be ridiculous or humiliating that they should be asked to set right a world that is out of joint. Knowledge kills action; action requires the veils of illusion.[15]

Though Nietzsche correctly discerned the significance of knowledge to modern man, he was too hasty in concluding that there is no modern tragedy. That conclusion fails to give credit to figures like Hamlet who do, after a long struggle, act in spite of the loss of illusion. He also underestimates the inhibitions of the more "active" Greek heroes, a point I will return to shortly.

By assuming that modern man can no longer act, Nietzsche has presented the most influential and dynamic argument against the existence of a modern tragic literature. Before analyzing that argument, however, I would like to adduce the views of Freud for two reasons: first, he is the only modern thinker to have an impact similar to Nietzsche's on our perception of our differences from the ancient Greek and, more important, his view of those differences is much like Nietzsche's, that is, flawed in many of the same ways. Like Nietzsche, Freud located the roots of tragedy in man's primordial rituals. Modern man is more remote (not just in time, but in attitude) from those origins than his ancient counterpart. In *Totem and Taboo* Freud established analogies between the totemic system and ancient tragedy on the one hand and between modern and primitive man on the other. He regarded the totemic system as a form of repression that allowed a compromise, reconciling fathers and sons for their parts in the Oedipal crime: sons receive protection from their fathers as well as expiation and a means of forgetting their crimes, while the fathers gain the promise that the crimes won't be repeated. Freud likened the tragic hero to the totem and the Chorus to the feast celebrants. The hero, having rebelled against divine authority and thus taken on tragic guilt and suffering, represents for Freud, "the primal father, the Hero of the great primeval tragedy . . . and the tragic guilt was the guilt which he had to take on himself in order to relieve the Chorus from theirs."[16]

In Freud's mind, then, the ancient tragic hero is much like René Girard's "surrogate victim,"[17] sacrificing himself for his community. But it is clear that his actions are instinctive; he is not burdened by consciousness as is Hamlet. The modern hero is less willing to act since, as Nietzsche would say, he has been stripped of his illusions and is less sure his actions "will change anything in the eternal nature of things."

While the ancient tragic hero is like the primitive man of sacrifice, willing to act to restore order to his community, modern man, according to Freud, has the characteristics of the neurotic:

> The neurotics are above all *inhibited* in their actions; with them the thought is a complete substitute for the deed. Primitive man, on the other hand, are *uninhibited:* thought passes directly into action. With them it is rather the deed that is a substitute for the thought. And that is why . . . it may safely be assumed that . . . "in the beginning was the deed."[18]

Like Nietzsche, Freud is suggesting that modern man can no longer act as his predecessors did, for increased consciousness inhibits him. Consciousness imprisons the modern protagonist in his own mind, the battle to overcome inhibition taking precedence over external objectives. The inhibitions of the neurotic are in fact similar to Hamlet's, though he finally triumphs over his inhibitions.[19] The neurotic fears action because he is preoccupied with its potential consequences. By meditating at length on those consequences, the neurotic defers action indefinitely.

Freud's comparison might seem to negate the possibility of a modern tragic hero. The hero, as traditionally conceived, is a man of action, uninhibited and certainly not neurotic. His heroism, as Freud says, lies in his rebellion against a father figure (perhaps God or Fate) who censors and prohibits man's freedom. But modern man has internalized this conflict and, in doing so, has not diminished its importance at all. Freud himself expounded this view at length in his later works. The new antagonist modern man faces is the mind itself, replete with myriad doubts and fears that accompany increased consciousness. For modern man the burdens of consciousness are prohibiting and censorious; consciousness, we might say, is the new "superego" against which one must rebel in order to avoid submitting to his inhibitions. The greatness of the modern protagonist lies principally in his struggle against those inhibitions that he must ultimately overcome if he is to take any decisive action.

Nietzsche's and Freud's views of the ancient Greeks are equally flawed. It seems that both fell prey to a tendency common among the Romantics: a fond, nostalgic, but critically naive view of a remote period. When the present seems unbearably degenerate, this tendency is natural, even among the most perspicacious thinkers. Nonetheless, Nietzsche's sentimental portrait of the ancient Greeks has distorted the similarities shared by ancient and modern tragic literature.

Having lived longer with the problems of modernity, we may now see our relationship to the Greeks with a greater objectivity that makes Nietzsche's views particularly suspect. He depicted the brief flowering of Greek tragedy as a time of erotic union between the two great opposing forces in art and life, the Apollonian and Dionysian. This consumation produced, for Nietzsche, a highly expressive culture (as opposed to our more repressive one), culminating in a glorious offspring: Attic tragedy. Such a culture, aided by its art, permits a release of tensions that a mentally healthy society needs. Nietzsche, then, comes very close to Freud's view of ancient Greek culture as one that manifests man's primordial roots and, as such, is the antithesis of our neurotic society.

But repression and neurosis are more evident in Greek tragedy than either thinker presumes. One indicator of repression lies in the use (and rationalization) of madness. In classical tragedy madness is attributed to external causes. Bennet Simon, noting that the madness of the Greek tragic hero is always provoked by the gods, believes that this tendency "covers up the deep conflicts and guilt that must be at work somewhere in the life of the culture."[20] Thus, Greek Fate is itself a form of repression, a rationalization of widespread guilt. E. R. Dodds, similarly, speaks of madness being caused by "psychic interventions"[21]: in Greek tragedy irrational behavior results from "an interference with human life by nonhuman agencies which put something into a man and thereby influence his thought and conduct."[22] For Dodds also this assigning of the causation of mental problems to external forces suggests a refusal to face unconscious desires. In a Christian culture, says Dodds, guilt is a "disease of man's inner consciousness," whereas the sense of guilt in Sophocles "belongs to the world of external events, and operates with the same ruthless indifference to motive as a typhoid germ."[23]

This latter description would never suit the guilt found in Shakespeare's plays nor in other modern tragic works. Shakespeare faces guilt more straightforwardly, exposing conflicts to full view. When his characters go mad, we must look within their characters to find the source of their madness. The madness of Lady Macbeth or of Lear is not the work of Fate, but of an overwhelming sense of guilt or the inability to withstand the grotesque nature of human evil that their own actions have set in motion. Even Ophelia's madness, innocent as it seems, is predominantly internal: her Saint Valentine's day song (4.5.48–66)[24] reveals her guilt over having been in love with the man who killed her father. Inasmuch as the modern hero is neurotic or mad, he cannot blame supernatural forces for making him that way, while acquitting himself and his fellow man.

Through careful analysis of the plays and their cultural milieu, critics like Dodds and Simon explode Nietzsche's nostalgic myth about the healthy expressiveness of Greek tragedy.[25] They present the Greeks as a society with important similarities to ours. Theirs too was a troubled culture with deep psychic conflicts they could not easily reconcile or explain. Their literature, in accord with their world view, externalized such problems, while ours has tended to internalize them. But the similarity of the conflicts argues for a continuity between Greek and modern tragic literature. The Romantics were obsessed with man's newly gained knowledge and subsequent substitution of thought for deed. Furthermore, these problems have roots in Greek tragedy. The haziness of this connection may be ascribed to a misunderstanding of Greek tragedy, which Simon and Dodds help correct, and to a complicated process of evolution, stimulated, as we will see, by radical changes in the conditions of the tragic protagonist's world.

## III

One of the most important differences between Greek and Elizabethan tragedy, the replacement of the chorus by the soliloquy, plays an important role in the shift toward subjective tragedy. The chorus in Greek tragedy, bridging the gap between the audience and the hero, heightened the audience's empathy with the hero. Removal of this bridge allowed for a more intimate relationship between hero and audience. Instead of hearing from a third party about the hero's emotional state, the audience received a firsthand description of the hero's suffering. The soliloquy's intimacy is increased by the departure of other characters from the stage, allowing Shakespeare's heroes to express their anxieties, hopes, and fears with a candor unknown in the Greek theater.

For the Romantics no change of technique or genre was more important. The Shakespearean soliloquy is the forerunner of the tragic Romantic lyric that, as Langbaum notes, turns inward, making "the dramatic situation the occasion for lyric expression."[26] Walter Jackson Bate sees a similar fusion of dramatic elements in Keats's Odes: "But in the 'Nightingale' and the 'Grecian Urn' a second voice interplays with that of the odal hymn, questioning, reluctantly qualifying, and joining in a form of lyric debate that moves actively toward drama."[27] In the Shakespearean soliloquy we can see the emerging doubt, introspection, and vacillation that become trademarks of the Romantic lyric. Such fusions of dramatic and lyric elements are no accident: they provided the Romantics a means of utilizing their talents for drama while escaping the shadow of Shakespeare's influence.

In *Hamlet* the soliloquies reveal the hero's vulnerability, which contrasts sharply with the satiric and confident guise he presents in his more public moments. When we have seen Hamlet mocking Polonius's pomposity or punning with bitter eloquence about the king's cold advice not to grieve, the agony of his internal suffering becomes especially poignant. Hamlet's dilemma reminds one of Freud's description of "the tension between the demands of conscience and the actual performances of the ego."[28] His soliloquies repeatedly expose Hamlet's guilt over the disparity between the demands of his conscience and his performance, or more correctly, nonperformances, of duty. Hamlet becomes obsessed with conscience: not only does he feel that conscience makes him a coward, but he sets out to trap Claudius with "The Mousetrap" in order to catch the king's conscience, as though merely having his uncle's conscience revealed will somehow solve Hamlet's dilemma. The opposite, of course, proves true, for having the king's conscience exposed merely verifies the obligation to act.

Hamlet responds to the demand for action—and his inability to meet the demand—much like a Romantic poet in his moments of crisis, becoming melancholic and projecting his frustrations onto the object world. Repeatedly, he asserts the deadness or sterility of the world around him. Hamlet's anxieties are evident elsewhere. His dream fears are especially emblematic of his internal anxiety—though they prevent his suicide, he tells Rosencrantz and Guildenstern that bad dreams confine and imprison him: "I could be bounded in a nutshell and count myself a king of infinite space were it not that I had bad dreams" (2.2.260–62). The dreams, of course, signify the disturbances in Hamlet's unconscious. Like Wordsworth, among other Romantics, Hamlet fears his imagination.[29] Hamlet's principal conflict is with himself, not with Claudius. The severity of that conflict is most apparent in Hamlet's soliloquies.

Hamlet's soliloquies have various themes, but the dominant subject is thought—the nature of thought, its implications, and the tendency of his own thought to subdue action; the last is evident in the soliloquy that follows the player's speech on Hecuba, where Hamlet tries to goad himself to action with words. He runs through a catalogue of imagined insults that might be hurled at him for his lack of resolute action. But even this ploy disgusts Hamlet, for he realizes that a conventional heroic man would not need it. In his next soliloquy, in the very next scene, Hamlet reasons more calmly the causes of his inaction. He has considered suicide, an act to which he cannot prompt himself for fear of the unknown:

> Thus conscience does make cowards of us all,
> And thus the native hue of resolution
> Is sicklied o'er with the pale cast of thought,
> And enterprises of great pitch and moment
> With this regard their currents turn awry
> And lose the name of action.
>
> (3.1.83–88)

An important aspect of Hamlet's despair is his sense that resolution is man's more natural state and that its subjugation by an overweening conscience is a form of sickness. These sentiments are emblematic of modern heroes who seem time and again to recognize their inability to resolve any crisis; such futility becomes, as Hamlet knows, an illness of the modern age. Overwhelmed by thought, modern heroes find it difficult to "take arms against a sea of troubles" and, even when they do so, futility often overrides their actions. Here we see Freud's paradigm of the hero/neurotic. Not only is the modern hero unable to act with the uninhibited spontaneity of his predecessors, but the very nature of his preoccupation with conscience leads him to doubt the efficiency of action in ways that would never have occurred to earlier heroes.

Hamlet's low esteem for the passive man finds its fullest expression in the final soliloquy. When he has before him the example of Fortinbras, whose virtue he overestimates, Hamlet regards passive men like himself as mere beasts. Fortinbras is, in many respects, the man Hamlet feels he should have been. Just as Hamlet's father once outshone Fortinbras's father as a warrior, so now the young Fortinbras with his conquering spirit seems to outshine young Hamlet. The difference between the sons is clear to Hamlet, and it provides him with another occasion to see himself as an inadequate son.

Hamlet's attitude toward his father complicates his internal struggle even further. One aspect of Hamlet's Oedipus complex seems particularly characteristic of modern heroes: the question of one's worthiness to replace the father, which casts doubt on one's worthiness to be a hero. In Hamlet's case, every comment he makes about himself is antithetical to the lavish praises he heaps on his father.[30] While casting himself as "a rogue and peasant slave," he frequently describes his father as godlike,[31] particularly when he confronts his mother in her bedroom. Here is another distinction between Hamlet and classical heroes. Hamlet fears greatness. His fear is exacerbated by his sense of his father's extraordinary, unmatchable greatness.[32] He feels inadequate to replace his father in the same way that Bloom insists ephebe poets feel inadequate to replace their poetic fathers. For Hamlet to replace his father successfully, he must vanquish the one foe his father could not defeat, Claudius. To complicate matters, Hamlet cannot forget that Claudius has replaced his father not only as king, but as his mother's husband. Thus Hamlet is called on to do consciously what Oedipus did unconsciously—kill the man who occupies his father's bed.[33]

Hamlet's anxiety about greatness portends an ambivalence that characterizes many heroes of modern literature. Many a modern protagonist echoes Hamlet's fears of being called to greatness, a fear that makes many of these characters verge on the antiheroic. But this fear carries a less cowardly, less selfish insight with it. The modern hero often realizes the ultimate futility of action, and yet he finds a reason to act anyway. This makes motive more important than deed and, thus, the emphasis of modern tragedy falls not on the event that brings the hero to his recognition, but on the hero's way of dealing with the recognition. As Bayley's comment above indicates, this emphasis is found in Shakespearean tragedy. Hamlet himself develops a cynical attitude toward life,

but coinciding with that cynicism is an emerging defiance of traditional
authority which indicates that Hamlet is beginning to break his bond
with his father. Such defiance also associates Hamlet with the Romantics. We see more of Hamlet's "romanticism" when he expresses the
importance of freedom and individuality over rigid adherence to authority. Rosencrantz, that obsequious courtier, describes succinctly the
traditional view on this subject:

> The single and peculiar life is bound
> With all the strength and armor of the mind
> To keep itself from noyance, but much more
> The spirit upon whose weal depends and rests
> The lives of many.
>
> (3.3.11–15)

Rosencrantz is in accord with Aristotle, who would make every tragic
hero a man of a great house because such a hero's fate affects the lives of
many others. Hamlet's disgust with Rosencrantz, Guildenstern, and
Polonius indicates his contempt for this attitude. Hamlet, like his Romantic successors, believes all lives are significant, and much of his
heroic character lies in his demand that all life should be individuated.[34]

Hamlet's view of the individual and his role within society, then,
should be regarded as proleptic of a world view that the Romantic poets
celebrate enthusiastically. It should not diminish the significance of this
point that Hamlet himself is a prince; the very idea that a prince,
traditionally educated for complete submission to regal authority, would
challenge this tradition makes Hamlet all the more remarkable for his
intellectual and emotional honesty.[35] Perhaps the true fascination of this
play, especially for readers in a post-Romantic era, lies not so much in
Hamlet's celebrated procrastination, but in his defiance of authority.
Harold C. Goddard held a similar view of Hamlet's individuality: "Only
on the assumption that Hamlet ought not to have killed the king can the
play be fitted into what then becomes the unbroken progression of
Shakespeare's spiritual development."[36] Goddard not only recognizes
Hamlet's defiance of authority; he praises it as morally just. Hamlet,
thus, is the ur-Romantic, refusing to accept authority that is tainted by
corruption.

Hamlet's defiance of authority in all its forms (father, king, God)
indicates an important aspect of the play's mediation between ancient
and modern tragedy. In ancient tragedy a recognition of fickle fate or the
suffering endured by man reinforces existing social and religious traditions, for these traditions are ways of at least minimizing inexorable
chaos and suffering. When one attempts to alter these established traditions, as Creon does in *Antigone*, tragic consequences follow. *Hamlet*

inaugurates the tendency in modern literature to question the validity of prevailing religious and social institutions. Whereas Greek tragic heroes ultimately conclude that the gods must have their own way, modern heroes are likely to reach more pessimistic conclusions, often denying the existence of any god or moral order, and then to rage against the lack of any such source of stability and justice.

Modern tragedy, in short, tends to be even darker, more terrifying than classical tragedy, though the suffering endured by the modern hero is not necessarily greater. The darkness of modern tragedy stems largely from questions about the source of the hero's suffering; if the ancient gods tended to be fickle, easily angered, or jealous, they were nonetheless dependable in their presence. Because of the Greeks' willingness to accede to the authority of their gods, Greek tragedy may be understood in terms different from modern tragedy. Greek tragedy is much more closely allied with myth and ritual than modern tragedy is; hence, it assumes that the proper form of expiation will please the gods, who then will restore the community to normal. In Greek tragedy, for example, the threat posed to the community is often diverted by the sacrifice of a scapegoat whose alienation serves to represent the expiation of the community for its crimes. René Girard has interpreted Oedipus as such a scapegoat or "surrogate victim," substituted for every potential victim in the community. The tragic hero is then exiled, but, ironically, this outcast ultimately becomes a redeemer in the eyes of the community. Although he might have been regarded as the source of the community's ills, the hero has purged its members and restored harmony by accepting punishment. The tragic hero, in a sense, is repaid for his suffering by being deified by the community that once cast him out.[37] For example, in the Oedipus cycle we have *Oedipus at Colonus*, in which the once-great king finds himself again respected in spite of his crimes.

For the modern tragic hero, any such restitution is unlikely. Though Shakespeare generally maintained the tradition of offering some indication to his audience of reestablished order (as in the appearance, at the end of *Hamlet*, of Fortinbras), the hero of modern tragedy sometimes meets his end utterly disillusioned and defeated in the manner of Macbeth. It is interesting that in his last two tragedies, *King Lear* and *Macbeth*, Shakespeare did the least to signal a clearly reestablished order at the end. It seems as though he was creating an increasingly pessimistic tragic world especially appropriate to the modern sensibility. Modern tragic heroes often die with their conflicts unreconciled and without order restored to their worlds.

Isolation and alienation are at the heart of tragedies both ancient and modern. But the classical hero's alienation comes at the work's end, as his punishment for his transgressions. The modern hero shares with

Hamlet an early recognition of his alienation. Modern heroes often, in fact, impose alienation on themselves. Obsessed with self-consciousness and guilt, they may, like Conrad's Lord Jim, for example, find the company of those who know about their transgressions to be unbearable. Alienation is as much the cause of their woes as the punishment for their sins. While the Greek hero may take his integration into society for granted until his crime is revealed, the modern hero often assumes that he has no place in his society. For the Greek hero exile from his community is the worst form of punishment imaginable; Socrates, for one, preferred death to it. Many a modern hero, in contrast, actually seeks escape from his community and tries to reestablish himself in a new environment where he can keep the sins of his past a secret from his neighbors.

To read Shakespeare's tragedies (especially from a Romantic point of view) is to realize increased emphasis on character and rebellion against traditional forms of authority in his tragedies. The Romantics, drawn as they were to introspection and self-examination, could harldy ignore the innovations Shakespeare wrought on tragedy. We know from their testimony that when they read the plays, it was the *characters* of Hamlet, Lear, Macbeth, and Iago that the Romantics were drawn to. They sought to understand the motivations of these characters and to explain their ambivalences with a rigor unmatched by readers of previous ages. Then, when they came to write their own tragedies, many proved themselves to be what Bloom calls "strong poets" by revising, to the point of originality, the achievement of their great precursor and injecting into other genres (especially the lyric and the novel) a psychological depth and candor similar to that they had found in Shakespeare's works.

## Notes

1. Sigmund Freud, *The Standard Edition of the Complete Psychological Works of Sigmund Freud*, trans. and ed. James Strachey (London: Hogarth Press, 1962), 22:247.

2. Ibid.

3. Harold Bloom, *The Anxiety of Influence* (London: Oxford University Press, 1973), 20.

4. Bloom, *Anxiety*, 11.

5. George Steiner, *The Death of Tragedy* (New York: Hill, 1961), 121.

6. Though the Romantics were not great dramatists, their interest in drama surfaces in other genres. Joseph C. Sitterson, Jr., has argued this point effectively; he finds (with the help of Irene Chayes) a dramatic plot in many Romantic odes with the speaker acting as a protagonist who moves " 'to a Reversal or Discovery by what he himself says.' " "The Genre and Place of the Intimations Ode," *PMLA* 101 (1986): 25.

7. Steiner, 143. Romantic identification with Shakespeare and Hamlet, and anxiety about that relationship, is most evident in Keats. Early in his career, Keats

confided to B. R. Haydon that he considered Shakespeare his "good Genius." Nine months later, Keats expressed his anxiety of influence vis-à-vis Shakespeare: "I have great reason to be content, for thank God I can read and perhaps understand Shakespeare to his depths, and I have . . . many friends, who, if I fail, will attribute any change in my Life and Temper to Humbleness rather than to Pride—to a cowering under the Wings of great Poets rather than to a Bitterness that I am not appreciated." More than a year later (June 1819), Keats described Hamlet as an autobiographical figure: "The middle age of Shakespeare was all c[l]ouded over; his days were not more happy than Hamlet's who is perhaps more like Shakespeare himself in his common every day life than any other of his Characters. . . ." And in the same letter, another confession of anxiety: "I have been very idle lately, very averse to writing; both from the overpowering idea of our dead poets and from abatement of my love of fame." *Letters of John Keats* (Oxford: Oxford University Press, 1970), 12, 70, 259.

8. Mark Conroy defines Lacan's Other as a "potential community of listeners" (*Modernism and Authority: Strategies of Legitimation in Flaubert and Conrad* [Baltimore: Johns Hopkins University Press, 1985], 10). For Hamlet and his modern successors (both writers and heroes), no audience is more important than their precursors.

9. Jacques Lacan, "Desire and the Interpretation of Desire in *Hamlet*," trans. James Hulbert and ed. Jacques-Alain Miller, *Literature and Psychoanalysis: The Question of Reading: Otherwise*, ed. Shoshana Felman (Baltimore: Johns Hopkins University Press, 1982), 19. Lacan's italics.

10. Lacan, 43. Certainly Aeschylus, even more than Sophocles, understood the impact on the tragic hero of a crime's being passed on from the previous generation; this inheritance accounts in large part for the power of the Orestes cycle.

11. Harold Bloom, *A Map of Misreading* (Oxford: Oxford University Press, 1975), 35.

12. Modern thinkers tend to miss this shift of emphasis in Shakespeare. A typical modern response is Rollo May's: "Shakespeare wrote when English . . . had a special vitality and power which was characterized by the inseparability of intent and act" (*Love and Will* [New York: Dell, 1974], 240). As my argument stresses, Hamlet evinces the opposite—a separation of intent and act—which makes purposeful action problematical for later modern writers aware of his innovation.

13. Matthew Arnold, *Selected Prose*, ed. P. J. Keating (Harmondsworth: Penguin, 1970), 41.

14. John Bayley, *Shakespeare and Tragedy* (London: Routledge, 1981), 166.

15. Friedrich Nietzsche, *The Birth of Tragedy*, trans. Walter Kaufmann (New York: Vintage, 1967), 60. Nietzsche's italics.

16. Freud, 13:156.

17. René Girard, *Violence and the Sacred*, trans. Patrick Gregory (Baltimore: Johns Hopkins University Press, 1979), 93.

18. Freud, 23.

19. The arguments of Nietzsche and Freud, if fully accepted, can support a view of Hamlet as tragicomic figure, absurdist, or antihero. Clearly, I do not agree with those views, though I cannot dispute them in detail in this essay. For now I can only assert my belief that Hamlet is not such a figure but is a tragic hero most appropriate to the modern age, a period of speculation and hesitation, not action.

20. Bennet Simon, *Mind and Madness in Ancient Greece: The Classical Roots of Modern Psychiatry* (Ithaca: Cornell University Press, 1978), 93.

21. E. R. Dodds, *The Greeks and the Irrational* (Berkeley: University of California Press, 1951), 28.

22. Ibid., 46.

23. Ibid., 36.

24. References to Shakespeare's plays are to *The Complete Works*, ed. G. B. Harrison (New York: Harcourt, 1968).

25. Since I criticize Nietzsche for misinterpreting the Greeks, it is only fair that I credit his shrewd interpretation of *Hamlet*. As William Brashear phrases it, "Nietzsche's unique contribution to *Hamlet* criticism is that he sees unqualified strength and magnitude where others see weakness in strength and limitation in magnitude." To Nietzsche Hamlet's "view of life *is* the tragic view. To think deeply is to think tragically" (*The Gorgon's Head: A Study in Tragedy and Despair* [Athens: University of Georgia Press, 1977], 16).

26. Robert Langbaum, *The Poetry of Experience: The Dramatic Monologue in the Modern Literary Tradition* (New York: Norton, 1963), 200. For examples of lyrical drama and lyrical tragedy see, respectively, Jerome Christensen, " 'Thoughts That Do Often Lie Too Deep for Tears': Toward a Romantic Concept of Lyrical Drama," *The Wordsworth Circle* 12 (1981): 52–64; and B. L. Reid, *William Butler Yeats: The Lyric of Tragedy* (Norman: University of Oklahoma Press, 1961).

27. Walter Jackson Bate, *John Keats* (Cambridge: Harvard University Press, 1963), 500.

28. Freud, 20:37.

29. See Geoffrey Hartman, *Wordsworth's Poetry: 1787–1814* (New Haven: Yale University Press, 1964), 238–42.

30. David McDonald sees such moments as "instances of effacement through language, . . . scathing, self-annihilating attacks on [Hamlet's] own identity" ("Forms of Absence: Derrida and the Trace of Tragedy," *Helios* 7, new series, [1979–80]: 90). So great is Hamlet's self-loathing that he, like many a modern protagonist, longs at times to annihilate self; it is a testament to Hamlet's courage that he does not acquiesce to that desire.

31. Conroy's fine book indicates the logic linking Hamlet's feeling for his father and the polar language he uses when speaking of himself and his father. Conroy argues that language is derived from the father, who prescribes the boundaries of language for the child (Conroy, 10). It would seem that the elder Hamlet has bequeathed his son an inferiority complex, manifested in the son's language. Thus, Hamlet's conflict is not entirely with himself, but also with the spectre of his father, whose influence he has not yet overcome. This conflict precisely mirrors the one which Bloom describes in the poet-precursor relationship.

32. Without referring to Hamlet, Conroy describes the psychodynamics of this process (Conroy, 31–32). The son seeks to replace his father, yet even if he succeeds, he feels guilt and insecurity about his own status. The usurping son continues to feel inferior to the father, so being required to replace the father makes him feel like a phony. Conroy's point is validated by Freud's confession of his "disturbance" at Acropolis.

33. The first time we see both Claudius and Hamlet in the play (act 1, scene 2), considerable emphasis is given to their ambivalent relationship as "son" and "father." In his first statement to Claudius, Hamlet tells him that he is "too much i' the sun" (line 67). Later, after Hamlet has agreed not to return to Wittenberg, Claudius refers to Hamlet as "our son" (line 117). Hamlet is clearly aware of his

ambiguous kinship with his erstwhile uncle, now his stepfather. Uncles, it should be noted, often became second fathers to sons in the Middle Ages and Renaissance, assuming the responsibilities of fatherhood for the children of a deceased brother. Thus, Claudius does have some legitimate paternal relationship with Hamlet, and any reference by Claudius to Hamlet as his "son" is bound to stir in him the awareness that he has been asked to perform the Oedipal crime.

34. Richard Fly, "Accommodating Death: "The Ending of *Hamlet*," *SEL* 24 (1984): 268–69.

35. Bayley has remarked perceptively on Hamlet's candor, comparing the frankness of his language to the subtle and suave rhetoric of Claudius (Bayley, 167). See also Fly, *passim*.

36. Harold C. Goddard, *The Meaning of Shakespeare*, (Chicago: University of Chicago Press, 1951), 1:336.

37. Girard, 79–86.

# The Status of Women in *Othello*

## Elizabeth Wiley

**A** major characteristic that sets man apart from other animals is his ability to wonder. Apparently the topic man has wondered about most is—woman. She is obviously different from man: smaller, softer, rather less hairy, and considerably more attractive, at least to man. Aside from these external differences, other less obvious ones were detected by Elizabethan man. For one thing, man was controlled by the hot dry humor, associated with fire, strength, activity, and courage. Woman, on the other hand, was dominated by the cold moist humor, associated with water and the changeable moon; as a result, woman was "naturally fearful and timorous." Most authors, ancient and Renaissance, agreed that "since women are weak physically, they must be weak morally and mentally."[1] On the other side of the argument, perhaps woman was superior to man; after all, she was made of a finer substance (Adam's rib) than that which formed man (dust of the earth). As the culminating step in the plan of creation, too, was she not at the top of the hierarchy of creatures?[2]

Throughout the Middle Ages (according to Maurice Valency) woman had risen in the esteem of poets, being considered first as a source of good, then an example of earthly perfection, then a saint, and finally an angel.[3] This superhuman woman came into English poetic literature through Petrarch and other Italian poets; she was a creature of frightening powers. With her golden hair (alas for the brunette) she could ensnare men; with her eyes she could wound them fatally or bestow a healing smile, as she preferred. Writers struggling to describe her ransacked the real and imaginary worlds for examples. With all these "truths" the Elizabethan man was acquainted. But other, contradictory, "truths" were equally familiar to him.[4]

A certain John More once compared marrying a woman with taking, sight unseen, "Eeles out of a bag, wherein were twenty snakes for an Eele."[5] Such disparagement of woman was a popular after-dinner topic with gentlemen. Sir Roger Wilbraham related the following conversation. One guest told of a poor man who, lacking money to pay a priest, asked him to marry him on credit, as it were. When the priest came to collect his fee later, the husband refused, but he offered him "10 tymes as much to unmarie [them]." Another guest countered with an anecdote about the Vicar of Acton. A parishioner asked him "when he would bestow a wife on him that he might geve him thanks." The Vicar's response was "since I live by the fruits of my benefice; & have maried 1000 coples in this parishe; not one that ever came to geve me thanks."[6]

Writers, of course, took advantage of the common taste. Characters in plays had lines like, "A woman is an angel at ten, a saint at fifteen, a devil at forty, and a witch at eighty."[7] Another author claimed, "There are only two good days in marriage: the wedding day and the day the wife dies."[8] Such writers could call on Plato or Saint Thomas Aquinas as authorities for their view that woman was a "mill-second" of creation, somewhere between reasoning creatures and beasts.[9] The vices especially laid to woman were eroticism,[10] pride, and excessive fondness for fine clothes.[11] The general attitude toward woman as a weak and unpredictable creature caused some problems when men were forced by circumstances to accept a woman ruler.[12]

Despite a "very bad . . . press," woman has played a significant role in western culture throughout our era. Such women as the mother of Saint Louis of France, Countess Mathilda of Tuscany, and Eleanor of Aquitaine were outstanding in the Middle Ages.[13] And for every woman whose name has come down to us we may presume scores of prominent women whose histories are forever lost.

In English history, women in the Tudor period are better known to us than those of earlier periods, because records provide a clear picture at this time of rural and village as well as city life. Two classes of people lived in rural areas, landowners and laborers. The wife of a landowner, despite her circumscribed existence,[14] was pleasantly occupied in supervising a "galaxy of lady's maids, laundresses, needlewomen, and dairy maids, goose girls and hen wives" under her authority. At dinners and banquets she was served first; she might have engaged in sports and certainly did fancy work. She might even have read a book.[15] If she brewed beer for sale (like Skelton's Elinour Rumming), the profits were hers, to keep in her personal locked box.[16]

Women servants and wives of farm laborers had less pleasant lives. Farm hands were fed abundantly while working, but their wages were meager, usually just equal in value to the food they ate on the job. From this pittance their wives and children must be fed, the whole family clothed, and rent paid on their huts.[17] The family easily sank into poverty and debt; when conditions became too uncomfortable and their wives grew less attractive through slow starvation, many laborers simply deserted their homes and found work in other counties, leaving the parish to care for their dependents.[18] Their wives, to avoid being evicted from their hovels and driven from the parish, were forced to seek such menial and ill-paying work as they could do in their weakened health.[19] As they watched their children sicken and die, and as they felt themselves failing under privation and overwork, they had good reason to believe that men were correct in calling the woman a misbegotten creature.

Women in large towns, especially London, were in the most favorable positions. From Anglo-Saxon times the townspeople had been fairly independent of external pressures. The feudal system impressed upon England after the Conquest had little effect on the burghers and their wives, and women retained much of the independence they had enjoyed in earlier periods.[20] They held membership in several guilds, they worked as shop managers and clerks, and as widows they often continued the family businesses, especially printing and bookselling.[21] Housewives themselves were respected as responsible for their families' well-being and success through careful management of the income. To instruct women in the proper behavior and in the supervision of household matters, many books were written (by men, of course) on the duties of the wife.[22]

Foreign visitors to London were surprised by the freedom allowed English women. Frederick, Duke of Wurttenberg, quoted an old proverb: "England is a paradise for women, a prison for servants, and a hell or purgatory for horses."[23] But even visitors were aware of the restrictions. Plattner mentions the ducking stool, used to "put some curb upon [women's] pranks and machinations."[24] Van Meteren, the Dutch consul in London, felt that "wives in England are entirely in the power of their husbands, their lives only excepted." And, although married women had more freedom in England than in Spain, unmarried girls were kept more strictly than those in the Netherlands.[25] Just as the Elizabethan man considered his counterpart with mixed feelings, so visitors to England were undecided how to judge English women. On some points there was agreement: English women were beautiful,[26] although perhaps somewhat overdressed[27] and too forward at public gatherings.[28] One of the freedoms allowed wives was the privilege of greeting all visitors with a kiss, a practice that amazed—and delighted—Samuel Kiechel in 1585.[29] In *The Lawes Resolution of Womens Rights*, additional privileges for woman were discussed, including her right to inherit and dispose of land, and the limits of control her husband had over her: he could beat her for disobedience, but she could sue him to maintain the peace if he was too severe.[30] The townswoman, despite a mixed reputation, was beginning to come out of her servitude.

One bond that was breaking was ignorance. Although the vast majority of English women were illiterate, those who had the opportunity to read were eager to taste the New Learning that was exciting the age. Katherine of Aragon, herself a classics scholar, desired the same education for her daughter, Mary. Sir Thomas More also offered his daughters an education equal to any gentleman's. Anne Boleyn, Katherine Parr, and Lady Jane Grey came under the influence of Renaissance learning. But undoubtedly the epitome of feminine scholarship was the learned queen, Elizabeth I.[31] Even the women who could not master Latin or Greek wished to read and discuss literature available in English. Although they might hesitate to discuss translations of "the somewhat licentious works of writers like Boccaccio, free though manners and conversations were," they did appreciate the highly stylized works of Lyly and Sidney.[32]

Another significant cultural influence upon the women of London was the theater. Some historians feel that "few women and no young girls" attended playhouses,[33] but contemporary accounts often speak of women in the audience. Philip Julius, Duke of Stettin-Pomerania, noted in 1602 "there are always a good many people present, including many respectable women [ehrbare Frauen] because useful arguments, and many good doctrines, as we were told, are brought forth there."[34] The didactic value of plays was questioned by many Puritans, of course. John Northbrook reminded his readers that, in a biblical parallel, "Dina was ravished" through "hir curiositie," because she "would go forth and vnderstande the maners of the other folkes" and that "the nature of women is much infected by this vice." Therefore, it behoved them "to loue their husbands, to bring vp their children, and to be byders and tariers at home" instead.[35] Stephen Gosson spoke in greater detail of the harm that could come of women attending plays,[36] and recommended, "When you are greeved, passe the time with your neighbors in sober conference, or if you canne read, let bookes bee your comfort," rather than seeking "salve at playes or Theaters, lest that laboring to shun Silla you light on Charabdis."[37]

Despite these warnings, women did attend the plays, and they "comforted their consciences with the good lessons that the drama extracted from the doleful ends of . . . faithless wives, and other sinners whose dying speeches were filled with repentance and advice."[38] It was for this type of audience that Shakespeare wrote, and this audience, in Harbage's opinion "must be given much of the credit for the greatness of Shakespeare's plays."[39] From such an audience, and from his acquaintance with outstanding women of his age, he also drew the women characters of his plays: from "learned women like Lady Russell, clever women like Lady Raleigh and Lady Warwick; vengeful women like Lady Shrewsbury; a devout one in Lady Hoby, and a devoted one in her sister-in-law, Lady Sidney. Beautiful and vivacious Lady Rich, impetuous Lady Southampton and Lady Essex" also furnished him with models.[40]

If Shakespeare's plays may be considered observations of life around him and at the same time lessons in desirable conduct (often through negative examples), *Othello* might be considered a reflection of his attitude toward marriage and woman's role in society. One must recognize, however, that the *Othello* plot was not original with Shakespeare; his own contributions (and, therefore, his presumed opinion) may be determined by comparing his version of the story with that of his source. The generally recognized source of the plot of *Othello* is Novello VII, Third Decade, in Giovanbatista Giraldi Cinthio's *Hecatommithi*.[41] In the prose tale the women are portrayed quite differently from their counterparts in Shakespeare's play. In general, they are amplified in the play, their roles enlarged and individualized. In *Othello* they become increasingly prominent as the play progresses. Cinthio, on the contrary, makes them most prominent in the first third of the tale, then decreases their part as the plot develops. They are absent from the last sixth.

Their importance is played down in another way also. Although direct speeches of the Moor (Shakespeare's Othello), the Ensign (Iago), and the Captain (Cassio) are used extensively, Cinthio limits the women's words to thirty-five lines, representing Disdemona's speeches primarily. Even Disdemona's actions are related by other characters rather than being shown directly, for the most part. In general, the tale emphasizes the actions of the men; the women are used only to provide motivation.

Of the three women characters, Disdemona is obviously the most prominent. She has the distinction of a name; the other characters are designated only by rank or relationship. The plot, of course, concerns a presumed triangle of which she is the pivotal character. Yet she is not so strongly portrayed in Cinthio as in Shakespeare. Disdemona and the Moor, while marrying against her parents' wishes, do marry with their knowledge and (presumably) their reluctant consent. It is a braver girl who agrees to elope with Othello and "offend grevously"[42] her widowed father. Here is bold action, perhaps too bold to be completely respected by the Renaissance audience. So Shakespeare adds another quality to Desdemona's courage.

John M. Major calls attention to the frequent use Shakespeare makes of the Dido legend in his plays, and he suggests that the wooing of Desdemona has a parallel in Dido's "lovesick desires" to hear Aeneas's adventures:[43]

> Nec non et vario noctem sermone trahebat
> Infelix Dido, longumque bibebat amorem,
> Multa super Priamo rogitans, super Hector multo . . .
> (*Aeneid* 1.748–50)

And, like Desdemona, Dido requested him to start at the beginning:

> "Immo age, et a prima dic, hospes, origine nobis
> Insidia," inquit, "Danaum, casusque tuorum,
> Erroresque tuos . . ."
>
> (1.753–55)

Through an illusion to a tale widely known in Elizabethan England,[44] Shakespeare links Desdemona with Queen Dido, suggesting that the Venetian maiden "is no simple naive girl, moonstruck by the attentions of a great warrior, but a young woman of imagination and fire and a tender heart swept into tragedy in the way of one of the most splendid tragic heroines in literature."[45]

The confrontation scene (1.3) elaborates this suggestion of nobility in Desdemona. The speech declaring her new duty to her husband has a maturity not expected in an infatuated adolescent.

> My noble father,
> I do here perceive a divided duty,
> To you I am bound for life and education,
> My life and education both do learn me
> How to respect you. You are the lord of duty;
> I am hitherto your daughter. But here's my husband;
> And so much duty as my mother showed
> To you, preferring you before her father,
> So much I challenge that I may profess
> Due to the Moor my lord.
>
> (1.3.180–89)

The speech begins and continues in gravity and the formality of respect: "My noble father," the repetition of "life and education," create that mood. The argument, unexpectedly, is based on reason and custom, not on emotion. The word *love* never appears; the emphasis, instead, is on *duty* and *respect*, qualities suggesting an intellectual rather than an emotional approach to the problem. That Desdemona loves Othello is obvious, but that she has allowed her emotions to override her intellect is disproved by this speech. It might have shocked some Elizabethan gentlemen in the audience to consider that Desdemona, a mere woman, could reason so cogently and speak so fearlessly. Of this reaction Shakespeare would be aware.

Desdemona's courage is further demonstrated by the way her voyage to Cyprus is handled. Both Cinthio and Shakespeare tell of the wife's insistence on accompanying her husband, but the circumstances differ. In Cinthio, the Moor is sent, not as the general of troops in wartime, but as the commander of a peacetime occupation army. Disdemona, marshaling arguments for going along, emphasizes that they will travel together "in a safe and well-provided ship," and neither battle nor storm disturbs the journey, for they sail on "a perfectly tranquil sea."[46] There is no evidence of the "fair warrior" in Cinthio's heroine; Shakespeare's Desdemona alone deserves that appellation. ⌐

We know little of Disdemona's specific reaction to the Moor's jealousy, and so a comparison on this point is difficult. Cinthio includes one speech, however, that would be unworthy of Desdemona. Weeping bitterly, the Moor's wife tells her friend (the counterpart of Emilia), "I fear I shall prove a warning to young girls not to marry against the wishes of their parents, and that the Italian ladies may learn from me not to wed a man whose nature and habitude of life estrange from us."[47] So little does Desdemona subscribe to this sentiment that, when Emilia reminds her of the "many noble matches" she has forsaken to be treated harshly by Othello, she blames only her "wretched fortune" (4.2.126–29), not her marriage.

Later Emilia declares more strongly, "I would you had never seen him!" Cinthio's heroine would have agreed with her, but Desdemona retorts, "So would not I; my love doth so approve him, / That even his stubbornness, his checks, his frowns— / . . . have grace and favor in them" (4.3.18–21). This idea is echoed in Shakespeare's alteration of the "Willow Song," when Desdemona sings, "Let nobody blame him; his scorns I approve," rather than "Let nobody chide her, her scorns though I prove."[48] The change from prove to approve (almost reversing the meaning) would be noted by the Elizabethan audience familiar with the original. The point is underlined by Desdemona's "Nay, that's not next!" immediately after the altered line. (4.3.51–52).

Some significant contrasts between Cinthio's and Shakespeare's heroines appear in the death scenes. Disdemona is killed not by her husband but by the Ensign. When she calls to her husband and receives accusations rather than help, the poor woman "appeal[s] to the justice of Heaven, since justice here [has] failed her . . . and as she [is] thus calling Heaven to witness, the wicked Ensign inflict[s] a third blow, under which she [sinks] lifeless to the floor."[49] At this point Disdemona exits as a character in Cinthio's tale. The scene is altered significantly in Shakespeare's hands. If it is true that "Desdemona goes to her death in terror,"[50] it is equally true that even death is no barrier to her love. According to Heilman, Shakespeare recognizes "the utmost extent of 'nature' . . . [but] also knows when to stretch it or go beyond it," as he does in recalling Desdemona from the dead. By her posthumous speeches, "Desdemona becomes, rather than simply is, the saint." In the three speeches after death, she passes from an accusation of Othello (5.2.119), in Heilman's opinion "the most primitive impulse," to a "simple denial of wrongdong," (125). Then she leaps beyond the natural reaction to "the acting of goodness"[51] in her response to Emilia's horrified question: "Nobody: I myself. Farewell; / Commend me to my kind lord: O farewell!" (5.2.127,128). The speech falls into two parts: Desdemona's assumption of guilt for her own murder (incredible but touching), and an expression of love and forgiveness to Othello, her murderer. The key word in the second part is *kind*, and both meanings are present here. She can forgive Othello, because his deed was human, natural, though cruel; she can love him for the kindness, the gentleness that she first saw in him.[52]

Desdemona's name has been analyzed by several critics. The derivation, according to G. Wilson Knight, is from "dusdaimon . . . unhappy in her guardian, *daimon*" and probably signifies merely "ill-fortuned" or "ill-destined."[53] She herself speaks of her "wretched fortune," and Othello calls her an "ill-starred wench" (5.2.275). But in another sense, her name is appropriate to her fate. As a woman, she is under the control—guardianship—of her father until her marriage, and then the control of her husband. Not unless she should be widowed can she call herself her own mistress. And, more than most women, she is unfortunate in her guardians. The first, her father, hardly knows what sort of daughter he has. To him she is a tractable child, though somewhat petulant in refusing the "wealthy curle'd darlings" of Venice (1.2.68). It is unthinkable that she might entertain an affection so strong as to cause her to elope with a man her father would never consider a suitable husband. Desdemona, bereft of her logical confidante, her mother (Brabantio is widowed in the play although not in the tale), has no one to advise her in the desperate situation that provokes her rash action.

If she has hoped for greater understanding from her husband, she soon discovers that he is no more able than her father to comprehend her as a creature of reason and spirit. To Othello she is a goddess on a pedestal, or at least a rare being he cannot understand. To her father, she is a bewitched, mindless child; but from the beginning, Othello's picture of Desdemona is no more rational, his insight no more penetrating, than Brabantio's. Desdemona suffers from a paradox: at first, she is a romantic figure of superhuman qualities, devoid of blemish; yet, at the slightest seeming cause, she becomes (in Othello's eyes) the epitome of animal appetite and dishonor. His soliloquy in the last scene dramatizes the dichotomy of attitude effectively.

John Money, who has played Othello, analyzes the rhetorical effect of the passage (5.2.1–22), centering his attention on the word *chaste* in line two. Although Othello cannot name the Cause, his use of the word *chaste* is significant. It is the apparent lack of chastity for which he condemns Desdemona; the quality is emphasized by the images immediately following the line. Her skin is not merely white but also cold (through the association with *snow*); both whiteness and coldness are present in alabaster, also used to describe her skin. Othello is naming the kind of complexion most admired by Elizabethans, but he is also unconsciously linking it with the qualities of character required by any woman worthy of a pedestal. He hints at his awareness of the warmth and life in woman (that is, in Desdemona) by the image of plucking the rose. Money suggests the connection (as, for example, in *Roman de la Rose*) of the Rose with the lady's love, and plucking the rose with the consummation of love. He points out the duality of attitude toward love and chastity. It is as if a lover were to say, "O, that my love might be responsive and compliant, and yet somehow remain chaste and virginal."[54] That is, that she might be a mindless animal in obeying my wishes, without stepping down from her pedestal. The impossibility of satisfying such a wish would inevitably result in some degree of tragedy in the relationship of man and woman.

The marriage of Iago and Emilia is no less tragic. Emilia, as Shakespeare develops her from the anonymous Ensign's wife in Cinthio, is both humbler and greater than her original. She is of lower birth than Desdemona; the proofs are her position as Desdemona's maid, her marriage to a noncommissioned officer, her speech, and the mind and habits revealed in her words. The Ensign's wife in Cinthio, on the other hand, is a woman of good family, a person to whom Disdemona is drawn in friendship, presumably through common interests. Yet Emilia proves able to transcend her rude background and humble position as Iago's wife (and virtual slave, one feels), while the Ensign's wife sinks into dishonorable servility.

Emilia's loyalty to her mistress ennobles her, but the same loyalty produces an inner conflict stronger than Desdemona's problem. Desdemona recognizes, however vaguely, that her well-being is endangered by Othello's suspicions. But her conflict is an external one; she feels no division of loyalties, no temptation to become something other than she has been since her marriage, a faithful, obedient wife. But Emilia, bound by the same vows as Desdemona (however lightly she might speak of them at times), bound also by a real physical fear of Iago, demonstrates courage and even nobility in defending Desdemona's reputation against both Othello and Iago. The Ensign's wife in Cinthio is fully aware of the plot her husband has set in motion and, although "she could never consent to such a project [as helping her husband to defame Disdemona], dare[s] not for fear of her husband, disclose a single circumstance." She contents herself with merely advising her friend to "beware lest you give [the Moor] any cause of suspicion."[55] This advice must sound futile to her even as she offers it, but she does not dare to defy her husband. An Elizabethan audience would understand the problem. Even the courts recognized the fact. As late as 1634, a husband was convicted of selling saltpeter but his wife, although recognized equally guilty, was released because she was "a wyfe and subject to obey her husband."[56]

Emilia, on the other hand, is ignorant of Iago's plot; one suspects he knows better than to tell her. Her greatest guilt lies in having taken the handkerchief, the theft that (according to Heilman) is "half an accident."[57] Iago has "a hundred times / Wooed" her to steal it (his insistence might, in a woman, be called nagging); so, although she cannot imagine what he wants to do with it, her duty is "nothing but to please his fancy," so she picks up the handkerchief. Suddenly, when Iago snatches it from her, she realizes the value it holds for Desdemona. "Poor lady, she'll run mad / When she shall lack it." But it is too late; Iago has the handkerchief and Emilia has his command: "Be not acknown on't" (3.3.321).

Forced to deny any knowledge of the handkerchief when Desdemona asks about it, Emilia is "caught by an unwilling commitment, a fear of confession, and a hope that things will turn out all right," so she "works off her uneasiness by attacking men."[58] If men are "not ever jealous for the cause, / But jealous for they're jealous" (3.4.164–65), she cannot really blame herself for providing "cause" for Othello's jealousy. She has not been present to see Othello strike his wife (4.1.240), or she might be more alarmed at his interrogation in the following scene. But even unaware of his violence, Emilia is sufficiently moved to brave his displeasure by offering a spirited defense of her mistress (4.1.12–19). Significantly, she offers to "lay down [her] soul" that Desdemona is honest; later she does lay down her life in that cause. Heilman feels the theft of the handkerchief has "slipped below the threshold of consciousness";[59] at least she does not connect it with the present trouble. Certainly she does not suspect her husband of plotting to make Othello jealous, for she speaks boldly against the "eternal villain" who "devised the slander" and asserts that the "base, notorious knave" should be lashed "naked through the world / Even from the East to th' West" by "every honest hand." Even Iago seems a bit cowed by this fury, saying merely, "speak within door."

Emilia is by this time seriously concerned for her mistress's welfare, especially when Desdemona tells her that Othello wishes the maid dismissed for the night. Perhaps, in her uneasiness, Bianca's claim to be "of life as honest / As you" carries to her activated conscience a ring of condemnation; for, although Bianca means one thing by the word *honest*,

Emilia could be thinking of another. Possibly she is trying to spit the idea out of her mind with her "foh!" as well as to indicate the expected reaction of wives to whores. When she returns to report the duel to Othello, she faces the full horror of the situation she has inadvertently helped to create.

Emilia's sensitivity to her mistress's problem is suggested by her immediate awareness of a tragedy in the bedroom. Her "alas" (5.2.120) and the "out, and alas" (122) indicate something other than surprise at hearing Desdemona's voice. Her mistress's words, dramatic as they are, need not have upset the maid, because the topic of conversation is murder. Yet Emilia fears even before she opens the bedcurtains, and her question, "O, who hath done this deed?" indicates an immediate suspicion of foul play. When Othello challenges her to name the murderer (5.2.129), her answer is cautious. Not for a moment, however, does she accept Desdemona's confession; her response shows the contrast: "She said so: I must report the truth." Although she has not named the murderer, she is not surprised by Othello's admission. Her retort, "O, the more angel she, / And you the blacker devil!" sets up a series of contrasts, *folly* and *lies*, *false* and *rash*, *water* and *fire*. (The last pair suggests the theory of humors mentioned earlier.) If the last scene is a kind of perverted trial, this fiery dialogue might represent the verbal in-fighting of opposing attorneys. Although she is shaken by the discovery that her husband has been the villain who incited Othello's jealousy, she recovers from the shock after several speeches and resumes her con-demnation of Othello; no words can silence her now. And when her cries are answered by the arrival of help, she faces the greatest challenge of her courage: the entrance of Iago.

Emilia is still Iago's wife, obliged by a vow to obey and honor him. Hoping, perhaps, that there may yet be something honorable in Iago, she offers him an opportunity to deny his guilt. But when he admits saying Desdemona was false (as he must, with Othello present), his wife gives him the Lie Direct and again refuses to be silenced. She has often denounced men, either in self-defense or peevishness. Now she "raises the voice of justice" against the evil of men, scorning even the threat of death. She faces a crisis of divided loyalties. Her mistress is dead, in part because Emilia's loyalty to Iago forced her to take the handkerchief and keep silent about it. But the cause for which Desdemona died is still quite alive, and in that cause Emilia must deny her loyalty to Iago (5.2.200). When she finally confesses taking the handkerchief, it is too late to save Desdemona, but it serves to convict Iago. His shock at her disobedience forces him into the only forthright crime he commits, stabbing his wife. Her death passes unnoticed; only Othello and Emilia are in the room, and the Moor is brooding over his own tragedy. Perhaps she is not really conscious of anyone else. Her last words are addressed to Othello, but her thoughts are on the mistress to whom she has paid her final loyalty. No one pronounces an epitaph over Emilia, but in a way she speaks her own. If we alter one of her final speeches slightly, we might say of Iago, "what should such a fiend do with so good a wife?" In her death she illustrates the possibility that "even apparently commongrained members of society may be . . . capable of making right choices instead of scheming self-protection." Emilia, a product of the social class from which came women who were both petty and major criminals,[60] demonstrates through her "subordination of self in a moral crisis" that there is "hope for the survival of human quality."[61]

Compared with Desdemona and Emilia, Bianca plays a very small role in Othello; her counterpart in the Cinthio tale is hardly a character at all. Shakespeare may be said to have elevated even this prostitute above the generally accepted picture of a strumpet. Unlike other women in her position, she offers her love generously and is patient under Cassio's disdain. Ironically, Emilia, who insults Bianca in the customary manner of "honest" wives (5.1.121), herself suffers being called "whore" by both Othello and Iago; indeed, not even Desdemona escapes the pain of hearing that insult from her husband (4.2.82–90).

At no time in the play does any of the men look upon his wife or mistress in a manner different from the standard attitude displayed toward Elizabethan women. She is either an exalted creature incapable of human temptations and errors (Desdemona, in Othello's earlier view and perhaps at the very end), or she is an animal, usually docile but controlled by her low appetites. Man's lack of insight into the human limitations and desires of woman, his inability to recognize reason and will as influences on her behavior, create an inherently tragic situation; a catalyst, like Iago, merely accelerates and intensifies the tragedy. It is this inevitability that universalizes *Othello*: that a woman may love and forgive and be true, yet suffer death at the hand of the one she loves; that she suffers, not because she has given cause for suspicion but because she has been placed, at birth, in the category "weak creature, incapable of honor." By creating a plot in which the disregard of the potential qualities of woman causes both the major tragedy and the downfall of the villain, Shakespeare demonstrates the danger of underestimating woman. Does this demonstration prove that Shakespeare was a feminist? Heaven forbid! It does indicate, however, that out of years of observing his fellow men—and women—he formed some conclusions about the ways in which they destroyed each other. He displayed his findings to an audience eager to learn more about itself and to profit by examples. I wonder whether some of the Elizabethan gentlemen glanced at their wives during the performance and began to make new estimates of the strange creature, woman.

## Notes

1. Carroll Camden, *The Elizabethan Woman* (Houston, 1952), 18, 19.
2. Ibid., 17, 18.
3. Maurice Valency, *In Praise of Love* (New York, 1958), 240.
4. Louis B. Wright, *The Middle Class Culture in Elizabethan England* (Chapel Hill, 1935), 465, says: "While courtly Platonists and adapters of Petrarchan conventions were glorifying women in dainty verse, the Elizabethan shopkeeper found a literature on the same theme no less fascinating, albeit the works that interested him had a somewhat different point of view from those that delighted the aristocratic audience."
5. Quoted in William Camden, *Remains Concerning Britain* (London, 1870), 307.
6. Sir Roger Wilbraham, *Journal 1593–1616*, ed. Harold S. Scott (London, 1902), 18–19.
7. From "Swetnam, the Woman-Hater," 1620, quoted in Camden, 24.
8. Anthony Nixon, *The Dignitie of Man*, 1612, quoted in Camden, 83–84. Wright (473) lists six other books popular in the 1560s dealing with one side or the other of the controversy: *The deceyte of Women, Schole house of women, Defence of women, The proude wyves Paternoster, The seuen sorowes that women haue,* and *A proper treatyse of a merchantes wyfe.* Philip Stubbes, in *The Anatomie of Abuses* (1583) and *A Crystal Glass for Christian Women* (1591), writes on both sides of the issue.
9. Camden, 23.
10. Ibid., 27.
11. According to Arthur Dent, *The Plaine Man's Path-way to Heaven* (1601), 44–45, women spend ". . . a good part of the day in tricking and trimming, pricking and pinning, pranking and pouncing, girding and lacing, and brauing vp themselves in most exquisite manner, [and then] . . . out they come into the streetes with their pedlers shop about their backs, and carrie their crests very high, taking themselves to be little Angels: or at least somewhat more than other women; whereupon they so exceedingly swell with pride that it is to be feared, they will burst with it as they walk in the streetes . . . for it seemeth that they are altogether a lumpe of pride, a masse of pride, even altogether made of pride, and nothing else but pride, pride, pride." (quoted in Wright, 478–79.)
12. Some of them resorted to philosophical dodges to satisfy themselves in the matter. A reported conversation of Sir William Cecil demonstrates the problem and his solution:

Two years ago 1555 John Knox asked me in private conversation what I thought about the government of women. I candidly replied that, as it was a deviation from the original and proper order of nature, it was to be ranked, no less than slavery, among the punishments consequent upon the fall of man; but that there were occasionally women so endowed [that it was evident that they were] raised up by Divine authority.

Cecil adds that Queens, as "nursing mothers of the Church," were to be "distinguished from females in private life." As to the objection that women could not lead armies into battle, some women had in the past; the argument that woman "is not of so sound judgment as man," Cecil countered with "you can never show . . . so learned a Kyng as we have now a Queene." Quoted in Doris M. Stanton, *The English Woman in History.* (New York, 1957), 127.

13. Valency, 4. To them could be added such fifteenth-century English women as the mystic Margery Kempe, the first Englishwoman to have an autobiography (dictated to a man, since she—like most women of the period—was illiterate), and Margaret Paston, who acted as the agent for her absent husband in financial and legal matters, and even stood off a siege of the family homestead.

14. ". . . many people in Tudor England were born in a village, lived in it all their lives and died there without ever going farther, if as far, as the neighboring village a couple of miles or so away." G. E. Fussell and K. R. Fussell, *The English Country-Woman A.D. 1500–1900* (London, 1953), 17.

15. Ibid., 19, 20.

16. Ibid., 81, 82.

17. Alice Clark, *The Working Life of Women in the 17th Century* (New York, 1920), 69.

18. Ibid., 86. The average wage for farm laborers was sixpence a day; their huts rented for an average of a pound a year, about one-fifth of their wages.

19. "The fact that a woman was soon to have a baby, instead of appealing to [her townmen's] chivalry, seemed to them the best reason for . . . driving her from the village, even when a hedge was her only refuge." Ibid., 89.

20. Stanton, 121.

21. Wright, 204.

22. Ibid., 201.

23. Quoted in William B. Rye, ed. *England as Seen by Foreigners* (London, 1965), 14. Robert Burton said essentially the same thing in 1628, reversing the theme by calling Italy a "paradise for horses and a hell for women" (*Anatomy of Melancholy,* [New York, 1924], 631).

24. Fussell, 27.

25. Rye, 72, 73.

26. Ibid., 98, 90; and Fussell, 27.

27. Rye, 90.

28. Ibid.

29. Ibid.

30. Stanton, 62, 64.

31. Ibid., 122, 123.

32. Fussell, 25.

33. Quoted in Alfred Harbage, *Shakespeare's Audience* (New York, 1941), 74.

34. Ibid., 77–78.

35. John Northbrooke, *A Treatise against Dicing, Dauncing, Playes, and Interludes,* ca. 1577 (repr. London, 1843), 95.

36. Stephen Gosson, *The Schoole of Abuses,* 1578 (repr. London, 1841), 25.

37. Ibid., 50.

38. Wright, 608.

39. Harbage, 159.

40. Fussell, 25.

41. The translation I am using is printed in the *Variorum Edition of Shakespeare,* ed. H. H. Furness (Philadelphia, 1914), 6: 377–89. At least one critic feels that Cinthio was not Shakespeare's source; he posits a (lost) version that combines Cinthio's story with a Byzantine tale, *Digenis Akritas,* since some details of *Othello* fit that version better than they do Cinthio. I find four elements of *Othello* in

*Digenis* and not in Cinthio, five discrepancies in *Digenis,* and four elements that the three accounts have in common. No definite conclusion seems possible in the absence of an English version of either of the two proposed sources. (See Alexander H. Krappe, "A Byzantine Source of Shakespeare's *Othello*," *Modern Language Notes* 39 [1924]: 156–61.)

42. Becom, *The Booke of Matrimony,* RRrl^v, quoted in Camden, 85.

43. John M. Major, "Desdemona and Dido," *Shakespeare Quarterly* 10 (1959): 123–25.

44. Three English translations of the *Aeneid* were made in the sixteenth century, by Gawin Douglas, Surrey, and Richard Stanyhurst (the last an attempt to reproduce the quantitative hexameter of the original Latin).

45. Major, 125.

46. Cinthio, 378.

47. Ibid., 384.

48. Ernest Breenecke, "Nay, That's Not Next!" *Shakespeare Quarterly* 4 (1953): 36.

49. Cinthio, 387.

50. G. Wilson Knight, *The Sovereign Flower* (New York, 1958), 134.

51. Robert B. Heilman, *Magic in the Web* (Lexington, Ky., 1956), 215.

52. The relationship of this speech to what is known as the "First Word from the Cross" would be recognized by Shakespeare's audience, I believe.

53. Knight, 190.

54. John Money, "Othello's 'It is the Cause . . .': An Analyis" *Shakespeare Survey* 6 (1953): 94–105.

55. Cinthio, 384.

56. Clark, 34, 35.

57. Heilman, 83.

58. Ibid., 181.

59. Ibid., 182.

60. As early as the thirteenth and fourteenth centuries, names of women robbers and murderers appeared on the plea rolls (Stanton, 85); Robert Green's crime exposés give ample evidence of women in crime in lower class Elizabethan society.

61. Heilman, 262, n.87.

# Remembering Patriarchy in *As You Like It*

## Kay Stanton

*A*s *You Like It* has long been considered one of Shakespeare's most sublime achievements in comedy, with Rosalind widely praised as his finest female comedic character. Yet many commentators who have seen much to like have also seen much to dislike, and they have found themselves answered by others who have liked what they disliked, disliked what they liked. Also, as with most of Shakespeare's plays, every age has found its attitudes confirmed in the play. Critics in our age, concerned at last with the status of women in society, have begun to probe *As You Like It* for Shakespeare's attitudes on patriarchy and sexual politics.[1] In my study of these subjects, I have found these attitudes to be inextricably bound up with the concept of remembrance.

In the play's first lines, Orlando connects memory with patriarchy: "As I remember, Adam" (1.1.1).[2] What the youth remembers is his father's will regarding him: paltry in provision and null in execution. This society is not only a patriarchy; it is also one based upon primogeniture—Orlando's brother Oliver, the eldest though least virtuous son, is "nearer" their father's "reverence" (1.1.49–50). Yet the justice of primogeniture has been successfully challenged before the play has begun. A younger brother, Frederick, has seized power from and banished his older brother, Duke Senior, the rightful ruler. No doubt Orlando's decision to "mutiny against [his] servitude" (1.1.22) is subconsciously inspired, at least in part, by the model of Frederick. Duke Frederick's power is based not upon benevolent traditions but upon force. The most popular entertainment in Duke Frederick's court is wrestling; it, too, celebrates success through force.[3] Orlando employs force to extract from Oliver a promise of some of his inheritance, but Orlando also intends to try his fortune through force at court by wrestling Charles. Orlando suffers from ambivalence, however: the new way of power through force denies the virtue of his heritage. He sees the spirit of benevolent patriarchy more in himself than in his older brother, and he does not want that tradition to die out, even though it is closely

139

bound up with primogeniture. When he triumphs through Duke Frederick's own means in the new duke's court, he cannot bring himself to reject his heritage in order to accept preferment by the new standard. Since he would rather be dominated by his father's memory than be "adopted heir to Frederick" (1.2.224), he thus puts himself into danger.

Like Orlando, Rosalind in her first appearance is obsessed with the memory of her father. Her pain comes from her empathy at his humiliation but also, like Orlando's, from her own estate's diminished condition. There are no mothers in the play, and no character seems to remember—let alone mourn for—a mother.[4] Ironically, neither Duke Frederick nor Duke Senior has a son; no matter which is in power, it seems that in the future either patriarchy or primogeniture will have to be abandoned. Indeed, Celia envisions a matriarchal government following her father's death: "my father hath no child but I, nor none is like to have" (1.2.16–17). When Rosalind complains, "Unless you could teach me to forget a banished father, you must not learn me how to remember any extraordinary pleasure" (1.2.3–6), Celia responds by negating patriarchy and stressing feminine unity. Whereas Orlando and Rosalind are nostalgic for the past's benevolent patriarchy, subverted in the present, Celia makes little distinction between past and present representatives of patriarchy: "If my uncle, thy banished father, had banished thy uncle, the Duke my father, so thou hadst been still with me, I could have taught my love to take thy father for mine" (1.2.8–11). To Celia, any patriarch can abuse power; one can only trust in female solidarity.

Celia further intends that her matriarchy will rectify the evils of the present patriarchy: what Duke Frederick "hath taken away from thy father perforce, I will render thee again in affection" (1.2.18–20). Celia will accept power in order to deliver it to Rosalind. Although Rosalind has often been held up as a model of feminism,[5] it is actually Celia who is the play's source of feminism. Rosalind continually sees herself in relation to a man: obsessed with her father until she meets Orlando, from then on she is obsessed with Orlando. Through most of the play, however, Celia refuses to define herself through her father or a potential lover. Her matriarchal vision of the future does not include a husband. When Rosalind, cheered by Celia's vision, decides to devise sports, the first that occurs to her is falling in love, which Celia allows as a sport but rejects as a serious occupation.

Instead, Celia proposes that they "mock the good housewife Fortune from her wheel, that her gifts may henceforth be bestowed equally" (1.2.30–32). She thus reinforces her negation of patriarchy's powers, interpreting the course of human life as determined not from men's acts but from the feminine power of goddesses. As one man can overthrow another, she playfully suggests, she and Rosalind can overthrow Fortune and perform Fortune's job better themselves.

Their "political" revolution, however, will be performed through mockery, not force. In their discussion of Fortune's and Nature's powers, they seem to be rehearsing for Celia's promised matriarchy. Sharing the supreme power themselves, they would delegate authority to their female government members. But this exercise in imaginary rule is cut off by the entrance of Touchstone, who proceeds to instruct them in the fine points of oath-making. Celia had bound her promise of power to Rosalind with the oath "By mine honor" (1.2.20), which is the same oath that Touchstone uses. Rosalind's request to Touchstone for information about that oath implies her memory of Celia's use of it. Touchstone teaches his lesson by asking them to "Stand you both forth now. Stroke your chins, and swear by your beards that I am a knave" (1.2.69–70). When Celia does so, Touchstone corrects her: "if you swear by that that is not, you are not forsworn" (1.2.73–74). If Celia here swears by a beard that she does not have, she has done the same thing in her previous oath. Not of the sex that grows beards (and holds power), she has sworn power to Rosalind on the basis of "that that is not"; a matriarchy will not be allowed in this society.

In case Touchstone's lesson has not been enough to dissuade them from thinking that they can hold power, Rosalind and Celia then suffer a demonstration of male force, first through Le Beau's account of the wrestling and then by a match itself. Whereas Le Beau takes wrestling seriously, Rosalind and Celia respond through mockery at this male test of strength until they learn of the injuries that have occurred, with which they sympathize. Touchstone, ever politically conservative, declares that "breaking of ribs" is not "sport for ladies" (1.2.129–30). Although Rosalind and Celia do not agree with Touchstone, they do attempt to dissuade Orlando from wrestling, even though they do not as yet know his identity. After Orlando has triumphed, proclaimed himself Sir Rowland's son, and incurred Duke Frederick's displeasure, Celia disconnects herself from her father ("Were I my father, coz, would I do this?" [1.2.221]), but Rosalind affirms her connection with hers ("My father loved Sir Rowland as his soul / . . . / Had I before known this young man his son, / I should have given him tears unto entreaties / Ere he should thus have ventured" [1.2.225–29]). Although both Rosalind and Celia had admired Orlando before and during the match, once they learn his heritage Rosalind promptly finds herself in love with him and takes him to be hers.

If the wrestling has brought a crisis of allegiance for Orlando between old and new ways of power, it has also provided Rosalind with a male way to power as an alternative to Celia's offer of power through feminine allegiance. As a woman, Rosalind cannot compete with Frederick through force to regain the dukedom for her branch of the family. But an alliance with Orlando, who has demonstrated both strength and proper political association, might be able to effect the reinstatement. The idea, as yet only probably subconscious motivation for Rosalind's love, surely presents itself as a conscious formulation to Duke Frederick and is the true reason for the outbreak of his wrath against both Rosalind and Orlando.

When Duke Frederick banishes Rosalind, his stated reason is that "Thou art thy father's daughter, there's enough" (1.3.56)—with the obvious implication that the father's sins or virtues will be visited upon the offspring. Actually, just prior to Duke Frederick's entrance, Rosalind had used similar reasoning to rationalize her love for Orlando: "The Duke my father loved his father dearly" (1.3.29). Celia had pointed out the flaws in this kind of reasoning: although her father hated Orlando's father, she herself does not hate Orlando. In this scene Celia continues to reject the idea of inherited feelings, and in fact applies her reason against her father's forcefulness. Duke Frederick in turn employs a time-honored masculine strategy for breaking feminine unity by creating rivalry, insisting that Rosalind hurts Celia's popularity. Celia nullifies this idea, standing up to her father and declaring that he must banish her if he banishes Rosalind. Duke Frederick patronizes her before he departs: understanding little of her seriousness, he calls her a fool. Afterward, Celia repeats her idea of exchanging fathers, but this time she follows through; she will disown her own father so she can seek Rosalind's father in the forest. In order to do so, however, she must also revoke her claim to potential rule in the dukedom: "let my father seek another heir" (1.3.97).

In this scene, as in their previous appearance, Celia has shown more strength and flexibility than Rosalind, yet it is Rosalind who decides on a male disguise. Perhaps it is because Celia has so much confidence in herself as a woman that she does not feel a need for masculine imitation in order to assert herself. Rosalind's change of sex, however, can be seen as political. As she is in more danger, she needs more disguise; being more helpless, she needs the extra measure of strength that maleness seems to provide.[6]

Celia proclaims that she and Rosalind will go "To liberty, and not to banishment" (1.3.136), and immediately afterward we see how Duke Senior has reconciled the ideas of liberty and banishment. In his famous forest speech opening act 2.1, he celebrates the forest with metaphors of the court. Clearly, the patriarch, remembering his former life of power, is as yet ambivalent about the liberty of Arden. Although he refers to his companions as "co-mates and brothers in exile" (2.1.1), he retains the title of Duke and the position of leader. In this speech he produces a double perspective of himself as merely another man and as the forest's patriarch—especially through his comparison of himself to Adam, generic man and the father of all mankind. Erickson is right to note that in Duke Senior's all-male community of exile, the members have become somewhat feminized.[7] Indeed, further support can be found in Amiens's attributing the Duke's banishment to "the stubbornness of fortune" (2.1.19), following Celia's stated explanation for life's events, rather than remembering Duke Senior's impotence before Frederick's superior force. But Frederick's takeover is recalled in the account of Jaques and the deer, with Jaques reportedly having sworn that Duke Senior is as bad as Frederick, usurping the forest from the "native burghers" (2.1.23), the deer. Thus male demonstration of force—wrestling at Frederick's court— has its parallel in the killing of deer in the forest. But the deer *are* needed for food, and the Duke, somewhat feminized, does regret having to use force in nature.

The play's continued use of the deer motif, however, reinforces the connection between deer and human beings. When Orlando comes upon the Duke's party in act 2.7, he requests that they forgo feasting "Whiles, like a doe, I go to find my fawn / And give it food" (2.7.128–29). Orlando has triumphed by male standards but still lost everything, freeing him to become somewhat feminized himself. But this companion on his trip to Arden has been Adam, the servant who embodies "the constant service of the antique world" (2.3.57). Just as Adam sees Orlando as the "memory / Of old Sir Rowland" (2.3.3–4), so Adam serves to remind Orlando of a wish to maintain his father's world. And yet, when Duke Senior has witnessed the "effigies" of Sir Rowland as "living" in Orlando's face (2.7.193–94), Orlando, like Celia, "changes fathers." Adam, his former surrogate father figure, disappears once Orlando has found the new "Adam," Duke Senior.

Securely protected by a patriarchal figurehead from the revered and benevolent past, Orlando gives reign to his love for Rosalind, heir of that patriarch. But he expresses that love by abusing nature, carving her name and his love poems onto trees, actions criticized by Touchstone, Jaques, and Rosalind herself (as "Ganymede"). Thus in the play male violence against nature has been demonstrated on three levels: man against man, in the wrestling at Frederick's court; man against animal, in the hunting of deer by Duke Senior's group; and man against vegetation, in Orlando's love carvings. Each subsequent level is less serious than its predecessor, but the point seems to be that men continually make violence a part of their lives, even when in love. Orlando does further violence in love, denying Rosalind's humanity by presenting her as goddesslike and as a composite of the better parts of famous females.

According to one of his poems, she was not even born to his beloved Duke Senior and his duchess in the normal way, but was "devised" by "heavenly synod" (3.2.150). Because he appreciates Rosalind piecemeal, according to her "many parts" (3.2.149), he cannot recognize her when she is fully assembled before him. Of course, she greets him in masculine disguise, but, again, as his portraits of her only celebrate the most traditional "feminine" qualities, he fails to recognize her embodiment of traditionally "masculine" attributes that both sexes in actuality share.

Disguised as "Ganymede," Rosalind proposes to "cure" Orlando of love by the teachings of "an old religious uncle" (3.2.339). Rosalind has, indeed, an uncle—Frederick, who, though not demonstrably religious, could certainly be the source of the misogynistic comments that she spouts. She uses these slanders to test whether Orlando's love can overcome inherent patriarchal and traditional biases against women. As spokesperson for this stance, in a sense she becomes her own enemy. In fact, Celia will chastise her in act 4.1 for misusing her sex (192) and will threaten to undress her to "show the world what the bird hath done to her own nest" (4.1.194–95).

But audiences and readers of the play have no difficulty in perceiving an enormous difference between what Rosalind says to Orlando and what she means. Actually, this discrepancy is rooted in her first lines in the play, when she tells Celia, "Unless you could teach me to forget a banished father, you must not learn me how to remember any extraordinary pleasure" (1.2.3–6). When she remembers patriarchal concerns, she is unhappy and helpless; when she learns to forget the past and appreciate the pleasures of love in the present, she is happy and powerful. She uses the past's accounts of male–female interaction in order to exorcise them. Often she forgets that she is a daughter at all, even casually fleeing from her opportunity to put herself under her father's care.

Orlando, however, does not "forget" patriarchy as thoroughly as Rosalind does, dividing his loyalty and time between "Ganymede" and Duke Senior. Thus Rosalind's father is her rival for Orlando's affection. Orlando honors the past as much as the present, whereas Rosalind would wish that the past be abandoned in favor of full commitment to her. Directly after Orlando has left "Ganymede" for Duke Senior, we are presented with a striking picture of the male camaraderie that attracts the youth in the strange short scene of act 4.2. The Duke's men celebrate the lord who has killed a deer. Jaques suggests that they present him to the Duke "like a Roman conqueror" (4.2.3–4), connecting this killing to war's mass conquest. The group then makes the man into an animal before the audience's eyes, dressing him in the skin and horns of the deer. Furthermore, the all-male group finally remembers women, but only in the most negative stereotype of inevitably unfaithful wives who turn their husbands' horns of victory in the male realm of violence into horns of cuckoldry in the realm of marriage.[8]

Thus we are made to see the ugly underlying assumptions of supposedly benevolent male-dominated society. Men will abandon "feminine" qualities they themselves have developed (as shown in Jaques's turnabout from sympathy for the deer to congratulations for the killer) whenever an opportunity arises to demonstrate or celebrate "manliness" through violence. When they reject the feminine within themselves, they can treat females only with contempt, limiting women to their sexual function and then hating them for that very sexuality.

Male camaraderie and the violent capabilities in men are not always negative, however. The deer-killing celebration of act 4.2 is also, in a sense, an on-stage version of what is taking place off-stage, as Orlando triumphs over two animals—lioness and snake—to rescue his brother Oliver.[9] The sight of Orlando's blood on the napkin causes Rosalind to swoon, breaking down her "Ganymede" disguise. As "Ganymede," she has been an equal to Orlando, but the blood reminds her of the difference between the sexes. A napkin bearing his blood testifies to his capacity to use violence; a napkin bearing her blood would testify to her reproductive capacity. Although she will make a few noble efforts to maintain her equality to Orlando, after the incident of the bloody napkin, she knows that she will have to give up male privilege. She has remembered that she is a woman after all.

If, when she was happiest in love, Rosalind forgot patriarchy, then Celia, who had not much troubled herself about patriarchy, suddenly remembers it when she falls in love. She chooses to marry a man who is exactly like her own father, except that he has been redeemed—as, indeed, Frederick soon will be as well. After the audience has learned of Celia's love for Oliver, Celia never speaks again in the play. The voice of feminism has been silenced by sexual desire for a man who is simply a younger version of her father. On the other hand, marriage to Oliver will enable her to become in reality what she had pretended to be in the forest: Rosalind's sister.

As the play comes to a close, Rosalind remembers patriarchy more and more. It moves in upon her from all sides. The sight of "Ganymede" inspires Duke Senior to say, "I do remember in this shepherd boy / Some lively touches of my daughter's favor" (5.4.26–27). And she remembers him. In her initial entrance in act 5.4, as "Ganymede," she first addresses him, making sure that he will "bestow her on Orlando" (5.4.7), then asks Orlando for confirmation that he will "have her" (5.4.9). When she comes in as herself later in this scene, she speaks the same words, first to the Duke and then to Orlando: "To you I give myself, for I am yours" (5.4.116–17). She becomes a possession subject to either man's will—but she does so willingly. By speaking of "giving herself," she implies that she owns herself, at least at this moment. She inverts the usual pattern in weddings of the father giving his daughter to the groom.[10]

Before Rosalind "dwindles into a wife," however, she makes one last demonstration of power in the masque of Hymen. In her last appearance as "Ganymede," she states, "I have promised to make all this matter even" (5.4.18), and she repeats before she exits, "from hence I go, / To make these doubts all even" (5.4.24–25). Yet when Hymen appears, he speaks of "earthly things made even" (5.4.109), and claims that *he* has brought Rosalind "from heaven" (5.4.112). Shortly afterward, he announces, "Tis I must make conclusion / Of these most strange events" (5.4.126–27). Hymen is clearly given credit for what Rosalind has done. And what she has done is to use magic to invest her appearance as a woman with mystery and majesty. Supposedly, her teacher of this magic was that "old religious uncle," who, if not representing Frederick specifically, certainly represents woman-fearing patriarchy. Assuredly, this pageant will satisfy the males present. In particular, Duke Senior is honored by the presence of a "deity" who recognizes him as the head of the assembly. Also, Orlando's vision of Rosalind as "heavenly," not human, is confirmed. In Hymen's song, although "Wedding is great Juno's crown" (5.4.141), "Tis Hymen peoples every town" (5.4.143). The lesser male deity is made to seem more productive than the most powerful female deity. After she has remembered patriarchy, Rosalind has used powers developed through her assumption of male privilege in order to reconstruct a new patriarchy, with most of its cliches intact.

Although Rosalind surrenders to the strength of patriarchy here, Shakespeare does not allow the play itself to do so, as Erickson supposes.[11] Immediately after the masque, Jaques de Boys enters with news that upstages the pageant. Duke Frederick, in his invasion of the forest to destroy his enemies, met an "old religious man" (5.4.160) when in the "skirts of this wild wood" (5.4.159) and was quickly "converted / Both from his enterprise and from the world" (5.4.161–62). It seems as if Frederick met the "religious uncle" that Rosalind as "Ganymede" had invented or transformed out of her imaginative reconstruction of Frederick himself. The point is that the magical mood that Rosalind has created appears to have removed the threat of force and has provided the means for Duke Senior's return to power. Yet the Duke's subsequent act is to name Orlando, not Rosalind, as his successor. Thus patriarchy *and* primogeniture will be restored, as Orlando has now become the Duke's "son." This news seems to make for an even happier ending than Rosalind had accomplished through Hymen.

However, seeds of potential problems are already sown. Duke Frederick has abdicated the dukedom and will live in the forest. He has not only the followers who accompanied him into Arden, but also Jaques, who abandons Duke Senior to join Frederick. With a duke in the court and a duke in the forest, we are left with the same situation as we had at the beginning. Frederick might become as ambivalent as Duke Senior had been about life in the forest and might try another takeover. This potential problem is duplicated in the situation of the de Boys family. Oliver, after being "converted," thought that he was marrying a shepherd girl—"Aliena"—and gave all of his land and possessions to Orlando. Now that he knows "Aliena"'s true identity as Celia and the whereabouts of her father, he might join Frederick in a takeover attempt to become heir to the dukedom himself. Besides, there is the problem of Jaques de Boys: as second son, he rather than Orlando should be next in line for Oliver's wealth, so he could cause disruption when he learns all that has happened. The chances that these potential disruptions would occur would be slight if either Rosalind or Celia held power.

Rosalind and Celia have become simply wives: no more significant than Audrey and Phebe, as all receive the same amount of recognition in the pronouncements of Hymen and Jaques near the play's end. However, our sense of a happy ending is clouded by this diminishment in status, as well as by our worries over Audrey, who may soon be abandoned by Touchstone, and over Phebe, who was tricked into marrying a man whom she does not love. I suggest that Shakespeare meant for us to see this patriarchal closing-down of women's options as social criticism. The epilogue provides the key to this reading.

Although she might have seemed to abdicate her power to Hymen, to Duke Senior, and to Orlando when she removed her male disguise, in the epilogue Rosalind returns and, in a position of power, commands the audience. She states that she will use magic on them, and she does, creating confusion as to whether she is, ultimately, male or female. She calls herself a "lady" in the first line, later denies being one ("If I were a woman" [17]), then seems to be one again in her curtsy at the end. Of course, Shakespeare's audience knew that boys played female parts, but her remarks still unsettle the dramatic illusion. The audience must see her as a male who played a female who played a male who played a female who is now both a male and a female. This confusion reinforces the fact, demonstrated in the play, that either sex is capable of being a fully functioning member of a society.

Once she has disoriented the audience, she begins to "conjure" (11) them, and she begins with the women. They are to like as much of "this play" (13) as pleases them, for the love they bear to men. The men are then similarly entreated, except that her magic to them includes the promise of her sexual interaction with them *if* she were a woman, suggesting that men will only do something for a woman out of sexual desire. She then asks for approval of the play through sex, not begging. The pun on "this play" as sexual interplay has long been noted,[12] but its implications have not. "This play" will succeed *through sex.* In other words, the play has shown through Celia that women could rule successfully, and through Rosalind that a woman can do anything that a man can, with the possible exception of personal exertion of force. In the epilogue's opening lines, Rosalind declares that "It is not the fashion to see the lady the epilogue, but it is no more unhandsome than to see the lord the prologue." "Lords" have traditionally "spoken the prologue"—the past had been given to them. But the "lady" can speak the epilogue, the future—if "this play" can be made to please both. That is, sexual interaction between men and women holds the key to the establishment of equality between the sexes. Such a thing could be suggested to Shakespeare's audience only through magic and, sadly, although more conjuring has been accomplished by our time, Shakespeare's vision has yet to become a social reality. What prevents it is dependence on the forceful memory of the past of patriarchy. Unless we can be "taught to forget" this "father," we cannot "learn to remember" the "extraordinary pleasure" of lively, intelligent, creative women like Rosalind and Celia expressing their talents fully in society. The choice is there, if we would only like it.

## Notes

1. See especially Louis Adrian Montrose, "The Place of a Brother in *As You Like It:* Social Process and Comic Form," *Shakespeare Quarterly* 32 (1982): 28–54; and Peter B. Erickson, "Sexual Politics and the Social Structure in *As You Like It,*" *Massachusetts Review* 23 (1982): 65–83. Montrose provides excellent analysis of and documentation for the play's subjects of patriarchy and primogeniture. Erickson makes many insightful points in his discussion of the play's sexual politics, although I disagree with his conclusions. In this essay, I analyze aspects of patriarchy, primogeniture, and sexual politics not covered in these two fine articles.

2. All quotations from *As You Like It* are from the Signet Classic Edition, edited by Albert Gilman (New York: New American Library, 1963).

3. I agree with Harold C. Goddard, in *The Meaning of Shakespeare,* 2 vols. (Chicago: University of Chicago Press, 1951), *passim:* the essential conflict in Shakespeare's plays is between force and imagination.

4. The word "mother" is used only twice in the play: Charles asks, just before the wrestling match, "Come, where is this young gallant that is so desirous to lie with his mother earth?" (1.2.189–90); and Rosalind as "Ganymede" queries the disdainful Phebe, "Who might be your mother, / That you insult, exult, and all at once, / Over the wretched?" (3.5.35–37). Both present the idea of a mother negatively: the first suggests a mother as temptation to incest; the other criticizes a mother for allowing sexual superiority to develop in a daughter.

5. Notable exceptions are Erickson, cited above, and Clara Claiborne Park, "As We Like It: How a Girl Can Be Smart and Still Popular," *The American Scholar* 42 (1973): 262–78; reprinted, with revisions, in *The Woman's Part: Feminist Criticism of Shakespeare*, eds. Carol Ruth Swift Lenz, Gayle Greene, and Carol Thomas Neely (Urbana: University of Illinois Press, 1980), 100–116. Both Erickson and Park see Rosalind as playing into the hands of patriarchy. Neither, nor any other published commentator that I have found, discusses Celia as a feminist, though many praise her devotion to Rosalind.

6. See my "The Disguises of Shakespeare's *As You Like it*," *Iowa State Journal of Research* 59 (1985): 295–305.

7. Erickson, 75.

8. Coppelia Kahn in *Man's Estate: Masculine Identity in Shakespeare* (Berkeley: University of California Press, 1981), 125, states that "Rather than being exceptional, a monster, [a cuckold] shares the common lot of men; if women are all whores, men are all cuckolds, and therein brothers. Thus though cuckolding sets men against one another, cuckolder one-upping cuckold, it also creates a bond between men that, though it offsets rivalry to some degree, is based on shared humiliation." See also Joel Fineman, "Fratricide and Cuckoldry: Shakespeare's Doubles," *Psychoanalytic Review* 64 (1977): 409–53; reprinted in *Representing Shakespeare: New Psychoanalytic Essays*, eds. Murray M. Schwartz and Coppelia Kahn (Baltimore: John Hopkins University Press, 1980), 70–109.

9. See Majorie Garber, *Coming of Age in Shakespeare* (London: Methuen, 1981), 145–48, for a discussion of sexual implications involved in this rescue account.

10. Cf. Touchstone's response to Sir Oliver Martext's question of "Is there none here to give the woman?": "I will not take her on gift of any man" (3.3.65–66).

11. Erickson, 81–83.

12. This pun was first suggested by Charles Brooks, in "Shakespeare's Heroine-Actresses," *Shakespeare-Jahrbuch* 96 (1960): 140.

# Timon's Servant Takes a Wife

## Ann Jennalie Cook

*T*imon of Athens deals with money more explicitly than any of Shakespeare's other plays. Variously damned, praised, and explained away, *Timon*'s mosaic of scenes has been analyzed with a fair degree of rigor in recent years.[1] Yet a brief but crucial encounter in the drama's opening moments has either been ignored or completely misunderstood. Here, after the initial dialogue among the Merchant and the Jeweller, the Poet and the Painter, and after Timon generously agrees to pay a debt of five talents to release his friend Ventidius from prison, an old Athenian enters.

> *Old Man.* Lord Timon, hear me speak.
> *Timon.*                                         Freely, good father.
> *Old Man.* Thou hast a servant named Lucilius.
> *Timon.* I have so. What of him?
> *Old Man.* Most noble Timon, call the man before thee.
> *Timon.* Attends he here or no? Lucilius!
> *Lucilius.* Here, at your lordship's service.
> *Old Man.* This fellow here, Lord Timon, this thy creature,
>       By night frequents my house. I am a man
>       That from my first have been inclined to thrift,
>       And my estate deserves an heir more raised
>       Than one which holds a trencher.
> *Timon.*                                         Well; what further?
> *Old Man.* One only daughter have I, no kin else
>       On whom I may confer what I have got.
>       The maid is fair, o' th' youngest for a bride,
>       And I have bred her at my dearest cost
>       In qualities of the best. This man of thine
>       Attempts her love. I prithee, noble lord,
>       Join with me to forbid him her resort;
>       Myself have spoke in vain.
> *Timon.*                                         The man is honest.
> *Old Man.* Therefore he will be, Timon.
>       His honesty rewards him in itself;
>       It must not bear my daughter.
> *Timon.*                                         Does she love him?

*Old Man.* She is young and apt.
                  Our own precedent passions do instruct us
                  What levity's in youth.
*Timon.*                                      Love you the maid?
*Lucilius.* Ay, my good lord, and she accepts of it.
*Old Man.* If in her marriage,
                  I callpr thehe n gods to witneill wchoose
                  Mine heir from forth the beggars of the world
                  And dispossess her all.
*Timon.*                                      How shall she be endowed
                  If she be mated with an equal husband?
*Old Man.* Three talents on the present; in future, all.
*Timon.* This gentleman of mine hath served me long;
                  To build his fortune I will strain a little,
                  For 'tis a bond in men. Give him thy daughter:
                  What you bestow, in him I'll counterpoise,
                  And make him weigh with her.
*Old MCo Man.*
                  If in her maan.
                                             Most noble lord,
                  Pawn me to this your honor, she is his.
*Timon.* My hand to thee; mine honor on my promise.
*Lucilius.* Humbly I thank your lordship. Never may
                  That state or fortune fall into my keeping
                  Which is not owed to you!

                                             (1.1.110–51)

The few critics who comment on this interesting encounter applaud Timon's behavior. H. J. Oliver scores the Athenian father for opposing his daughter's marriage "for purely mercenary reasons" and sees in the master's generosity "nothing 'ridiculous' . . . nothing that is even open to criticism."[2] Others echo his views, claiming that Timon's actions "show immediate right feeling" and that he "serves the causes of romantic love and gratefulness by rewarding an honest and faithful retainer, Lucilius, with enough money to enable him to marry the daughter of a tight-fisted and snobbish old Athenian," "the girl he truly loves."[3] The play's most ardent champion, G. Wilson Knight, calls Timon "a Renaissance prince, benevolent and rich . . . anxious to help anyone of lower status."[4]

Such opinions reveal an astonishing ignorance of accepted behavior in Shakespeare's day. In the twentieth century love takes priority over every other consideration for entering into a marriage. Not so in Renaissance England, where matters of interest—money, social status, family advancement—took a decided precedence over matters of affection— love, physical attraction, compatibility.[5] Moreover, while the right to contract a union today rests solely with the couple themselves, in Shakespeare's time that right was vested in the parent or guardian. Under the canon law of 1603, no marriage could be entered into by a minor without parental consent, and it was considered a grave sin to marry after the age of twenty-one without such consent.[6] Private engagements, secret marriages, or elopements could and usually did incur harsh punishment—physical, financial, social.[7]

In the light of these courtship customs, the wooing of the old Athenian's daughter by Lucilius is considerably more than a case of romantic love thwarted by mere lack of money. To begin with, Lucilius has been resorting to the girl "at night," a time when the English especially feared stealthy meetings.[8] Margaret (disguised as Hero) and Juliet both talk with their lovers secretly at night, while darkness covers the elopements of Jessica, Bianca, and Desdemona. Honest suitors, like Petruchio and Paris, first approach the father in the daylight before wooing a prospective bride under any circumstances. As for Lucilius, though he merely "attempts" the girl's love, so far as her father knows, he not only loves the young woman but already "she accepts of it." In other words, they have a private engagement like that between Claudio and Julietta.[9]

The forbidden nature of the lovers' meetings is emphasized by the fact that Timon, who is responsible for his servant—"this thy creature"—as were all masters,[10] knows nothing of Lucilius's courtship. According to codes of ethical conduct, Lucilius should have asked for Timon's approval, as do Gratiano and Nerissa. In the present circumstance, the old Athenian begs that Timon "Join with me to forbid him her resort; / Myself have spoke in vain." Despite his master's protest that Lucilius is honest, the servant has deceived his lord, initially must have deceived the girl's father, and most recently has flatly defied the legitimate authority of the Athenian. The young woman's inexperience—she is, after all, "o'th' youngest for a bride"—may partly excuse her behavior, as it does Juliet's, but no such excuse prevails for Lucilius. Having served Timon long, he would presumably be old enough to understand the irregularity of his actions.

Moreover, the daughter's extreme youth simply reinforces the father's obligation to protect her future welfare and defend her against "What levity's in youth." For years he has "been inclined to thrift." Yet he has spared no expense on her education: "I have bred her at my dearest cost / In qualities of the best." At her marriage she will receive "Three talents on the present; in future, all," for "One only daughter have I, no kin else / On whom I may confer what I have got." Just barely of marriageable age, this heiress has ample beauty and wealth to attract a wide choice of prospective husbands, certainly a man "more raised / Than one which holds a trencher." The outraged father may echo the choleric Capulet in vowing to "dispossess her all" if she marries without his consent. But, unlike *Romeo and Juliet*, the audience here lacks the extenuating knowledge of a prior marriage, sympathetically presented. Not only is the old Athenian well within his rights as the parent of a minor and as a man whose entire life has been dedicated to his daughter's worldly advancement, but what other weapon save disinheritance remains to him?

Timon's proper response to such a tale from such a father—its truth freely admitted by Lucilius—should be a sound chastisement of his servant. Indeed, the man merits dismissal from Timon's service. Yet the master hands out a munificent reward rather than severe punishment, promising to provide an amount equal to the bride's resources. Most of the critics limit this sum to three talents,[11] the dowry offered at the time of marriage. Alas, Timon actually pledges, "What you bestow, in him I'll counterpoise, / And make him weigh with her"—that is, the dowry plus the amount of the father's lifelong accumulation of wealth that she will eventually inherit. By comparison, the five talents for Ventidius's debt is a pittance. No wonder Timon says, "To build his fortune I will *strain* a little."

And well he might strain. The estimates for the equivalent value of three talents, all of them out of date, range from £750 to $6,000 to $7,950 (though no one provides any basis for these calculations).[12] In contemporary terms, the pledge was immense. Ordinary working men, even the most skilled, would expect to earn no more than £10 a year. Schoolmasters' and clerics' salaries ranged from £10 to £20. Even a gentleman retainer—and Lucilius is perhaps derogatively termed a trencherbearer—looked for no more, often for less.[13] Lucilius and his bride will enjoy an uncommonly comfortable existence, in effect twice as luxurious as the old Athenian's. Shakespeare himself never approached such an income.

Now what is the point of introducing a vignette about a servant's irregular courtship into *Timon of Athens?* I think the scene is intended to show almost from Timon's first appearance that he is gravely flawed in the exercise of his benevolence. Later scenes amply demonstrate the folly of his prodigality and the ingratitude of his friends. But this brief encounter has already stamped Timon as a man who uses wealth to overturn social conventions and to reward questionable behavior. Defenders of Timon's character, who see him cruelly victimized for embodying the old ideals of munificence in the face of a cold new commercial world, fail to recognize his subversion of both monetary and marital codes in the scene with Lucilius. Timon's princely endowment of a man who has done much to merit disapproval and who has done nothing to merit a fortune except to serve his master for a long time should raise doubts about the worth of other recipients of Timon's generosity. Immediately one wonders whether Ventidius, who has just been released from imprisonment for debt, deserves such relief. The Lucilius incident serves admirably as a bridge between what first seems to be a laudable act of friendship and the onslaught of more obvious opportunists. Shakespeare apparently intends his audience to question both the wisdom and the ethics of Timon's actions from the outset.

Moreover, the link between money and love, introduced so clearly in this brief scene, is one of the dominant motifs of the play. Except for the Steward, all love is reduced to what can be bought, to a pervasive, perverted form of prostitution. There is every reason to suppose that Lucilius is attracted as much by his beloved's wealth as by her beauty and that he is taking advantage of her youth to further his own financial interests. And the father is willing enough to hand over his daughter, even to a man whose conduct has been less than honorable, if the price is right. Thus Timon's house is clearly established as a place where money buys love and where love is denied if it is not paid for. The very language of the master and the father points to the commercial nature of their transaction:

> Timon.                            Give him thy daughter;
>         What you *bestow*, in him I'll *counterpoise*,
>         And make him *weigh* with her.
> Old Man.                      Most noble lord,
>         *Pawn* me to this your honor, she is his.
>
>                                            (italics mine)

The subsequent appearance of the usurers' servants, called "bawds between gold and want," of the Fool who serves a brothelkeeper, and of two prostitutes makes explicit what Shakespeare has already indicated more subtly. Timon is in the business of buying and selling love—for himself and for other people. Not surprisingly, when the money runs out and the business folds, Lucilius deserts Timon, just like all the other whore-friends. When he vows "Never may / that state or fortune fall into my keeping / Which is not owed to you!"—these are Lucilius's last words. Timon never sees him again.

## Notes

1. See, for example, David Cook, "*Timon of Athens*," *Shakespeare Survey* 16 (1963): 83–94; Francelia Butler, *The Strange Critical Fortunes of Shakespeare's "Timon of Athens"* (Ames: Iowa State University Press, 1966); Ann Lancashire, "*Timon of Athens:* Shakespeare's *Dr. Faustus*," *Shakespeare Quarterly* 21 (1970): 35–44; Michael Tinker, "Theme in *Timon of Athens*," in *Shakespeare's Last Plays*, eds. Richard C. Tobias and Paul G. Zolbrod (Athens: Ohio University Press, 1974); James C. Bulman, "The Date and Production of *Timon* Reconsidered," *Shakespeare Survey* 27 (1974): 111–27, and "Shakespeare's Use of the *Timon* Comedy," *Shakespeare Survey* 29 (1976): 103–16; Robert C. Fulton, "Timon, Cupid, and the Amazons," *Shakespeare Studies* 9 (1976): 283–99; William W. E. Slights, "*Genera mixta* and *Timon of*

*Athens," Studies in Philology* 74 (1977): 39–62; Lewis Walker, "Fortune and Friendship in *Timon of Athens," Texas Studies in Language and Literature* 18 (1977): 577–600; G. Wilson Knight, *Shakespeare's Dramatic Challenge* (New York: Harper and Row, 1977); Ruth Levitsky, "Timon: Shakespeare's *Magnyfycence* and an Embryonic Lear," *Shakespeare Studies* 11 (1978): 107–21; Rolf Soellner, "Timon of Athens," *Shakespeare's Pessimistic Tragedy, with a Stage History by Gary Jay Williams* (Columbus: Ohio State University Press, 1979); Peter Pauls, "Shakespeare's *Timon of Athens* and Renaissance Diogeniana," *The Upstart Crow* 3 (Fall, 1980): 54–66; Clifford Davidson, "Timon of Athens: The Iconography of False Friendship," *Huntington Library Quarterly* 43 (1980): 181–200; Lewis Walker, "Timon of Athens and the Morality Tradition," *Shakespeare Studies* 12 (1979): 159–78; Leo Paul S. de Alvarez, "Timon of Athens," *Shakespeare as Political Thinker* (Durham: Carolina Academic Press, 1981), 157–79; Agostino Lombard, "The Two Utopias of *Timon of Athens," Shakespeare-Jahrbuch* 120 (1984): 85–89; William O. Scott, "The Paradox of TImon's Self-Cursing," *Shakespeare Quarterly* 35 (1984): 290–304; Natalie Shainess, "Shakespeare's *Timon of Athens*: The Progress from Naivete to Cynicism," *Journal of the American Academy of Psychoanalysis* 12 (July 1984): 425–40.

2. H. J. Oliver, ed., *Timon of Athens*, New Arden Shakespeare (London: Methuen, 1959).

3. Cook, 88; Ramsey, 164; Charlton Hinman, ed., *The Life of Timon of Athens*, in *William Shakespeare The Complete Works*, ed. Alfred Harbage (Baltimore: Penguin, 1969), 1136.

4. Knight, 115.

5. See Lawrence Stone, "Marriage among the English Nobility in the 16th and 17th Centuries," *Comparative Studies in Society and History* 3 (1960-61): 182–206; *The Crisis of the Aristocracy, 1558–1641* (Oxford: Clarendon Press, 1965), esp. 175–78, 192–95, 589–671; *The Family, Sex and Marriage in England, 1500–1800* (New York: Harper and Row, 1977), esp. 3–62, 85–218; Peter Laslett, *The World We Have Lost* (New York: Scribner's, 1965), esp. 81–106; *Family Life and Illicit Love in Earlier Generations* (Cambridge: Cambridge University Press, 1977), esp. 1–49, 102–73.

6. Stone, *Family*. 151, 171–72; *Crisis*, 594–99, 608–9, 619; "Marriage," 182–85. For the 1603 canons, see E. Gibson, *Codex Juris Ecclesiastici Anglicani* (London: Clarendon Press, 1761), 421.

7. Stone, *Crisis*, 605–6, 609–10; *Family*, 103–4, 181; "Marriage," 186; G. R. Hibbard, "Love, Marriage and Money in Shakespeare's Theatre and Shakespeare's England," *The Elizabethan Theatre VI* (Hamden, Conn.: Archon Books, 1977), 135–36.

8. For example, objections to night performances of plays mentioned the evil conduct that could be cloaked by darkness:

> If they be dangerous on the day time, more daungerous on the night certainely: if on a stage, & in open courtes, much more in chambers and private houses. For there are manie roumes beside that where the play is, & peradventure the strangeness of the place & lacke of light to guide them, causeth error in their way, more than good Christians should in their houses suffer.

Gervase Babington, *A Very Fruitful Exposition of the Commandements*, in E. K. Chambers, *The Elizabethan Stage* (Oxford: Clarendon Press, 1923), 4:225.

9. On the technicalities of private contracts, see W. W. Lawrence, *Shakespeare's Problem Comedies*, 2nd ed. (1931; rpt. New York: Frederick Ungar, 1960), 95–96; Harding P. Davis, "Elizabethan Betrothals and *Measure for Measure," JEGP* 49 (1950): 139–58; J. Birje-Patil, "Marriage Contracts in *Measure for Measure,"*

*Shakespeare Studies* 5 (1969): 106–11; A. D. Nuttall, *"Measure for Measure:* The Bed-Trick," *Shakespeare Survey* 28 (1975): 51–56; Ernest Schanzer, "The Marriage Contracts in *Measure for Measure," Shakespeare Survey* 13 (1960): 85–86; S. Nagarajan, *"Measure for Measure* and Elizabethan Betrothals," *Shakespeare Quarterly* 14 (1963): 115–19; Karl P. Wentersdorf, "The Marriage Contracts in *Measure for Measure:* A Reconsideration," *Shakespeare Survey* 32 (1979): 129–44.

10. For a full analysis of the master-servant relationship that provided the basis for the English social system, see Laslett, *The World We Have Lost.*

11. See, for example, Terence Spencer, "Shakespeare Learns the Value of Money: The Dramatist at Work on *Timon of Athens," Shakespeare Survey* 6 (1953): 76.

12. Ibid., Hinman, 1143n; Lewis Walker, "Money in *Timon of Athens," Philological Quarterly* 57 (1978): 269.

13. See Paul L. Hughes and James F. Larkin, eds., *Tudor Royal Proclamations* (New Haven: Yale University Press, 1969), 2:401–3, 422–23; 3:22–25, 40–42, 59; G. R. Batho, ed., *The Household Papers of Henry Percy, Ninth Earl of Northumberland (1564–1632),* Camden Society Publications, 3rd ser. 93 (1962): 149ff; William Harrison, *The Description of England,* ed. Georges Edelen (Ithaca: Cornell University Press, 1968), 28; Kenneth Charlton, *Education in Renaissance England* (London: Routledge and Kegan Paul, 1965), 161–62; M. E. Finch, *The Wealth of Five Northamptonshire Families, 1540–1640,* Publications of the Northamptonshire Record Society 19 (1954–55): 121, 127; Lisle C. John, "Roland Whyte, Elizabethan Letter-Writer," *Studies in the Renaissance* 8 (1961): 219.

# Puck's Headless Bear—Revisited

## Charles A. Rahter

When Puck sets out after the Athenian hempen home-spuns "through bog, through bush, through brake, through brier," he tells us that he will assume just about as many shapes as Proteus himself:

> Sometimes a horse I'll be, sometime a hound,
> A hog, a headless bear, sometime a fire,
> And neigh, and bark, and grunt, and roar and burn,
> Like horse, hound, hog, bear, fire, at every turn.
>
> (*MND* 3.1.111–14)

Editors and emendators have been troubled by the "headless bear," suggesting in its place "heedless" (Delius's emendation, which Percy Simpson says "must have been symptomatic of his own state of mind"), "curbless," and so forth. In *Studies in Elizabethan Drama* Simpson reprinted an earlier piece of his, "The 'Headless Bear' in Shakespeare and Burton," in which he pointed out that "during Shakespeare's lifetime the headless bear appeared in a more realistic setting than any that his art could furnish," and cites a pamphlet, published in 1614 by John Trundle under the title *A Miracle of Miracles, etc.*, which purports to be an account of some strange and wonderful events that took place in Sommersetshire in September 1613.[1] The pamphlet has the running-title *Strange News out of Sommersetshire* and is bound together with two other tracts; one having to do with a prophesy and return from the dead by a young girl in Germany, the other recounting a disastrous flood in Lincolnshire, both events having occurred, it is claimed, in 1613 also. Together the three pieces comprise STC /14068. The title page of the volume includes a woodcut showing a woman in bed, surrounded by five persons (three men and two women), a child angel, and a huge headless bear. The bear is the Devil in animal form, we learn, who, for reasons not explained, had been pursuing this poor woman, one Margaret Cooper. Then follows a preface "To My Friends and Readers in London," signed "Your Friend, T.I."

Professor Simpson summarizes the material in *Strange News out of*

*Sommersetshire* and then points out that Burton undoubtedly owned the copy that now rests in the Bodleian Library,[2] for it bears his initials and his mark on the title page. And to the third edition of *The Anatomy of Melancholy*, 1628, Burton prefixed some verses entitled "The Authors Abstract of Melancholy," in which he describes the fantastic forms, shapes, and ideas that come into the melancholic brain, among them

> Methinks I heare, methinks I see
> Ghosts, Goblins, fiends; my phantasie
> Presents a thousand ugly shapes
> Headless bears, black men, and apes. . . .

"This," says Simpson, "is a suggestive parallel to Shakespeare, and Burton may have derived it from his own copy of T.I.'s pamphlet."[3] But what about Shakespeare? *A Midsummer Night's Dream* was written in the mid-nineties. Was Puck's "headless bear," then, a compositor's error or the invention of Shakespeare's unbridled fancy? Neither. The purpose of this note is to reinforce Simpson's suggestion that headless bears were well known when Shakespeare wrote *A Midsummer Night's Dream* and to resolve a conjecture made in a footnote in the article referred to about the activities of Trundle as a publisher and author.

When one examines STC /5681, *A true and most Dreadfull discourse of a woman possessed with the Deuill . . . 1584 . . . Imprinted at London for Thomas Nelson*, one discovers Trundle's *Strange News out of Sommersetshire* in toto and verbatim, allowing for the inevitable variants in the resetting of the type and the changing of dates and time indicators. For example, Nelson's account begins, "Vpon the nineth day of May last past *Anno*. 1584. There was a Yeoman of honest reputation, dwelling in the Towne of *Dichet*, etc." Trundle's, on the other hand, begins, "Vpon the ninth day of Septemb. last past, there was a Yeoman of honest reputation, dwelling in the Towne of Dichet, etc." But essentially the pamphlets are the same, right down to "the names of the Witnesses, that this is most true."[4] Both are in black letter, Nelson's "To the Reader," however, being in italic, Trundle's, in roman type. Nelson's pamphlet is a single gathering octavo, while Trundle's small book is a quarto of four gatherings, *Strange News* comprising Sigs. A——B3r. Trundle's title page is much more elaborate: it contains the titles of all three pamphlets in the volume, as well as the elaborate woodcut described above. Nelson's title page reads as follows: *A true and most Dreadfull discourse of a woman possessed with the Deuill: who in the likeness of a headlesse Beare fetched her out of her Bedd, and in the presence of seuen persons, most straungely roulled her thorow three Chambers, and doune a high paire of staiers, on the fower and twentie of May Last. 1584. At Dichet in Sommersetshire. A matter as miracu-*

*lous as euer was seen in our time.* [Ornament: A woodcut of a headless, tailless animal, presumably a bear, in profile, going on all fours.] *Imprinted at London for Thomas Nelson.*

Here, then, is the source of Puck's headless bear. In circulation long before the composition of *A Midsummer Night's Dream*, Nelson's pamphlet with its delightful title page must surely have caught the omnivorous eye of Puck's creator, who stored it away in his memory against the day when he needed just such an image. That of all the monstrosities and prodigies recounted in the popular press of the late sixteenth century the headless bear was a favorite is indicated by Trundle's reprinting almost thirty years after the appearance of Nelson's pamphlet—and passing it off as having occurred within the year—this account of one; and the bear, in Simpson's words, "had a new lease on life in 1641 when John Thomas revived the pamphlet in a garbled form and published it with a new title page: *Most Fearefull and Strange Newes from the Bishopprick of Durham, Being a true Relation of one Margret Hooper of Edenbyres, neere the River Darwent in the said Bishopprickes. Who was most fearfully possessed and tormented with the Devill, as also in what ugly shape he first appeared unto her, how lamentably she was handled with this evill spirit, and at last how wonderfully the Lord delivered her. Affirmed by these Cridible witnesses there present. November the fifteenth. 1641.*

| | |
|---|---|
| *Stephen Hooper.* | *Alexander Egleston.* |
| *John Hooper.* | *Anthony Westgarth.* |
| *John Sley.* | *Aliee Egleston.* |

*And divers others.*

*London, Printed for John Thomas, 1641.*[5]

This version, moreover, was reprinted at Newcastle in 1843, with a preface by one M.A.R., who maintains that the names used in the 1641 version were those of actual inhabitants of Edmondbyres and Huntsworth, the locales to which Dichet and Rockhampton were changed in that version.[6] And finally, as Professor Simpson reminds us, the monster is not extinct even in modern times: did he not appear as late as 1889 in *Silvie and Bruno?*

> He thought he saw a Coach-and-Four
>     That stood beside his bed:
> He looked again, and found it was
>     A Bear without a Head.
> 'Poor thing,' he said, 'poor silly thing!
>     It's waiting to be fed.'

"Did Lewis Carroll draw on some forgotten folk-lore or take a hint from Shakespeare or from Burton . . .? Or was this an unconscious recoinage of his own? In any case the practical suggestion that the gaping orifice required feeding was both original and characteristic; it sprang from a mind as logical as it was imaginative."[7]

The preface to Trundle's little book, signed T.I., admonishes us that these miracles and disasters were sent by God as warnings to the wicked. T.I. cites the specific case of a man and his wife at Holnhurst in Hampshire, both of whom were executed by God Himself with His holy fire from heaven. This incident had been written up by John Hilliard, a minister, earlier in 1613, and published by Trundle a short time before he published *A Miracle of Miracles*. Simpson has suggested that the T.I. who wrote the preface was probably Trundle himself, using his initials reversed, something common enough at the time, and that he did so to advertise Hilliard's book, *Fire from Heaven. Burning the body of one John Hitchell of Holnehurst, within the parish of Christ-church, in the county of Southampton, the 26. of June last 1613, who by the same was consumed to ashes, and no fire seene, lying therein smoaking and smothering three dayes and three nights, not to be quenched by water, nor the help of man's hand.* "If so," says Simpson, "He adroitly caught a suggestion of the clerical manner."[8] This is an interesting conjecture, half of which is borne out by the facts, half not so. Trundle did indeed take the opportunity to advertise Hilliard's book by making a slight alteration in the preface to his *A Miracle of Miracles* that he got, again, verbatim from the earlier publication by Nelson, *A true and most Dreadfull discourse.* In the preface to Nelson's pamphlet, which is not signed, the passage in question reads:

> Many are the woonders which hath lately happened, as of suddaine and straunge death vpon periured persons, straunge sights in the Aier, straunge birthes on the Earth: Earth quakes, commetts and fiery Impressions, and all to put vs in mynde of God, whose woorkes are wonderfull.
>
> Remember the late storme of haylstones in which many thinges were slaine and beaten to the ground, which Hailestones were equall in greatnesse to a Goose Egge, of eight inches about. (Sig. A 2v)

Trundle, or T.I., has altered this to read as follows:

> Many are the wonders which haue lately happened, as of soadine and strange death vpon periured persons, strange sights in the Ayre, strange births on the Earth, Earthquakes, Commets, and fierie Impressions, with the execution of God himself from his holy fire in heauen, on the wretched man and his wife, at *Holnhurst* in Hampshire; written by that worthy Minister maister *Hilliard;* and all to put vs in minde of God, whose workes are wonderfull. (Sig. A 3v)

Both then conclude with the following paragraph:

These and suche like examples (good Reader) warneth vs to be watchfull for the day of the Lorde which is at hand, least sodainly his wrath be kindled against vs. Let vs therefore pray to almightie God to hold back his Rod, to be mercifull to vs, and to forgiue vs all that is past: that through the assistaunce of his Spirte, we maie with penitent hartes liue in his feare to our liues ende. Finis. (Nelson, Sig. A 2v)

It is evident, then, that Trundle, or T.I., did not derive the clerical manner from Hilliard; it was in the preface that Trundle picked up with the pamphlet from Thomas Nelson.[9] The diction and imagery and tone of this preface can be found in countless other admonitions in countless other tracts and pamphlets published before and after Trundle's *A Miracle of Miracles*. In 1595, for example, William Barley published a fairly long tract, compiled interestingly by one T.I., entitled *A World of wonders. A Masse of Murthers. A Couie of Cosonages. Containing many of the moste notablest Wonders, horrible Murthers and detestable Cosonages that haue beene within this Land.*, in the preface to which T.I. says that he has made this compilation to "stirre and moue vs vp to prayer to God to amendment of our sinful liues, to the horror of such wicked actions and such like." Compare this with the preface to the 1584 *A true and most Dreadfull discourse* and Trundle's *A Miracle of Miracles*: "Let not this which is here declared seeme a fained fable vnto thee, but assure they selfe that such thinges are sent as warnignes for our wickednesse and to put vs in mynd of the staie of our saluation, which is an assured faith in Christ Iesus: from which piller if wee once shrinke, the Tempter is redie to driue vs into dispaier of Gods mercie" (Nelson, Sig. A 3r-v). As the puritan spirit and the emerging middle class came more and more into prominence and power during Elizabeth I's reign and throughout the first half of the seventeenth century, books and pamphlets dealing with low-life, monstrosities and prodigies of nature, murder, and witchcraft were more and more in demand; and they appeared to meet the demand, almost always prefaced by a solemn admonition to the reader to consider the contents of the book or pamphlet as a sign of God's punishment of sinners and a warning to him to prepare his soul for that day of judgment that was close at hand.[10] Neither Shakespeare nor Burton was either a puritan or a middle-class tradesman, but both had, apparently, a keen interest in this mass of ephemeral reading—as exemplified by *Strange News out of Sommersetshire*—and derived from it, one suspects, great delight also.

### Notes

1. Percy Simpson, *Studies in Elizabethan Drama* (Oxford: Oxford University Press, 1955), 89. "The 'Headless Bear' in Shakespeare and Burton," 89–94, in this volume originally appeared in the *Queen's Quarterly* of Canada in 1932.

2. Pollard and Redgrave locate only two copies: in the British Museum and in the Bodleian Library.

3. Simpson, 94.

4. Nelson, Sig. A 8r.

5. Simpson, 94.

6. Ibid., 93.

7. Ibid., 94.

8. Ibid., 90n.

9. Actually, there is no way of proving that Trundle got the preface or the story from Nelson's pamphlet; he may very well have picked it up from a later pirating or reprinting of the Nelson pamphlet. The important point is that the story of the headless bear was in print no later than 1584 and, when the mass of this popular literature is properly surveyed and recorded, it may turn out to be much older than that.

10. For a full study of the popular literature of the period, the reader is referred to Louis B. Wright's *Middle-Class Culture in Elizabethan England* (Chapel Hill: University of North Carolina Press, 1935), especially to chap. 12, "Ephemeral Reading."

# Textual Double Knots:
# "make rope's in such a scarre"

## Gary Taylor

*Dia.* I see that men make rope's in such a scarre,
That wee'l forsake our selues. Giue me that Ring.
*(All's Well That Ends Well,* 2063–64)

This is one of the most famous cruxes in the Shakespeare canon. The Old Cambridge editors record twenty-five conjectural emendations; none of these, or several subsequent conjectures, has achieved wide currency, for most are wildly implausible, and many editors, in despair, simply print the passage as it stands in the Folio. The sources of this difficulty are self-evident. Diana's first line contains at least two errors that affect the two key terms in the image or thought; the solution to one error must therefore cohere with the solution to the other, and yet neither term can give us any guidance in finding its companion; the precise location of one error is disputable; the first error offers limited scope for emendation based on the *ductus litterarum,* while the second could be a misreading of so many different words that conjecture hardly knows where to begin. In these circumstances it may prove impossible to rectify the corruption. But before coming to this hopeless conclusion, we should examine exhaustively the evidence. As it happens, I believe I have found a reasonably satisfactory solution. Others before me have found what they thought were solutions; let me emphasize at the outset that I am less concerned with advocating my own solution than with understanding the problems such a crux presents and their effect on the methodology and philosophy of emendation.

The evidence is of two kinds, *signifiant* and structural. By *signifiant* I mean the evidence of grammar, syntax, meter, word-meaning, and dramatic context; all that defines the possible "meaning" of the correct restoration as a linguistic sign: its grammatical function and semantic content. By structural I mean the evidence that helps us to reconstruct the literal shape of that sign as physical object: the letters of which it was composed. These two categories resemble in some, but not all, respects

163

the familiar linguistic categories of signified and signifier, and the familiar bibliographical categories of substantives and accidentals (or incidentals).[1]

We begin with the *signifiant* evidence.

1. Both *make rope's* and *scarre* appear to be corrupt. At the very least, the apostrophe in *rope's,* if meant to signify either the possessive singular or an elision of *us,* cannot coexist with *make;* and no known usage of *scarre* produces satisfactory sense.[2] It is possible that an emendation of *make rope's* would create a new context in which *scarre* would be satisfactory, but no such emendation has been produced, and the requirements of the larger context make it unlikely that any meaning of *scarre* could be satisfactory however *make rope's* was emended. Thus the passage contains two cruxes and requires two emendations, and, though these obviously will be related, it is valuable logically to keep them distinct. I will refer to *make rope's* as crux X and *scarre* as crux Y.

2. Metrically, the emendation of *rope's* must be a word of one syllable;[3] that of *scarre,* either of one syllable or, if of two, accented on the first.

3. Crux X offers two alternative syntactical possibilities, depending on which term we emend: *may* + verb + *us,* or *make* + [plural?] noun.

4. *In* may mean either *in* or *e'en.*[4] These are alternative interpretations of an ambiguous spelling; *e'en* would not be an emendation, but a modernization. To my knowledge, no one has remarked on this alternative.

5. The construction *such a [Y]* requires that Y be a noun; the exact relation of this noun to crux X will depend upon our interpretation of *in.* If *in* equals *e'en,* and *make* is retained, then the sentence can describe a transformation: "I see that men turn X into Y."[5] If it does not describe a transformation, then the *e'en* is merely intensive. But if *make* is emended, and/or *in* = *in* (as all conjectures hitherto have assumed), then the sentence must be paraphrased "I see that men do X in such a fashion" or "in such a quantity," or the *in* clause must describe the locale for the action of the verb X.

These first five conditions are rudimentary, and almost all conjectures satisfy them. (That editors have not mentioned the *in/e'en* possibility in no way invalidates their conjectures; we are concerned at the moment with defining the range of permissible meanings.) But the remaining conditions have usually not been satisfied.

6. *That* in line 2064 is ambiguous, and can relate to actual consequence or mere motive; the sentence can be construed either as "I see that men X in *such* a Y *that* we do forsake ourselves" or "I see that men X in such a Y *so that* we will forsake ourselves." The *in/e'en* ambiguity is exclusive; we must choose one or the other. The ambiguity of *that* is not

exclusive and can be retained as part of the symbolic finished statement; it is also, as we shall see, possibly related to ambiguities in the larger context.

7. The word *forsake*, in Shakespeare, contains—often explicitly and literally, but always at least implicitly—the idea of "movement away from."[6] Whatever image or thought we supply for X-Y must be consistent with this; that is, it must at least *permit* this meaning, and preferably it should anticipate or encourage or relate to this meaning. Movement away from our selves could have one of two motives, fear or temptation. If Diana means that women are frightened out of themselves, she must be speaking facetiously, and the preceding sentence would have to be construed:

(a) I see that men make Xs (which are good)
  e'en *such* a Y (which is bad, or frightening)
  that we'll forsake our selves
or (b) I see that men do X in such a (frightening or aggressive manner)
  Y that we'll forsake our selves.
or (c) I see that men may put [?] us in such a scare that we'll forsake
  ourselves

None of these interpretations seems likely, though they are possible. More probably, Diana means that men tempt women to forsake themselves, by means of something attractive, some bait or lure.

8. Shakespeare uses the verbal formula of "forsaking one's self" on only three other occasions. We have no guarantee that these other occasions illuminate the thought behind this passage, but as collateral evidence these parallels deserve attention.

> "Is thine own heart to thine own face affected?
> Can thy right hand seize love upon thy left?
> Then woo thyself, be of thyself rejected;
> Steal thine own freedom, and complain on theft.
>   Narcissus so himself himself forsook,
>   And died to kiss his shadow in the brook."
> (*Venus and Adonis*, 157–62)

> Beshrew that heart that makes my heart to groan
> For that deep wound it gives my friend and me!
> Is't not enough to torture me alone,
> But slave to slavery my sweet'st friend must be?
> Me from my self thy cruel eye hath taken,
> And my next self thou harder hast engrossed;
> Of him, my self, and thee, I am forsaken;
> A torment thrice three-fold thus to be crossed.
> Prison my heart in thy steel bosom's ward,

But then my friend's heart let my poor heart bail;
Whoe'er keeps me, let my heart be his guard;
Thou canst not then use rigour in my gaol.
   And yet thou wilt; for I, being pent in thee,
   Perforce am thine, and all that is in me.

                               (Sonnet 133)

And in this aim there is such thwarting strife
That one for all or all for one we gage:
As life for honour in fell battle's rage;
   Honour for wealth; and oft that wealth doth cost
   The death of all, and all together lost.

So that in vent'ring ill we leave to be
The things we are for that which we expect;
And this ambitious foul infirmity,
In having much, torments us with defect
Of that we have; so then we do neglect
   The thing we have and, all for want of wit,
   Make something nothing by augmenting it.

Such hazard now must doting Tarquin make,
Pawning his honour to obtain his lust;
And for himself himself he must forsake— . . .

             (*The Rape of Lucrece*, 143–57)

All three of these parallels, it must be conceded, are from nondramatic poems. But they are, nonetheless, possible clues to a pattern of thought or verbal association in Shakespeare's mind. As such, the fact that all four occurrences relate this image to a debasing sexual love seems more important than the fact that three of the passages occur in poems and only one in a play. The *Venus and Adonis* parallel is of little use for its subject matter, though stylistically it resembles the other two as a rhetorically balanced succession of paradoxes based upon analytical distinctions, and there are a number of other parallels between the play and the poem.[7] The sonnet is more troubling: its meaning is more convoluted and elliptical; in itself it does not tell us why the speaker has been led to forsake himself, only that he has; it describes, complains of, expands upon, extrapolates from that situation. In *All's Well* we need a motive for the forsaking; therefore, this sonnet is of little use. The passage from *Lucrece*, however, is unmistakably related to *All's Well*: in particular, the line that immediately precedes "himself . . . forsake"—"Pawning his honour to obtain his lust"—describes what Bertram is doing in this scene, especially his relinquishing of the ring—the very action initiated in Diana's next words, "Give me that Ring." The parallel is striking, and it would be reasonable to suppose that the thought behind the corrupt line in *All's Well* is similar to that in the preserved lines of *Lucrece*. Tarquin forsakes himself because he "Make(s) something nothing," substitutes lust for honor, hazards honor for wealth. These images, of exchanging or confusing a good with a bad, and of forsaking oneself as a consequence, strongly favor the construction "make X [a bad] e'en such a Y [a good]." That the passage in *All's Well* is capable of this construction further strengthens the force of the parallel.

If it is likely that the same thought underlies the passages in *All's Well* and *Lucrece*, it is equally probable, given the imaginative habits of Shakespeare's mind—which have been minutely explored[8]—that certain words or images might be associated with forsaking oneself. Beyond the context of romantic love, the only such associations all three parallels share are commercial or monetary: steal, theft (*Venus*), engrossed, bail (Sonnet 133), gage, wealth, wealth, cost, vent'ring, having, want, augmenting, hazard, pawning, obtain (*Lucrece*). These images are most insistent in the passage offering the closest parallel; but there are few such images in the *All's Well* scene, as it stands, until after this point; then, in relation to Bertram's ring, they become abundant and important.

9. Diana's sentence must indicate to Bertram (if he hears it) that she is weakening; but, as the audience knows that her real intentions are to deceive him, her words might be expected to have another meaning for spectators.

10. Diana's sentence must (if Bertram hears it) offer an explanation for her weakening ("that we'll forsake our selves"); yet we would also expect or prefer it to offer an explanation—at least to the audience—for her sudden, apparently unmotivated demand for Bertram's ring.

11. Given the ambiguities of 9 and 10, it seems unlikely that the existing ambiguity of *that* is fortuitous; it would be most economical, verbally and logically, if the ambiguities of 9 and 10 sprang from variant interpretations of *that*.

12. Whatever Diana says here must fit her character, what she would have been likely to say on this particular occasion—a desire for appropriateness beyond the minimal dramatic expectations of 9 and 10. Diana's character has many facets—simplicity, stubbornness, irony, and (especially under Helena's tutelage) a riddling intellectuality—any one of which might seem "right" at any given moment. Just as, in performance, individual actresses may interpret particular moments in opposite ways, yet each convince us of the appropriateness of her chosen way,[9] so very different emendations might equally satisfy our desire for appropriateness to Diana's character. What the editor must resist is giving one possible interpretation of the character a veto over emendation or interpretation of the crux—as, for instance, by saying Diana "isn't the type of girl to speak in asides" or "would never use a word like *grope*."

13. To a degree, the entire play acts as a super-context to the corrupt line, but the play as a whole is of little use in searching for a solution, though it may be of value in confirming a solution.

Before we proceed to a full examination of the structural evidence, we must consider several recent conjectures. The first, Dover Wilson's "make rapes in such a scour," has been accepted by no subsequent editor, and even Wilson did not insert it in his text.[10] It is a very easy error graphically, but it falls impossibly short of sense. There is no reason for Diana to speak of *rapes;* there are no Shakespearean parallels for either conjecture; "make rapes" is awkward; the resulting sentence does not cohere with the explicit meaning of *forsake* or its imaginative and intellectual connotations for Shakespeare; the emendations do little to resolve ambiguities and difficulties of the larger context.

The second, P. A. Daniel's conjecture "may rope's in such a snare," has been accepted by C. J. Sisson (1954), John Munro (1958), and Jonas A. Barish (1969) and therefore must be considered the only emendation with any real contemporary following.[11] *Snare* for *scarre* is very easy, graphically. But *may* for *make* presupposes a different kind of error—compositorial memorial assimilation to "make ropes"—though an error Compositor B, who set this passage, was no doubt capable of.[12] Although B nowhere else set *make* for *may,* Compositor E set *make knowne* at *King Lear* 248, where Q, rightly or wrongly, had *may know.* In both readings the second word agrees with the first. And at *Richard III* 1.3.71, where Q1 (like F1) has "make pray," Q3 alters to "may prey." Though the emendation is certainly not so easy as *snare* for *scarre,* we would be justified in positing a nonce error, if the resulting emendation produced exactly the right sense. But this emendation does not. To begin with, though *rope* is acceptable as a verb, you do not *rope* someone in a *snare*—you catch them, or trap them, or entangle them. There is no parallel for this forced construction in Shakespeare's—or, so far as I know, anyone else's—use of *snare* or of *rope.*[13] Secondly, *snare* provides exactly the wrong image to explain *forsake.* A snare traps you, it prevents you from moving; Diana might be lured to forsake herself, then snared, but as an image the forsaking cannot intelligibly postdate the snaring. Finally, Daniel's conjecture does not explain Diana's sudden demand for the ring, nor does it resemble the parallel passage from *Lucrece.* These objections are, in combination, insuperable.

Barbara Everett, most recently, has conjectured "make vows in such a flame."[14] *Vowes* could be misread as *rope's* only if the compositor confused the ascender of the *s* or *l* of *selves* (in the line below) as a descender from the *w,* which then could be misread as a *p.* But Compositor B had already set correctly *vowes, vow,* and *vow'd* within the last thirty lines.

Moreover, in a context given over to oaths and vows, is it likely that a compositor—particularly B, who tended to pay too much attention to the sense of what he was setting—would misinterpret the obvious *vowes* for an unaccountable *rope's*? As for *flame*, it requires the compositor to misread the ascending *l* as a *c*—or alternatively (and more plausibly) to misread *l* as *k*, and then normalize to his own preferred spelling *c*. These explanations for the misreading are persuasive, but the other passages Everett cites for the use of *flame* are not: "in so true a flame of liking" (1.3.206), "The honour, sir, that flames in your fair eyes" (2.3.79), " 'Let me not live,' quoth he, / 'After my flame lacks oil, to be the snuff / Of younger spirits' " (1.2.59). What warrant do these passages, which all involve quite traditional images, give for describing vows as made "in such a flame"? Why should this particular image have been chosen here? According to Everett, Diana deliberately and facetiously adopts Bertram's romantic vocabulary, seeming to slip into the conventional poeticism of the world of "Fontybell"; but this would be easier to believe if Bertram himself had used the word, or if there were closer parallels, inside and outside Shakespeare, for the meaning Diana here must give to it.[15] More generally, the emendation neither prepares for nor easily combines with *forsake*; it does not relate in style, vocabulary, or substance to any of the three parallel passages; it does not make use of the ambiguity of *that*; it does not explain Diana's sudden demand for the ring; and it leaves the disparity between Diana's apparent and her real meaning to our inference that what Bertram takes seriously she means facetiously. Underlying all these objections is another: the resulting thought ("men make vows so ardently that we'll forsake ourselves") seems, to me, disappointingly shallow. As an explanation of human sexual corruption, it explains nothing. Why should the vows, why should the ardency, succeed? The passage demands an idea more complex, morally and intellectually; and the three parallels for *forsake ourselves* reinforce this expectation.

I have as yet presumed—as have these three editors, and all others—that the line is doubly corrupt. But Anne Lancashire, more than a decade ago, defended both *rope's* and *scarre*.[16] As she pointed out, *rope* in a number of other contemporary passages seems to have a bawdy significance, most probably as a slang synonym for penis; *scar* can mean "crack, chink" (*OED* sb.[3]), which might take a complementary sexual sense; and *rope* as a verb meaning "cry out" is recorded as late as 1549.

> On the surface, then, Diana is saying, "I see that men make ropes (cries of lamentation, distress) in such a scare (plight, panic, alarm) that we (women) will forsake ourselves (give in, yield up our virtue)." The word "ropes" for "outcries" . . . is doubtless used by Shakespeare for the sake of the sexual pun involved. (244)

Although Lancashire successfully demonstrates the sexual sense of *rope* elsewhere, her explanation of this crux remains unconvincing. Even granting that *rope* equals penis, there are no parallels for *make ropes* as "have intercourse" or "put penises" [in a chink]. Although *chink* or *crack* or *crevice* might have sexual senses, that in itself would not prove that *scar* ever did; or that *scare* and *scar* were homonyms to be punned upon. This sexual interpretation disregards the conclusion of Diana's sentence—or does she see that men have intercourse with women *so that* women will forsake themselves? Moreover, it requires that we disregard the primary and obvious sense of both *rope* and *make rope*. Finally, although Diana has "used sexual language in this scene" (244), sexual vulgarity is uncharacteristic. Such notions of what a character would or would not say are hardly the best guidelines, but there is a difference between Diana's "Ay, so you serve us / Till we serve you" and the language of Dromio, Grumio, and Juliet's Nurse; between the traditional imagery of the barbed retort in "but when you have our roses / You barely leave our thorns to prick ourselves" and the unprompted and graphic vulgarity of rope-tricks in chinks. And if, for all these reasons, the proposed sexual innuendo is unconvincing, then that in itself undermines Lancashire's reading of the surface sense. For, as she concedes, the noun *ropes* (as "cries of distress") is last recorded in the fourteenth century, more than two hundred years before the composition of *All's Well*; and even as a verb, the word is not recorded after 1549—and then in *The Complaynt of Scotland* ("The ropeen of the rauynis gart the crans crope"), which can hardly reflect mainstream mid-sixteenth-century English usage. Given weak linguistic evidence for Lancashire's intepretation, one is justified also in pointing out its dramatic and aesthetic deficiencies: it provides only an indirect introduction for the forsaking image; it does not explain the sudden demand for the ring; it makes no use of the speech's dramatic and grammatical ambiguities. Nor does it relate, in content or imagery, to the three parallels for *forsake ourselves*. If there were later parallels for the required surface sense of *ropes*, and if parallels could be found for the scare/scar pun and the scar/vulva innuendo, and if the sexual allusions could be integrated in the whole sentence, these aesthetic objections would have to yield to the historical evidence; but, as it is, both the historical and the aesthetic objections to Lancashire's defense are, to my mind, insuperable.

Another possiblity, which to my knowledge has not been considered, is that given *in* for "e'en" *scarre* may be correct. Bertram has just urged "give thyself unto my sick desires, / Who then recovers"; Diana might reply that men make their desires into wounds, so that women will forsake themselves in order to heal them. If this interpretation is satisfactory, crux Y need not be emended, and in crux X we could substitute *loue* or *lust* for *rope's*—not the most plausible emendation graphically, but possible, especially as we would only be required to posit one misreading instead of two. Despite its initial attractiveness, this solution must be rejected. A scar is not a wound but a wound already healed, and consequently can provide no excuse for the "physic" of physical love. Even if we could read "make love e'en such a wound," which would of course involve emending both cruxes—in which case nothing has been gained—women's motive for forsaking themselves would be left entirely implicit and the larger ambiguities of the context unresolved.

The *signifiant* evidence can only define the perimeter of a satisfactory solution. It can help us to reject proposed solutions; it does not help us to invent new ones. In itself it cannot, at least in this instance, tell us which words to put in place of those the Folio offers. Only the structural evidence can help us to reconstruct these. This structural evidence divides into nongraphic and graphic categories.

By nongraphic evidence I mean evidence of an error that could have resulted not from misreading, but from some physical or mental error in the act of composition: foul case, transposed letters, turned letters, dittography, assimilation, aural or memorial error, misinterpreted proofreader's instructions.[17] There are five opportunities for that kind of explanation here. The *p* of *ropes*, which is quite similar to an upsidedown *d*, might have been mistakenly distributed into the *d* box.[18] *Make rode* is an intelligible phrase with Shakespearean parallels, but this emendation, with its hostile and aggressive intention, restricts the range of solutions available for crux Y and imposes the least likely construction on the whole passage: "men make road in such a [frightening] way that we forsake ourselves [out of fear]"—an interpretation that suffers from many of the same deficiencies as Wilson's "rapes in such a scour." No other apparent emendations based on a type-error are plausible. Another possibility is the well-attested aural error of *p* for *b*,[19] which would presume a manuscript *robes*, which of course does not make sense. Another conceivable aural error, *make gropes* or *may grope's*, also produces nonsense. *Ropes* and *scarre* cannot have resulted from assimilation or dittography triggered by anything in the context, and the only plausible candidate for some kind of memorial error is *may* for *make*. Once *may rope's* is discredited, as I think it has been, then reading *may* for *make* requires us to suppose a further error in *ropes*, which drastically reduces the probabilities and removes Sisson's explanation for *make* (assimilation to *rope's*). If we could find a verb to replace *rope* which would allow us to retain *scarre* (or *scare*), such a construction might be entertained, for it puts the two errors in the line side by side. I have not found any such verb, and even if it were found its suitability to the larger context would be doubtful. I therefore assume that *make* is right and *rope's* wrong. The "*may* + verb + *us*" pattern can thus be eliminated as a syntactical option. This means that the Folio's apostrophe must be an error or a mere spelling variant, whatever our solution to crux X. Nor should this surprise us unduly, for such "errors" occur often enough elsewhere in B's work.[20]

As presumed misreadings, crux X and crux Y present quite different problems. X, because of the medial *p* and the monosyllabic dictates of meter, offers limited possibilities; Y, a scrawl of minims of either one or two syllables, offers an almost unlimited range, bounded only by the small number of misreadings possible for the initial *s*.

The letters of *rope's* could be misreadings of the following:[21]

      r:    c, i, l, m, n, t, u, v, w

      o:    a, e

      p:    f (?), g(?), x, y(?)

      e:    d, l, t, [o], [y]

      s:    t, [r]

The bracketed letters can be effectively eliminated, because of the need for a monosyllable. The resulting word must be a noun.

The real difficulty, of course, is the third letter. X, the letter most plausibly misread as *p*, does not produce a noun with any combination of the other letters. In *Sir Thomas More* on at least one occasion *f* might be misread as *p*, and at least one misprint in a Shakespearean foul paper text seems to derive from such confusion.[22] I have included *g* and *y* simply because they are tailed; so is *h*, but it produces nothing useful in combination with the other letters. The value of the resulting list—its *only* value—is as a concordance of letter combinations bearing some graphic resemblance to *rope's*. The degree of that graphic resemblance and the mechanical plausibility of emendations resulting from it vary widely.

Most of these letter combinations produce nonsense. The only nouns that result are cogs, coyls, iapes, ioyes, laps, mopes, mops, napes, naps, nayls, rags, rapes, raps, tapes, taps, tops, toyes, voyds, wayes. (If Compositor B misinterpreted four letters as *rops*, he would probably have inserted the *e* himself, regarding it as a mere normalization: hence B's *e* is simply ignored in "cogs," etc.)

Of course, most of these words cannot be fitted into the context at all. The only real possibilities are *iapes* and *toyes*—to which we may add *vowes*, accepting the possible confusion posited by Everett. The graphic probability of *vowes* has already been discussed. It can construe with *in* or *e'en*: if *in*, "men make vows in such a [attractive quantity or quality]"; if *e'en*, "men transform vows into [something attractive, which in some way contrasts with vows]." Becket long ago conjectured *iapes* (in the phrase "make japes of such a scathe"), but it has never been adopted, despite its graphic similarity to *rope's*: in terms of purely mechanical criteria of "ease of misreading," *iapes* is the most plausible of the three readings under discussion, and one of the most plausible imaginable. But Shakespeare never elsewhere used the word, which was in several of its senses obsolescent. It could mean "A trick, or device to deceive or cheat" (*sb*. 1; last example 1501), or "A trifle, toy, trinket" (*sb*. 3; last example 1570, Scots); although these meanings might be pertinent, neither is demonstrably current ca. 1600. More promising are "a jest, joke, gibe" (*sb*. 2; examples 1340–1882) and "sexual intercourse" (*sb*. 1c; last example ca. 1600; last example of parallel sense of the verb 1589). This pun is potentially relevant to the dialogue, and *iapes* is an easier misreading than *vowes*, both absolutely and in this particular context (where the word has not previously been used, and hence is less likely to have been recognized again by the compositor).

The third possibility, *toyes*, involves less common misreadings than *iapes*. By contrast with *vowes* it has the advantages of a tailed third letter and of the word's unfamiliarity in the immediate context; it has the disadvantage of a more unusual misreading of the initial letter. Because *r* and *t* are so often and easily confused in foul case, it is difficult to establish, on errors in printed books alone, how readily the two letters were confusable in Shakespeare's hand (though they are confusable in many contemporary secretary, or mixed, hands). Both letters can be misread as terminal *s*; *t* can occasionally, like *r*, be misread as minims. Confusion of *r* and *t* is therefore certainly possible, though not as common a misreading of *r* as *v*. I would therefore judge that, in descending order of probability, *iupes* is clearly easiest, with *toyes* marginally more likely in this context than *vowes*.

Unlike *japes*, the word *toy(s)* occurs thirty-five times in Shakespeare, in a variety of pertinent senses: "amorous sport, dallying" (*sb*. 1), "antic, trick" (*sb*. 2), "a frivolous or mocking speech; a foolish or idle tale . . . a jest, joke" (*sb*. 3), "foolish or idle fancy; a fantastic notion, odd conceit" (*sb*. 4), "A thing of little or no value or importance, a trifle" (*sb*. 5), "a plaything" (*sb*. 6), "A small article of little intrinsic value, but prized as an ornament or curiosity" (*sb*. 7). In short, *toyes* offers all of the pertinent meanings supplied by *iupes*, and several others in addition; *vowes*, by contrast, offers only one meaning, which is present in the context anyway. Within the *signifiant* requirements, then (as opposed to the purely structural ones), the order of attractiveness of these three candidates is clear: *toyes* (often used by Shakespeare in many pertinent senses), *iapes* (never used by Shakespeare, but current in some pertinent senses), and *vowes* (often used by Shakespeare, but in only one pertinent—and redundant—sense). Thus, in my judgment, *vowes* is the least probable of the three in both categories; *toyes* and *iapes* are finely balanced, depending upon whether we give more importance to structural or to *signifiant* evidence.

We now can search among the variety of probable misreadings that could result in *scarre*.[23]

```
s:   f

c:   k,  l,  i,  n,  u,  r,  t  ⎫
                                ⎬   m,w
a:   o,  u,  c,  i,  r,   n     ⎭

r:   c,  i,  l,  n,  t,  u,  z  ⎫
                                ⎬   m,  w
r:   c,  i,  l,  n,  t,  u,  z  ⎭

e:   d,  t,  y,  [o],  [l]
```

A further complication: even if his copy read *scar, scarr, skarre,* or *scare,* Compositor B may well have set *scarre*.[24] As the letter combinations here are staggering, I went through the concordance checking all the words under possible combinations of the first two letters (fi, fl, fr, fu, sc, si, sk, sl, sn, st, su, sw), recording those plausible as minim misreadings for *scar(re)*. Of the resulting list, only about a dozen seemed remotely possible: flame, flatterer(?), flaw, flud, fury, score, sieve, sin, stain, store, storm, suit, sum, surance, sweet.

For *vowes,* five possibilities exist. One is an indifferent or neutral term: "men make vows in such a suit" or even "in such affairs" (Rowe's suggestion). This choice contributes little to the context and does nothing to explain *forsake* or the demand for Bertram's ring. The second alternative is to read *in* and conjecture a word expressing the quantity or quality of the thing: in such a flood, such a flow, such a fury, such a score, such a store, such a storm, such a sum. Shakespeare often speaks of hyperbolic quantities of *oaths* (not generally of *vows*); but there are no parallels for any of these constructions, and again they contribute very little. *In such a flame,* which also belongs to this group, has been discussed (and rejected) earlier. Third, men might "make vowes in such a sieue"; although the sieve image is an expressive one that Shakespeare elsewhere uses, it is only tangentially relevant here. Besides, the phrasing is awkward—one would expect "pour vows"—and the sense conveyed almost opposite to that required: the image suggests futility, not success. Fourth, interpreting *in* as *e'en*, men might make vows into a *flatterer* or a *flattery*. Neither of these long words seems especially attractive paleographically; *flatterer* does not fit the plural of *vows*, and *flattery* phrases awkwardly an awkward image. Finally, and most attractively, Diana might see that "men make vowes e'en such a surance / That wee'l forsake our selves." But even this does not seem adequate. How has Bertram made his vows a surance? Why should surance, in itself, tempt us out of ourselves? Hence, *vowes*, intrinsically the weakest of the three chief candidates in crux X, offers no attractive combination with any of the paleographically plausible solutions to crux Y. But of the possibilities, "vows e'en such a surance" is the most appealing.

For *iapes*, the possible combinations are similar and suffer from the same disadvantages: blandness ("japes in such affairs," "japes in such a flood," etc.) or unparalleled contortions ("japes e'en such a flattery"). The most attractive pairing, again, is with *surance*; but *surance* makes better sense with *iapes* than with *vowes*, for to "make japes e'en such a surance" is to "turn a joke (or a bit of sexual dalliance) into something you rely on." The question still remains, why should "japes" have the power to tempt women to forsake themselves?

Finally, for *toyes* the range of possible solutions to crux Y is more limited. Because *make vowes* and *make iapes* are idiomatic predicates, they permit a variety of qualifiers, and hence a variety of interpretations of the remainder of the sentence. But *toyes* would force us to interpret the syntax as transformational: "make X e'en such a Y." Of the available candidates for crux Y, only *surance* makes any sense with *toyes*. Whichever of the three most plausible candidates for crux X we choose, *surance* is the preferred pairing.

Shakespeare uses *surance* once elsewhere (*Titus* 5.2.46); he uses *assurance* thirty-one times; as conjecturally emended, *a surance* is of course aurally ambiguous, and could represent either form. In any case, *surance* is a formation from *assurance*, "of which it may be sometimes merely an aphetic form" (*OED*); the range of meanings is identical. An *assurance* (or *a surance*) is "a formal pledge . . . or guarantee" (*sb.* 1), "A marriage engagement, betrothal" (2), "A positive declaration intended to give confidence" (3), "the conveyance of lands or tenements by deed" (4), "security" (7), "certitude; confidence, trust" (8). All these meanings are well attested in the period and used by Shakespeare. (The collocation "make . . . assurance" occurs at *Shrew* 2.1.387, 2.1.396, 3.2.134 and at *Macbeth* 4.1.83.) Diana would be saying that men make [japes, or toys, or vows] into a guarantee, or betrothal, or legally binding covenant, or something trusted, or something intrinsically reliable, in order to make women forsake themselves. Whichever word we choose in crux X, the

basic sense would be the same: "men transform—or appear to transform—something unreliable into something reliable." Shakespeare's
other uses of *assurance* and of the verb *assure* encourage this construction:

> rather like a dream than an assurance (*Tempest* 1.2.45)
> jealousy shall be called assurance (*Ado* 2.2.49)
> Thy now usurped assurance (*John* 2.1.470–1)
> Incertainties now crown themselves assured (Sonnet 107.7)
> The ills that were not, grew to faults assured (Sonnet 118.10)
> Most ignorant of what he's most assured (*Measure* 2.2.119)

In all these passages something *not* assured is contrasted with something that *is;* in most of them, the uncertainty is apparently transformed
into a (false) assurance. Indeed, the plot of *The Taming of the Shrew* turns
upon an actual "counterfeit assurance" (4.4.92). These parallels reinforce
the conclusion that *surance* is the most attractive solution so far offered
for the Folio's *scarre:* an easy misreading that makes good sense and pairs
well with the most attractive solutions to crux Y.

If we therefore take *surance* as the likeliest solution to crux Y, it should
help us to arbitrate between the three short-listed candidates for crux X.
As indicated, "vows e'en such a surance" makes a sense, but not a rich,
wholly satisfying sense, and *surance* does not alter the fact that *vowes* is
intrinsically the least attractive of the three candidates. All senses that
*iapes* offers in relation to *surance, toyes* can also offer; but *toyes* can offer
other senses, too. Most important, *toyes,* unlike either alternative, offers
an explicit temptation, a bait, a lure: something insubstantial but appealing, which might attract us to forsake ourselves. Thus, Tarquin, driven
on by his lust, "sells eternity to get a toy" (*Lucrece* 214) fifty-seven lines
after concluding that "for himself himself he must forsake" (157). *Toyes*
are more obviously inconsequential by nature than *vowes* (which should
be, and often are, serious and trustworthy); *toyes* are indeed a stereotype
of triviality. Hence, after Duncan's death "All is but toys" (*Macbeth*
2.3.94); Theseus dismisses the "fairy toys' of "Lovers and madmen" (*A
Midsummer's Night Dream* 5.1.3–4); Julia sets "As little by such toys as may
be possible" (*Two Gentlemen of Verona* 1.2.79). Because they serve as
images of inconsequentiality, Shakespeare elsewhere uses *toys* in opposition to more substantial things: "Triumphs for nothing, and lament-
ing toys, / Is jollity for apes, and griefs for boys" (*Cymbeline* 4.2.193–94);
"making misery their mirth, and affliction a toy to jest at" (*Kinsmen*
2.1.34–35). In the second passage, something serious is transformed into
a toy; a similar metamorphosis occurs in *Love's Labours Lost:*

> To see a king transformed to a gnat!
> To see great Hercules whipping a gig,

And profound Solomon to tune a jig,
And Nestor play at push-pin with the boys,
And critic Timon laugh at idle toys!

(4.3.164–68)

In this passage, as in *All's Well*, it is specifically love and/or sexual desire that works this transformation.

*Toyes* has three additional advantages over its rivals. First, in *The Taming of the Shrew*, Shakespeare juxtaposes "a toy" (2.1.402) with "make assurance" (2.1.387, 396). Secondly, because a *toy* is something of "no value," it brings into the passage the evaluative fiscal imagery found in all three parallel passages for the conceit of "forsaking oneself." This range of associations is also present in *a surance; toyes* and *surance* in combination reinforce one another in insinuating the expected image complex. Finally, as a "small material object" of little financial but considerable emotional value, a *toy* leads naturally to a *ring:* the emendation thus prepares, as does no other, for Diana's demand for Bertram's ring: a *toy* that will serve as a *surance* (or betrothal).

In short, *toyes* operates verbally at more levels than any other conjecture. Diana sees that men "make [sexual play; antics; tricks; fantastic frivolous speeches; idle fancies; trifles; playthings] appear to be such [a formal betrothal; a guarantee; a legal transfer of property; something trustworthy and dependable] that women, tempted, forsake their own integrity." Diana's words have another meaning of which Bertram (but not the audience) is unaware: Diana sees that men themselves "transform [what they should not value] into [something of momentous and binding consequence], in order to make women forsake themselves." Diana appears to say that women should not trust men; but her words also, to the audience, suggest that men should not trust their own lust, which lures them into consequences they had not foreseen. By appearing to believe him, Diana contrives to deceive him. His ring (which, by comparison with sexual satisfaction, he regards as a mere toy) and sexual play (which he regards as mere toying) will in fact constitute a genuine and binding surance (betrothal to Helena). In contrast to *vowes* and *iapes*, *toyes* makes use of and contributes to all the ambiguities of the speech and situation.

This riddling style, moreover, is entirely in character for Diana and the whole play; the emendation matches two of the play's thematic preoccupations. The first, false language, is announced by Parolles's very name and sustained by him throughout the play; it also sounds in the apparent artificiality of Bertram's acquiescence in the marriage, in his and Parolles's excuses for leaving Paris and sending Helena ahead, and in Bertram's later confession of his supposed love for Maudlin. But this preoccupation appears most explicitly in the first three scenes of act 4. In the first and third, Parolles is deceived by an invented mock-language; in between, Diana is (apparently) deceived by the (artificial) mock-language of her false lover.[25] As emended, Diana at the turning point of the scene remarks on men's ability to make something valueless appear valuable, something insecure appear reliable—a moral commonplace of calling a vice by the name of a related virtue, or vice versa.[26] This sort of misprision characterizes the entire plot: Bertram's of Helena, Bertram's of Parolles, and (perhaps) Helena's of Bertram. The bed trick itself is a mistaking. Characteristic, too, is the description of love in terms of value. This theme and its imagery have been discussed elsewhere,[27] but three passages between this scene and the end of the play are worth quoting.

> [*to Bertram*]                    Our rash faults,
> Make triuiall price of serious things we haue,
> Not knowing them, vntill we know their graue.
> Oft our displeasure to our selues uniust . . .
>
> (2767–70)

> *Dia<na>* . . .
> He might haue bought me at a common price.
> Do not beleeue him. O behold this Ring . . .
>
> (2913–14)

> *Ros<sillion>*   Her [infinite cunning] with her moderne grace,
> Subdu'e me to her rate, she got the Ring,
> And I had that which any inferiour might
> At Market price haue bought.
>
> (2943–46)

All three are remarkable for their similarity of thought, context, and wording. Moreover, the very next scene contains three more close parallels to the thought, and attendant imagery, of this conjecture.

> . . . he hath giuen her his monumentall Ring, and
> thinkes himselfe made in the vnchaste composition.
>
> (2122–24)

> *Cap. G.* How mightily sometimes, we make vs comforts of our losses.
> *Cap. E.* And how mightily some other times, wee drowne our gaine in
> teares.
>
> (2171–74)

In both cases, it is Bertram who is being discussed; in the first, it is Bertram, Diana, and the ring. And between these two statements comes, in one of the play's best-known lines, an echo of "forsake our selves":

> . . . as we are our selues, what things are we.
> *Cap. E.* Meerely our own traitours.

(2125–27)

To these parallels can be added, finally, Helena's reflection on the bed trick,

>          . . . But O strange men,
> That can such sweet use make of what they hate.
>          . . . so lust doth play
> With what it loathes . . .

(2463–67)

These parallels are the most persuasive confirmation that the syntax of transformation and the imagery of misplaced value represent the most appropriate solutions to the great crux in act 4, scene 2.

Among the *signifiant* criteria, "toys e'en such a surance" makes better sense of the crux than any available conjecture. For crux Y, presupposing an easy set of minim misreadings produces a word—*surance*—that fits perfectly the requirements of the sense. For crux X, some sense can be extracted by three conjectures, of varying degrees of paleographical probability. Of these three, *vowes* can now be dismissed as an unsatisfactory second or third best in every category. Either of the two others is possible and in some ways attractive. But *iapes* is unparalleled in Shakespeare's works, and only carries a few appropriate senses; *toyes* is demonstrably Shakespearean and exploits dramatic and verbal nuances. All other things being equal, an editor would have no difficulty choosing which word to adopt. But all other things are not quite equal: *iapes* presupposes two of the simplest of misreadings (ia/ro), while *toyes* presumes two possible but less usual misreadings (t/r, y/p). The manifold critical superiority of *toyes* outweighs its relative inferiority in paleographical terms. I therefore adopt *toyes* in my own edition—a decision less important than the principle that underlies it, a principle of relevance to other cruxes and other authors. Thus, before leaving my own conjectures to their editorial fate, I return to methodological issues, which the reader has no doubt long since lost sight of in the foregoing welter of argumentative detail.

The lists of possible misreadings or printing errors could be extended, either by explaining the possibility of a letter misread or an additional foul-case error or another potential combination of the available letters, or by positing for *scarre* an emendation involving a word that does not elsewhere appear in Shakespeare's vocabulary (and thus did not occur in the concordance), or by showing that some other combination of the existing X + Y possibilities makes sense, or by showing, on the basis of additional lexical evidence, that one of the emended terms makes sense. There remains a large field for continued speculation, and the free play of intelligence for anyone dissatisfied with my proposal. But I have at least provided a framework for such investigation. If editors share their labors, then at least our successors will be in a position to build and refine our efforts, rather than each time starting, despairingly, from scratch.

This crux is unusual, though by no means unique, in being open-ended: *both* key terms of the thought and/or the image are corrupt. For most emendations we are either reasonably sure of what Shakespeare wanted to say (would he have said it this way, or that way?) or the text says one thing, when we believe the author probably wanted to say another. Here we know only that Shakespeare wanted to give, within several possible syntactical frameworks, the cause for a given effect; we have to rediscover that cause ourselves, for it is by no means self-evident. We are thus forced to introduce into the text of Shakespeare a "new" thought—although, we hope, that thought, though new to us, will be what Shakespeare thought 380 years ago. In aspiring toward this meeting of minds, we are guided by two distinct kinds of evidence, *signifiant* and structural. Both are important, but their uses are clearly different. The *signifiant* requirements *must* be satisfied; structural evidence, on the other hand, simply defines a perimeter of probable solutions based upon kinds of probable corruption. Within the field of words bounded by the structural requirements, we search for a combination that will satisfy all the *signifiant* requirements. It is logically possible that more than one solution might do this, and then we must decide which is better. It is possible, however, as in this case, that in the field of variants produced by the strictest construction of the structural evidence, no combination that fully satisfies the *signifiant* requirements may be found. In these circumstances, we must gradually expand the perimeters until we find one. It is axiomatic that there *is* a solution; and if that solution cannot be found among the variants produced by the most probable kinds of corruption, then it must exist among the variants produced by relatively less probable corruptions.

This situation, in a simplified form, can be represented geometrically. If A and B are two *signifiant* requirements, and the solution to crux X must satisfy both, we might imagine this solution as representing a point $X^1$, where the lines from A and B intersect. We can then regard the crux X as the center of a circle defined by the radius p (for *probability*). The structural evidence, strictly construed, will define this radius. But if our point $X^1$ does not lie within this first circle, then we must gradually increase the radius of probability until we have produced a circle that *does* include point $X^1$. A graph somewhat misrepresents the problem, because on the graph A and B only intersect at one point. Our model would be closer to the editorial reality if A and B were lines on the surface of a sphere, which would thus intersect at two points, $X^1$ and $X^2$; the proper solution would then be the point that was closest to crux X— the point, that is, that could be contained within the shorter radius of probability.

I apologize for resorting to geometry, but it is the simplest way of illustrating the logical inevitability of this procedure. It also helps to make obvious the two methodological imperatives imposed by such a crux: one, the *signifiant* requirements must be comprehensively described; two, *all* of the variants within the initial strict radius of probability must be scanned and eliminated before one can justify expanding the radius.

One consequence of these imperatives is the length of this essay. Despite Dr. Johnson's often quoted dictum about an argument's length being in inverse proportion to its plausibility (an epigram that justifies his own epigrammatic style of criticism), for cruxes such as these an argument can only be persuasive by being properly exhaustive. And this fact in turn affects what might be called the rhetoric of emendation. The "great" emendations have an irresistible neatness; they are like Elizabethan perspectives or a magician's trick: "here is nonsense, but change one letter, *voila*, a phrase of genius." One could reasonably describe such emendations, at their best, as being *witty*. And this wit is essential to most emendations, for the ease and neatness and superiority of the emendation help to persuade us that the text indeed needs emending. In a crux such as this one, there can be no doubt that the text needs emending; it is only a matter of finding the most plausible emendation possible. Of course, even in such cases we would like to pull a rabbit out of the hat, to satisfy that desire for an irresistible neatness, to preserve that illusion of a careless editorial *sprezzatura,* but sometimes there is no rabbit in the first hat, and we have to search through a whole millinery to find it. We must learn to dissociate the logic of emendation from its rhetoric; we must realize that an emendation is no less right for not being "witty." Oscar Wilde is not the only arbiter of editorial principle.

### Notes

1. For I. A. Shapiro's valuable suggestion that the misleading term "accidentals" be replaced by "incidentals," see *The Library* 5, (1978): 33, 335.
2. Hilda Hulme, in *Explorations in Shakespeare's Language* (London, 1962) ar-

gues that *scarre* means "splice," and that *splice* figuratively means "to marry" (264–66). The lexical arguments are in themselves unconvincing, and the interpretation is in any case wildly awkward in this context.

3. This in itself argues against H. W. Jones's proposal,"may compass's in such a snare" (*MLR* 55 (1960): 241–42). Of course, one does often find an extra unstressed syllable at the caesura, but here the caesural pause is not strongly marked, and would if anything come much more naturally after *men*. Graphically, *cōpas* could be misread as *ropes*, but aurally this leads to absorption of the all-important *'s*. Moreover, by abandoning *ropes* (the inadequacy of which he rightly sees) Jones is forced to presuppose *three* errors in the line, while removing Sisson's original explanation for the first, and most unusual, substitution (*may* for *makes*). Finally, as I try to demonstrate, *snare* is itself unsatisfactory.

4. *E'en* is spelled *in* at *Comedy of Errors* 2.2.202, *All's Well That Ends Well* 3.2.18 (and probably 1.3.42), *Romeo and Juliet* 5.1.24 (Q2), *Antony and Cleopatra* 4.15.73— all autograph texts. In positing that *in* might stand for *e'en*, I am thus assuming that *in* was an idiosyncratic spelling that compositors would usually have normalized, and that Compositor B did not do so here only because he did not realize that *in* here stood for *e'en*.

5. Though there are no exact parallels for this construction in Shakespeare, the two syntactical patterns that it combines are common enough. The first pattern, *e'en* or *even* before *such*, is often followed by a noun, and sometimes by an explanatory clause: "e'en such as you speak to me" (*AWW* 4.1.13), "Even such a husband / Hast thou of me as she is for [a] wife" (*MV* 3.5.83), "with a love even such" (*WT* 3.2.65), "companions; / Even such, they say, as stand in narrow lanes" (*R2* 5.3.8), "Even such a man, so faint, so spiritless, / So dull, so dead in look, so woe-begone, / Drew . . . " (*2H4* 1.1.70), "Even such a passion doth embrace my love" (*TRO* 3.2.35), "even such delight . . . shall you" (*ROM* 1.2.28), "these penciled figures are / Even such as they give out" (*TIM* 1.1.160), "Ay, even such heaps and sums of love and wealth / As shall to thee blot out what wrongs were theirs" (*TIM* 5.1.152), "Eros, thy captain is / Even such a body" (*ANT* 4.14.13), "even such our griefs are" (*PER* 1.4.7), "Even such a beauty as you master now" (*SON* 106.8). In most of these cases, meter requires elision of the *even*. The second pattern involves *make* as a verb of transformation, with the transformed object being described as "such a [noun]": "made such a sinner of his memory" (*TMP* 1.2.101), "he shall never make me such a fool" (*ADO* 2.3.26), "You would not make me such an argument" (*MND* 3.2.242), "And makes a god of such a cullion" (*SHR* 4.2.20), "Make such unconstant children of ourselves, / As . . ." (*JN* 3.1.243). There seems no great or uncharacteristic difficulty in combining these two constructions.

6. *OED forsake* (*v.* 4) "To abandon, leave entirely, withdraw from; *esp.* to withdraw one's presence and help or companionship from; to desert." Shakespearean passages in which this sense is uppermost include: *WT* 1.2.362 (I must / Forsake the court), *OTH* 5.2.330 (You must forsake this room and go with us), *ANT* 2.7.38 (Forsake thy seat), *VEN* 321 (swiftly doth forsake him).

7. Muriel Bradbrook, in *Shakespeare and Elizabethan Poetry* (London, 1951), has compared Bertram to Adonis (169), and Michael Jamieson, in "The Problem Plays, 1920–76: A Retrospect" (*SS* 25 [1972]: 1–10) has compared Helena to Venus (3).

8. The best-known studies of Shakespeare's associations are Caroline Spurgeon's *Shakespeare's Imagery* (Cambridge, 1935) and E. A. Armstrong's *Shakespeare's Imagination: A Study of the Psychology of Association and Inspiration* (London, 1946; rev. ed. Gloucester, Mass., 1963).

9. For a fuller discussion of this species of ambiguity, see the chapter on Viola in my *To Analyze Delight: A Hedonist Criticism of Shakespeare* (Newark, 1985).

10. J. D. Wilson, *All's Well That Ends Well*, New Shakespeare (Cambridge, 1929), 168.

11. William Shakespeare, *The Complete Works*, ed. C. J. Sisson (London, 1954); *The London Shakespeare*, ed. John Munro, 4 vols. (London, 1958); *All's Well That Ends Well*, ed. Jonas A. Barish, New Pelican Shakespeare (Baltimore, 1969).

12. For the attribution to Compositor B, see Charlton Hinman's *The Printing and Proofreading of the First Folio of Shakespeare*, 2 vols. (Oxford, 1963), 2:515. For B's memorial substitutions, see Paul Werstine, "Folio Editors, Folio Compositors, and the Folio Text of *King Lear*," *The Division of the Kingdoms: Shakespeare's Two Versions of "King Lear*," ed. Gary Taylor and Michael Warren (Oxford, 1983), 247–312.

13. This assertion is based on the evidence of *OED* and its Supplements, with the addenda to *OED* contained in all the Revels Plays (Methuen, and Mancheser University Press), in R. W. Bailey's *Early Modern English* (Hildesheim, 1978), in *The Plays and Poems of Philip Massinger*, ed. Philip Edwards and Colin Gibson, 5 vols. (Oxford, 1976), and in Jurgen Schafer's *Documentation in the O.E.D.: Shakespeare and Nashe as Test Cases* (Oxford, 1980). I have also checked *The Harvard Shakespeare Concordance*, ed. Marvin Spevack (Cambridge, Mass., 1974).

14. *All's Well That Ends Well*, New Penguin Shakespeare (Harmondsworth, 1970), 198.

15. *In such a flame* must mean "with such ardour, in such an intense and passionate way." *OED* (sb 2 *fig*) defines *in a flame* as "inflamed with anger, passion, or zeal," but its first example of this usage is from 1685, and even that is not exactly parallel ("What a flame had your negligency put me into"). Likewise, under the sense "a burning feeling or passion" (6a), there are no parallels for the absolute sense until 1702; until then, *flame* is always qualified to indicate this specific sense (flame of love, of delight, of charity, of zeal, of liking). In Shakespeare's own use, too, the image is usually—though not invariably—qualified. The closest parallel to Everett's emendation is from *Twelfth Night*: "If I did love you in my master's flame" (1.5.264); this is the only absolute use with *in*. But even here, the linking of the adverbial phrase *in my master's flame* to the verb *love* makes the image traditional and easy to follow; one has only to substitute "If I did make vows in my master's flame" to see the relative difficulty of Everett's interpretation.

16. "Lyly and Shakespeare on the Ropes," *JEGP* (1969), 237–44. Subsequent editors have either overlooked or deliberately disregarded this article; Brian Morris, in his recent new Arden edition of *Romeo and Juliet* (London, 1980), cites it, and cross-references all of Lancashire's parallels *except* this one in *All's Well*.

17. For this last category of error, and the evidence for foul proofing generally, see Peter W. M. Blayney's *The Texts of "King Lear" and their Origins*, 2 vols. (Cambridge), vol. 1, *Nicholas Okes and the First Quarto* (1982): 188–257.

18. Compare *OTH* 4.1.107: pow'r (Q1), dowre (F1).

19. Compare Q1's error *pillows* for correct *billows* in *2 Henry IV* 3.1.127.

20. Alice Walker, in "Compositor Determination and Other Problems in Shakespearian Texts" (*SB* 7 [1955]: 11), has remarked upon "the frequency with which erroneous apostrophes occur in the work of Jaggard B. . . . All the erroneous apostrophes in *3 Henry VI* and *Richard III*, for instance, are in his stints." (The stints to which she refers have not been challenged by subsequent investigators.)

21. This list and the one following are based upon the discussions of graphic confusion in J. D. Wilson, *The Manuscript of Shakespeare's "Hamlet"*, 2 vols. (Cam-

bridge, 1934),1: 106–14; R. B. McKerrow, *An Introduction to Bibliography for Literary Students* (Oxford, 1927), 341–50; W. S. B. Buck, *Examples of Handwriting 1550–1650* (London, 1973), 66–67. Other than the specific confusions discussed in the following paragraph, I have added to the confusabilia in these reference works the misreading of *l* as *r*, a misreading supported by: *R3* 1.1.133 (*F1* play; *edd* prey), *MAC* 1.1.13 (*F1* gallowgrosses; *edd* gallowglasses), *OTH* 5.1.1. (*F1* barke; *Q1* bulk), and *1H6* 4.4.16 (*F1* Regions; *edd* legions). This last mistake is repeated in the errata for Philip of Mornai's *A Treatise of the Church* (STC 18162), sig. L14ᵛ line 24, and the errata for the 1606 translation of Suetonius (STC 23422) at sig. B6ʳ line b14 corrects *groria* to *gloria* (Blayney,1: 617, 621). The many instances in Shakespeare and elsewhere of *l* being misread as *i* and *c* also testify to its being indistinguishable from a minim when, as often,the ascender did not ascend very high.

22. *HAM* 5.2.9 Q2(u) *pall*, Q2(c) *fall*. See also Hamlet 3.1.143, where F1's *pace* is clearly an error for Q2's *face*. I take it that Folio *Hamlet* was not set from an annotated copy of Q2, but from a manuscript instead: see my "The Folio Copy for *Hamlet, King Lear,* and *Othello,*" *Shakespeare Quarterly* 34 (1983): 44–61, and "Folio Compositors and Folio Copy: *King Lear* and Its Context," *PBSA* 79 (1985): 17–74. *Richard III* 5.3.13 (F1 faction/Q1-6 partie) may be another example; though the variant could of course arise from memorial error, if we assume the use of a tilde the two words would be easily confusable, given the p/f similarity in *More*. The relevant reading in *Sir Thomas More* is the word *for* at II.c.98 ("for to the king"). Similar errors outside of Shakespeare occur in John Blagrave's *The Art of Dyalling* (STC 3116), sig. M4ʳ 29, where the errata list informs us that for "C. F." we should read "C. P.," and in Thomas Sparke's *A Brotherly Persuasion to Unitie* (STC 23019.5), where the uncorrected errata list has *fit* (line 7) for *put* in the corrected state.

23. Leon Kellner, in *Restoring Shakespeare* (London, 1925) contends that long-s could be a misreading of *l, st,* or *t,* but his examples are not convincing, and I know of no Shakespearean parallels. I have likewise disregarded his assertion that *p* could be a misreading of *pl, pr,* or *r;* even if he were right, only the third would be relevant anyway,because of the need for a monosyllable in crux X.

24. Compare *Winter's Tale* 1507 (F1 scarr'd, Rowe scar'd), *3 Henry VI* 1404 (F1 scarre,F3 scare), *Antony and Cleopatra* 2221 (F1 scarre's, F2 scars)—all set by Compositor B. The last also illustrates his use of redundant apostrophes. B spelled the word *scar* as *scarre* fifteen times, using *scar* only once, in a justified line (*All's Well* 2577).

25. Joseph Price, *The Unfortunate Comedy: A Study of "All's Well That Ends Well" and its Critics* (Liverpool and Toronto, 1968), 164.

26. For an extended use of this trope, see the first of Wyatt's "Satires." Shakespeare uses it often: *R2* 1.2.29 (patience/despair), *2H4* 2.1.123 (honourable boldness/impudent sauciness), *H5* 3.2.42 (steal/purchase), *TRO* 1.3.150 (slander/imitation), 1.3.197 (policy/cowardice), 2.3.87 (melancholy/pride), *COR* 3.1.137 (cares/fears), 3.1.245 (manhood/foolery), *MAC* 5.2.14 (mad/valiant fury), *LR* 1.1.129 (pride/plainness), 1.4.214 (shame/discreet proceeding), *TN* 3.1.99 (lowly feigning/compliment), *JC* 2.1.180 (purgers/murderers), *SON* 105.1 (love/idolatry), *MV* 1.3.51 (well-won thrift/interest), *HAM* 3.4.42 (virtue/hypocrite). Even more relevant are parallels involving *make*, in the sense "make out to be," "make seem" as here: see *LLL* 2.1.59 ("he hath wit to make an ill shape good"), 5.1.140 (the grace "to make an offence gracious"), *AWW* 2.3.2 ("to make modern and familiar, things supernatural and causeless"), 2.3.4 ("make trifles of terrors"), 4.3.65 ("make us comforts of our losses"), 5.3.61 ("make trivial price of serious things"),

*TN* 3.3.2 ("make your pleasure of your pains"), *WT* 2.2.17 ("here's such ado to make no stain a stain"), *TRO* 2.2.57 ("make the service greater than the god"), 3.2.59 ("fears make devils of cherubims"), *TGV* 3.1.368 ("that word makes the faults gracious"), *LLL* 5.2.374 ("your wits makes wise things foolish"), *SHR* 4.2.20 ("makes a god of such a cullion").

27. The play's economic imagery has generally been alluded to in relation to the theme of value, which is integral to the structural debate between Bertram's inherited and Helena's "native worth" (M. C Bradbrook, "Virtue is the True Nobility," *R.E.S.* N.S. 1 [1950]: 289–301).

# "Dumb Significants": The Poetics of Shakespeare's *Henry VI* Trilogy

## Richard Fly

> In dumb significants proclaim your thoughts.
> (*1Henry VI* 2.4.26)

### I

The world of the *Henry VI* plays is noisy, crowded, action-packed; and Shakespeare, as Mark Van Doren supposes, "must have learned invaluable lessons from the experience of writing so busy a work."[1] Certainly he had to confront great difficulties in subordinating such disorderly and volatile chronicle materials to a coherent artistic purpose. The tragic career of Henry the Sixth could prove especially instructive to the young playwright, since artist and child-king—both novices in the art of rule—occupy analogous positions. Both men must use what talent they possess to establish unity, to mediate alliance and cooperation among their subjects' atomistic impulses. Both struggle for authoritative expression capable of modulating cacophonous declamation and lamentation into some semblance of harmony.[2] The "invaluable lessons" Shakespeare learned from this identification with the king, and their contribution to his development as a poetic dramatist, is the subject of this essay.

Subordination, modulation, mediation—these qualities are not much in evidence in either the trilogy's content or structure. Consequently, neither king nor playwright finally masters the anarchic energies at war in the land. For just as King Henry's subjects insist on standing as self-sufficient rebels from authority, so too do Shakespeare's scenes and episodes demand the fullest self-assertion at every moment—refusing to sacrifice instant gratifications for long-range goals.[3] The rebellious impulse is so general that we can hear in the harried king's exasperated words echoes of the dramatist's self-commentary. The king's frustration with his unruly nobles, that is, includes the playwright's frustration with his stubbornly recalcitrant chronicle materials. One such instance of dual reference occurs in the Hawking Scene of *2 Henry VI*. Henry voices

186

disappointment with his quarrelsome lords in language as appropriate to the artist as to the monarch:

> The winds grow high; so do your stomachs, lords.
> How irksome is this music to my heart!
> When such strings jar, what hope of harmony?
> I pray, my lords, let me compound this strife.
>
> (2.1.56–59)[4]

Henry's figurative language seems simultaneously to describe the discordant behavior of the peers and the stylistic excesses of the plays. And the ease with which his offer to arbitrate is ignored underscores the ungovernable nature of both kingdom and play-world.

The *Henry VI* plays dramatize the inexorable disintegration of a unified and heroic kingdom. Neither in the Hawking Scene nor elsewhere does King Henry succeed in calming the gathering storm of civil war. In fact, the tempest builds in direct inverse ratio to his increasing impotence as a mediator. His failures to "compound this strife" culminate in the most anarchic moment in the trilogy—the battle of Towton—where the helpless king sits alone on a molehill and describes the elemental chaos of warfare sweeping unchecked over his desolate land:

> Now sways it this way, like a mighty sea
> Forced by the tide to combat with the wind,
> Now sways it that way, like the selfsame sea
> Forced to retire by fury of the wind.
> Sometime the flood prevails, and then the wind;
> Now one the better, then another best;
> Both tugging to be victors, breast to breast;
> Yet neither conqueror nor conqueréd.
> So is the equal poise of this fell war.
>
> (*Part 3* 2.5. 5–13)[5]

With the king unable to function as a mediating center, the world of the play has collapsed into universal antagonism—a self-destructive dialectic involving only unarbitrated extremes. Differentiations blur into irreconcilable conflicts, making it impossible to distinguish between the warfare of wind and sea and that of Lancaster and York. A father has murdered his son and a son has murdered his father. Everywhere opposites are locked "breast to breast" in a self-annihilating fury, even on the blood-spotted pale cheeks of a murdered son. "The red rose and the white are on his face," Henry observes, "the fatal colors of our striving houses" (97–98). The battlefield becomes for Henry a hall of mirrors reflecting only appalling images of his failure as king.

So absolute is Henry's isolation that his passionless commentary on

his country's disintegration can stand as an indictment of the very
structure of the play that contains him. *3 Henry VI's* burgeoning cast of
indistinguishable characters, its accelerating ebb and flow of political
fortunes, its refusal to subject historical sequence to formal control—all
these factors seem to extend Henry's vision of unmediated strife to the
play's overall structure. One can explain these formal defects by arguing,
as Edward Berry does, that "the vicissitudes of the play's action serve as a
structural mimicry of the vicissitudes of the wars catalogued by the
chroniclers."⁶ Shakespeare may be exploiting artistically his received
materials' formlessness. But I think the young playwright is also finding
in the king's failure of rule analogues to his own difficulties in mediating
among the seemingly antipathic elements of his craft. For as Henry's
kingdom gradually decomposes into "the interminability of conflict, a
ceaseless flux in which victory and defeat eventually lose all meaning,"⁷
so too, it would seem, does Shakespeare's trilogy. We can pursue further
this possible relationship between politics and poetics by turning to the
opening play of the series.

## II

The first two acts of *1 Henry VI* locate the source of England's troubles
in the vicious quarrels that erupt between Winchester and Gloucester
and between Somerset and York. Shakespeare delays Henry's initial
appearance until the third act so the young king can enter the play at a
moment when these squabbles have intensified to a point where they
threaten, as an observer puts it, "to slay your sovereign and destroy the
realm" (3.1.114). Thus King Henry's first words illustrate the mediating
role he is forced to play in his country's affairs:

> Uncles of Gloucester and of Winchester,
> The special watchmen of our English weal,
> I would prevail, if prayers might prevail,
> To join your hearts in love and amity.
>
> (3.1.65–68)

Though the last line perfectly summarizes Henry's dramatic function in
the trilogy, the general effect of the speech is not promising: the king's
use of the subjunctive mood in combination with the qualifying "if"
clause drains the royal gesture of its power. Nevertheless, Henry does
bring about a truce of sorts between his truculent nobles. Gloucester
gives in first, saying "Here, Winchester, I offer thee my hand," and the
Bishop responds in kind, "Love for thy love and hand for hand I give"
(126, 135). But the falsity of this alliance and the naïveté in Henry's
expression of accomplishment ("How joyful am I made by this con-

tract!") surface in Winchester's instant confession (to the audience) of implacable hatred of Gloucester. The scene ends gloomily with the choric Exeter left alone onstage to expose the true quality of the reconciliation:

> This late dissension grown betwixt the peers
> Burns under feignéd ashes of forged love
> And will at last break out into a flame.
>
> (3.1.189–91)

The king's contribution to this scene's dramatic structure is no more successful than his contribution to the political situation. Of the scene's two hundred lines, for instance, only thirty-five—those allotted to the perfunctory restoration of York's dukedom—actually further the plot. The rest are used to display inveterate hostility between various factions: Gloucester against Winchester, Warwick (as York's surrogate) against Somerset, the Protector's tawny-coated servants against the Bishop's blue-coated servants. Without the king's presence and his would-be peacemaking, the scene would be a static exfoliation of unmediated confrontations—a Towton battlefield in miniature. What little forward impetus the scene has and what rudimentary motions it makes toward dramatic continuity are generated solely by the king's intervention.

More disturbing dramaturgical consequences of Henry's inadequacy as a mediator appear in the busy coronation scene that opens the fourth act. This time it is the smoldering hatred between Somerset and York that disrupts the ceremonial proceedings and halts the action's forward movement, but now the combatants have found a powerful new way to invigorate and protract their quarrel. Their followers have signified their allegiances by displaying red and white roses, and they have found in the properties of these roses (i.e., their colors, smells, thorns) opportunities for boundless invective. Henry listens to a sampling of these "forged quaint conceits" and exclaims in shocked disbelief:

> Good Lord, what madness rules in brainsick men
> When for so slight and frivolous a cause
> Such factious emulations shall arise!
>
> (4.1.111–13)

To Henry, beleaguered by national and international problems, the roses are no more than "a toy, a thing of no regard" (145). And in the longest and most forceful speech he makes in the trilogy, the newly crowned monarch dismisses these divisive tokens, trying instead to direct his subjects' attention to the realities of their perilous situation. "Remember where you are," he pleads, "In France, amongst a fickle wavering nation" (137–38). Henry's self-indulgent courtiers are so obsessed with symbols and so intoxicated with figurative expression that they lost sight of the real world's larger dangers.

The king's annoyance is understandable; but his effort to correct their fault by denying *any* symbolic meaning resident in the roses will prove ruinous for him and England. His blindness becomes unmistakable when he intervenes, a supposedly impartial "umpire" who demonstrates his contempt for symbols by donning a red rose:

> Let me be umpire in this doubtful strife.
> I see no reason, if I wear this rose, [Puts on a red rose]
> That any one should therefore be suspicious
> I more incline to Somerset than York.
> Both are my kinsmen, and I love them both.
>
> (4.1.151–55)

The entire speech is Henry's finest moment in the trilogy. But the disparity between what his words say and what his putting on the red rose signifies complicates the conflict he wants to resolve. Shakespeare directs attention to this fatal disjunction between word and act by leaving Warwick and York alone on stage to comment. "The king," Warwick says, "Prettily, methought did play the orator." "And so he did," York answers, "but yet I like it not, / In that he wears the badge of Somerset" (174–77). Henry's dramatic gesture undermines the force of his rhetoric, for he can hardly expect to serve as an "umpire" while wearing the insignia of a competing party.

Act 4's other scenes dramatize the tragic consequences of Henry's flawed attempts to bring together the disjointed kingdom. Henry's battlefield surrogate, Sir William Lucy, fails in his mission to unite the forces of Somerset and York and bring them to the rescue of Lord Talbot and his son, who have been entrapped by the French. The Talbots fight bravely, but it is clear from the context that they are anachronisms in an increasingly polarized world. Killed by "the fraud of England, not the force of France" (4.4.36), they become the first casualties in the emergent Wars of the Roses. As they die in each other's arms, they celebrate a unity of mind and behavior that remains an unobtainable ideal in the fragmented world they leave behind:

> Thou antic Death, which laugh'st us here to scorn,
> Anon, from thy insulting tyranny,
> Coupled in bonds of perpetuity,
> Two Talbots wingéd through the lither sky,
> In thy despite shall scape mortality.
>
> (4.7.18–22)

Death becomes a benign force that releases these heroes from the labyrinth of earthly existence and allows their souls to ascend, like Daedalus and Icarus, into a realm of glory where they will forever remain "Coupled in bonds of perpetuity."

All other bonds remain uncoupled. Indeed, the movement of events in *1 Henry VI*, from the cumulative demonstrations of the king's inadequacy to the eulogistic nature of the Talbots' demise, suggests that the only effective mediator of England's problems is Death. Henry V is dead as the play opens, and the deaths of his great generals, Salisbury and Bedford, figure prominently in the early scenes. An elegaic atmosphere permeates the landscape, reminding us that some essential glory has departed the earth. But it is in the scene placed immediately before Henry's first appearance that the idea of Death as mediator between intolerable existence and spiritual rest receives its explicit expression. Here the enfeebled Edmund Mortimer, claimant to the throne, comes forth to describe the "loathsome sequestration" of his long incarceration, to inventory his physical deterioration, and to announce his deliverer's arrival:

> But now the arbitrator of despairs,
> Just Death, kind umpire of men's miseries,
> With sweet enlargement doth dismiss me hence.
>
> (2.5.28–30)

"Here dies the dusky torch of Mortimer" (122), York says, as the body of his uncle is carried from the stage. Within seven lines of Mortimer's death the young king will enter the play to make his arbitrational gestures. But Mortimer's evocation of Death as "kind umpire of men's miseries" throws an ominous shadow over the events that follow—from the king's several attempts to "be umpire in this doubtful strife" to the eventual collapse of all mediation in the Talbots' massacre.

As the *Henry VI* trilogy unfolds its dismal patterns of failure, Death fills the space vacated by inadequate human mediation. It triumphs on the battlefields of Wakefield, Towton, and Tewkesbury. In *3 Henry VI*'s penultimate scene, the miserable Henry finds himself, like old Mortimer, imprisoned, powerless, awaiting in despair his deliverer's arrival. Death, by this time the only clear "arbitrator of despairs," materializes in the grisly form of Richard of Gloucester, and Henry dies, like Talbot, comparing himself and his murdered son to Daedalus and Icarus.

### III

The king's failure as a mediator calls forth the deadly hump-backed apparition that eventually destroys him and devastates his country. A grim dialectic structures Henry's fortunes and those of his ultimate antagonist, Richard: as the king's speech reveals its incapacity to shape events, Richard's diabolical actions slowly gain control. Richard embodies that corrupting action Henry introduced by tainting his reconciliation speech with putting on the Lancastrian rose. From their first appearance in the Temple Garden scene of *Part 1*, the red and white roses are "dumb significants" (as Richard's father describes them) capable of representing and releasing forces hostile to language's mediating power. Shakespeare imagines these mute symbols as the originating cause of the civil wars. Hence Henry's fatal adoption of the sanguine rose becomes the opening shot (a self-inflicted wound) in what will be a victorious campaign against authoritative language. The king inadvertently releases a force that strengthens as the trilogy progresses, until it crystallizes in the savagery of his assassin Richard.

The target of Richard's aggression is language as much as Lancastrians. Disproportioned in every part, "Like to a chaos, or unlicked bear-whelp" (*Part 3*.3.2.161), he exists as a walking emblem of anarchy: a "dumb significant" grown powerful enough to function as the exterminator of authoritative speech. "I'll hear no more," he shouts as his dagger cuts short Henry's final words, "die, prophet, in thy speech" (*Part 3*.5.6.57). But his very first utterance in the trilogy—"And if words will not, then our weapons shall" (*Part 2*.5.1.140)—reveals his priorities and points the direction his development will take. When occasion demands, Richard can play orator with the best of them, but he would prefer to let his actions speak for themselves. At the beginning of *3 Henry VI*, for instance, he executes a shocking theatrical *coup,* suddenly tossing Somerset's bloody head into the midst of bragging Yorkists and curtly announcing "Speak thou for me, and tell them what I did" (1.1.16). Even this horrific gesture is prologue to the swelling acts he will perform as he pursues the imperial theme. As the trilogy draws to its barbaric close, his behavior is increasingly fueled by an obsessive hatred of speech, especially when associated with Henry. Captured during the battle of Tewkesbury, Henry's son denounces his captors, saying "Suppose that I am now my father's mouth." "By heaven, brat," Richard responds as he stabs him to death, "I'll plague ye for that word" (5.5.18,27). Richard then turns his remorseless weapon on Henry's Queen, asking those assembled "why should she live to fill the world with words?" (43). But this time Richard is restrained, and so must hurry away to feast in the Tower on his "bloody supper"—Henry. Richard's last action is to kiss his brother's young heir, Prince Edward, while reminding us that "so Judas kissed his master" (5.6.53–54). Thus, our final glimpse of Richard reveals his identification with the archetypal betrayer of the Logos. After what we have been through, the analogy does not seem forced.

Language is anathema to Richard because his essential being is communicated through his visual appearance. His fundamentally different presentation is underscored at the climactic instance of Henry's murder. "Teeth hadst thou in thy head when thou wast born," Henry says as Richard's knife flashes, "To signify thou cam'st to bite the world." "And so I was," Richard recalls, "which plainly signified / That I should snarl, and bite, and play the dog" (5.6.53–54, 76–77). Such mute signification is the rule of his dramatic life; from his initial appearance onward, his role is prefigured in his physical deformity. The first words he speaks draw from Old Clifford the stinging rebuke, "Hence, heap of wrath, foul indigested lump, / As crooked in thy manners as thy shape!" (*Part 2*.5.1.157–58). Later, he confesses that "This shoulder was ordained so thick to heave, / And heave it shall some weight, or break my back" (*Part 3*.5.7.23–24). As a "foul stigmatic" whose character is "plainly signified" by nonlinguistic means, Richard freely pursues a dazzling exploitation of language. The other characters present themselves immediately and unequivocally through their public utterances, while Richard manipulates language as a disguise and strategic weapon.[8] Consequently, he sees the arena of public discourse as primarily a stage for displays of personal perversity:

> Why, I can smile, and murder whiles I smile,
> And cry "Content!" to that which grieves my heart,
> And wet my cheeks with artificial tears,
> And frame my face to all occasions.
>
> (*Part 3*.3.2.182–85)

Language is merely a wardrobe from which Richard can select the appropriate garment, not an extension of his being. As an actor who can "change shapes with Proteus for advantages" (192), he maintains a cynical detachment from his exploitative words. Any hint of an ontological freedom, however, has been rejected beforehand by the quasi-allegorical conception of his character and role. Like a criminal branded with the mark of his crime, his essential nature is always and unmistakably on full display.

By the time Henry lays aside his book of devotion to face his killer, he has been reduced to a disembodied and isolated voice unable to influence the course of events but increasingly eloquent in his suffering commentary. Indeed, his authority as a prophetic witness, as spokesman for truths beyond the reach of his countrymen, grows in proportion to his waning ability to make his voice heard above the din of factional disputes. After the defeat of the Lancastrians at Towton, Henry, separated from his scattered supporters, is helpless. Yet the Keeper who arrests him as he wanders alone and in disguise can identify him because, as he explains, "Thou talk'st as if you wert a king" (*Part 3*.3.1.59). As the symbols of his former dignity fall away, only his royal utterance remains. But even this defining idiom modulates toward the oracular during the brief period in act 4 when Warwick and Clarence try to return him to the throne. Henry immediately turns over all power to the two men and chooses "to lead a private life / And in devotion to spend my latter days" (4.6.42–43). Having stripped himself of secular authority, he launches into an impressive "presaging prophecy" concerning the bright future he envisages for young Henry Tudor, the Earl of Richmond: "If secret powers / Suggest but truth to my divining thoughts," he announces, "This pretty lad will prove our country's bliss" (68–70). Henry's final pronouncement in the oracular mode is addressed to his assassin and is much less appreciated. "And thus I prophesy," Henry says, as he begins to catalogue the disasters Richard will unleash on England. "I'll hear no more," Richard interrupts, "Die, prophet, in thy speech" (5.6.35–36). For once Richard's epithet is absolutely correct.

Since Henry and Richard represent polar extremes of language, silencing the king and his concept of effective speech means licensing Richard and his concept of anarchic action. Two episodes late in the trilogy demonstrate this complete, gradual transfer of power. In the confrontation at the outset of *Part 3*, Henry attempts a bold show of verbal authority. "Peace thou! and give King Henry leave to speak" (1.1.120), he shouts, as he gathers himself to chastize and discipline the Yorkists who have invaded his Parliament to dethrone him. But the defiant tone cannot be sustained, and after only fifty lines of debate concerning his right to rule, the king is reduced to abject pleas for permission even to speak at all: "My Lord of Warwick," he begs, "hear me but one word" (174). Crushed by his opponents, Henry averts a bloody showdown in Parliament only by disinheriting his son and proclaiming York his heir. The sorry business ends with Henry abandoned by his disgusted supporters and under a withering tongue-lashing from Queen Margaret. "I shame to hear thee speak," she says, as she prepares to take command of the royal army. Henry's weak response—"Stay, gentle Margaret, and hear me speak"—only draws from the exasperated Queen the sharp rebuke, "Thou has spoke too much already: get thee gone" (258–65). Henry's verbal impotence and social isolation now are nearly total.

The final blow to the king's authority, however, comes in the verbal skirmishes preceding the battle of Towton. Henry is with the Lancastrian army despite Young Clifford's request that "I would your highness would depart the field," and he insists on making one last attempt to mediate linguistically the devastation that is about to overwhelm his kingdom. This time it is not his enemies but his own party who makes it impossible for him to commence:

> *King Henry.* Have done with words, my lords, and hear me
> speak.
> *Queen Margaret.* Defy them then, or else hold close thy lips.
> *King Henry.* I prithee give no limit to my tongue:
> I am a king and privileged to speak.
> *Clifford.* My liege, the wound that bred this meeting here
> Cannot be cured with words. Therefore be still.
> (*Part* 3.2.2.117–22)

Clifford's brusque command to his king—"be still"—makes it clear that
Henry's "bookish rule" is over and that the disease afflicting England
"cannot be cured with words." From now on the edge of the sword will
arbitrate differences—a fact underscored by Richard's instantaneous response to Clifford's rebuke: "Then, executioner, unsheathe thy sword"
(123). Richard's brother Edward explicitly links eruption of civil war to
silencing the king's word: "Since thou deniest the gentle King to speak,"
he reasons, "Sound trumpets! Let our bloody colors wave!" (172–73). The
brothers' reaction brings into sharp outline the dialectical pattern I am
trying to clarify. With the king's mode of discourse discredited and
stifled, the combatants are left to proclaim their homicidal thoughts only
in the "dumb significants" of sword, trumpet, and bloody colors.
Richard's mode of action triumphs; gruesome battles are underway and,
as Mortimer foresaw in *Part 1*, the only "arbitrator of despairs" left in
England is Death.

Silenced and driven from the battlefield, Henry—who thought he was
"a king, and privileged to speak"—will never again be directly engaged
in the action. Even when captured by the Yorkists in act 4, he is quickly
and silently hustled off to prison. "Hence with him to the Tower,"
Edward orders, "let him not speak" (4.8.57). There, as we have seen, his
final silencing awaits him in the person of Richard.

## IV

The logic binding the collapse of the king's language to the ascent of
Richard, its "executioner," helps us to understand the mix of linguistic
perversion and theatrical sensationalism making up most of *3 Henry VI*.
Brutal actions expand to fill the void left by effective speech. The dominant pattern emerges early in the play when Young Clifford seizes the
Yorkist child Rutland during the battle of Wakefield. Rutland begs,
"Sweet Clifford, hear me speak before I die," but the word-annihilating
warrior cuts short his petition: "In vain thou speak'st, poor boy," he says,
"my father's blood / Hath stopped the passage where thy words should
enter" (1.3.18–22). As stone-deaf to Rutland's pleas as he will be to his
king's words of reconciliation, and driven by the bloodlust that drums in

his ears, Clifford mercilessly stabs to death the defenseless child. But in the capricious world of this play not many scenes pass before Clifford himself staggers on stage (with an arrow lodged appropriately in his throat) to die at the feet of Rutland's momentarily victorious brothers. The shifting fortunes of war bring no improvement in verbal behavior, however, as the brothers combine their abusive speech to "vex him with eager words" (2.6.68). But the Yorkists' invective is just as useless as was Rutland's plea, since, as Warwick disappointedly explains, "He nor sees, nor hears us what we say" (63). Richard's response to Clifford's immunity to his insult illuminates the level to which both action and language have sunk. "By my soul," he says,

> If this right hand would buy two hours' life,
> That I (in all despite) might rail at him,
> This hand should chop it off, and with the issuing blood
> Stifle the villain. . . .

$$(2.6.79-83)^9$$

Horrible as they are, Richard's words reinforce the play's recurrent imagery of blood suffocating normal human discourse. Finally, it is the play itself that "stifles" on this surfeit of blood.

The Yorkists' ludicrous attempt to communicate with Clifford's dead body gauges the efficacy of language in the trilogy's final play. Although the air rings with the clangor of vaunts and taunts, ultimatums and lamentations, we seldom hear anything resembling what Hamlet will call "the accent of Christians." In the torrent, tempest, and whirlwind of their passion, not much modulation away from the hyperbolic norm is possible. Hence a dismal *sameness* of expression envelops the knights as they bellow and strut their way to a common end. Somerset's report to Warwick of his brother Montague's death provides both a good example and a precise commentary on this indiscriminate style:

> Ah! Warwick! Montague hath breathed his last!
> And to the latest gasp cried out for Warwick,
> And said, "Commend me to my valiant brother,"
> And more he would have said, and more he spoke,
> Which sounded like a cannon in a vault
> That mought not be distinguished.

$$(5.2.40-45)$$

Like Montague, the people of 3 *Henry VI* always seem to have something more to say, especially when suspended on the point of death. But all too often their speech sounds "like a cannon in a vault," splitting the ears of the audience with indistinguishable noise and destroying their capacity to differentiate among the characters.

The fact that Shakespeare supplied the critically useful commentary on Montague's dying speech suggests that he is aware of his play's linguistic deficiencies. Such moments may remind us of Sigurd Burckhardt's conviction that Shakespeare, even in this early work, "has mastered the trick of making the style he employs comment upon itself."[10] It does seem evident—from the many instances of crude casuistry, perverted embassages, insidious displays of rhetoric, oaths and pledges cynically sworn and opportunistically broken, obscene delight in sexual innuendo, and volleys of bombastic invective—that Shakespeare knows of, and is calling our attention to, the degenerative nature of his play's language. This awareness is accompanied by a further recognition that the only kind of communication capable of surviving in this sordid linguistic environment is the dumb-show sign language of brandished swords, battle flags, and hectic skirmishes—the primitive expressive mode of Richard of Gloucester. As the sanguinary gladiators sink to the level of what Queen Margaret calls "Butchers and villains! bloody cannibals" (5.5.59), their language undergoes a similar diminution and brutalization until it becomes indistinguishable from the subhuman acts they so eagerly inflict on each other. What makes this general collapse poetically significant is Shakespeare's understanding of his own complicity in it: his tacit acknowledgment that it has come as a result of the king's failure, and his own, to enact an effective mediation between language and action.

Genuine dramatic interplay between speech and action are virtually nonexistent in 3 Henry VI because speech, as an instrument of social integration, is severely circumscribed, restricted to the incompetent King Henry, and then quarantined from the play's action. With language shrunken in scope and powerless, the play increasingly falls back upon appeals to the audience's appetite for crude theatrical sensationalism: displays of bloodied swords, garish banners, and severed head; staged instances of homicide, parricide, infanticide, and regicide; spectacles of mock paper crownings on mole-hills, heads impaled on city gates, and dying warriors with arrows in their necks; exhibits of red and white roses on hats and other insignias of allegiance; and so on. Such disproportionate reliance on these simple stage effects makes 3 Henry VI a noteworthy exception to Shakespeare's usual stagecraft. "One is struck in performance," J. P. Brockbank says, "by the expressive force of the mere dumb-show and noise,"[11] but Brockbank ignores the degree to which this "expressive force" has usurped the function of speech and coarsened the quality of the play. With the rejection of the king's language and the erosion of knightly civilities comes a disheartening insistence on gestures toward those who Hamlet will later identify as "capable of nothing but inexplicable dumb shows and noise."

V

The poetic dramatist, as Hamlet noted in a famous passage, must "suit the action to the word, the word to the action," taking care to "o'er-step not the modesty of nature"(3.2.16–23). Like other well-meaning theorists of the theater, Hamlet prescribes a poetic often more honored in the breach than the observance—as he himself will learn when his modest playlet, "The Murder of Gonzago," polarizes into crude dumb-show and wordy oration. The seemingly easy challenge of suiting words to actions is one Shakespeare will return to in his long career, never resting content with whatever temporary alliance he can effect. He will have remarkable success, of course; but there will be times when it will seem to him that poetic language and mute spectacle cannot be brought together without one corrupting the other. This antipathy will appear in the tragic experiences of Brutus, Hamlet, and Angelo when they fail at crucial moments to find an accommodation between their words and their actions. Thus we watch Brutus proclaiming "Peace, freedom, liberty!" while his hands drip with the blood of the murdered Caesar, Hamlet asserting his determination to "speak daggers to her, but use none" just before stabbing Polonius in his mother's chamber, and Angelo mouthing pious sentiments of personal purity even as he maneuvers to deflower Isabella and behead her brother. Such failures to integrate aspects of character into a unified personality offer profound insights into the human condition. They also reflect, I believe, Shakespeare's own prolonged struggle to master the divided legacy of poetic drama.

I have tried to show how the artist's sensitivity to his complex medium is an important factor in the *Henry VI* plays, concentrating on the formal implications of the interplay between King Henry and Richard of Gloucester. Richard's triumph suggests that Shakespeare has not yet evolved a poetic language that can hold its own against the simpler appeals of stage action. As the trilogy unfolds, consequently, the weak and ineffectual "word" of the king capitulates before the "action" of Richard, leaving the plays' participants with little to rely on but bombastic rhetoric and crude spectacle. Shakespeare is aware of this damaging imbalance between language and action and is prepared to follow its formal consequences to the dismal culmination in *3 Henry VI*. Indeed, it is that peculiarly Shakespearean alertness to the difficulties inherent in play-making, along with a willingness to project such concerns into the content of his work, that allows the young playwright eventually to master the full resources of poetic drama. The *Henry VI* plays would not satisfy the judicious Prince of Denmark, but neither he nor his brilliant insight into the "purpose of playing" could exist had not his creator willingly suffered the educative experience of these plays.

## Notes

1. *Shakespeare* (New York: Henry Holt, 1939), 17.

2. In his essay "'I Am but Shadow of Myself': Ceremony and Design in *1 Henry VI*," Sigurd Burckhardt imagines Shakespeare saying "Am I not in the position of Henry VI, a child, a mere beginner in the art of governing this play-world, surrounded by powerful and headstrong nobles, pleading helplessly for peace and amity, for subordination to the common purpose?" (*Shakespearean Meanings* [Princeton: Princeton University Press, 1968], 58). James L. Calderwood elaborates on this point: "If Henry VI is figured as a dramatist staging the play of state, how he does and fails to do this can tell us something about how that royal dramatist Shakespeare—in whose theatrical realm actors are courtiers, and groundlings in the pit are subjects as potentially rebellious as Jack Cade's unworthies—regards his role in ordering his fictional commonwealth" (*Shakespearean Metadrama* [Minneapolis: University of Minnesota Press, 1971], 6). The conclusions Burckhardt draws from this identification are quite different from my own, and Calderwood does not develop his point. Nevertheless, my approach to the *Henry VI* plays owes much to the work of these two critics.

3. Clifford Leech describes the *Henry VI* plays as "an anecdotal kind of drama in which incidents are presented in turn for the sake of immediate dramatic effect rather than for their contributions to a total pattern" (*William Shakespeare: The Chronicles* [London: Methuen, 1962], 14). Mark Rose says that "*1 Henry VI* is above all a play of individual scenes," and "the result is that the play as a whole lacks articulation" (*Shakespearean Design* [Cambridge: Harvard University Press, 1972], 127, 129). See also Burckhardt, 54.

4. All quotations from the plays are taken from *William Shakespeare: The Complete Works*, ed. Alfred Harbage (Baltimore: Penguin Books, 1969).

5. Notice how Henry's description of the madness of the battlefield anticipates Gertrude's description of Hamlet as "Mad as the sea and wind when both contend / Which is the mightier" (4.1.7–8).

6. *Patterns of Decay: Shakespeare's Early Histories* (Charlottesville: University of Virginia Press, 1975), 53.

7. Ibid., 54.

8. For an excellent discussion of how character is presented through public utterances in the history plays, see Arthur Sewell, *Character and Society in Shakespeare* (Oxford: Oxford University Press, 1951), 38–52.

9. Compare this passage with the spine-tingling exchange late in *Part 3* between the recently crowned King Edward and his former ally Warwick. Edward is chiding Warwick for switching his allegiance to the Lancastrians and commanding him once more to kneel in obedience:

*Warwick.* I had rather chop this hand off at a blow
And with the other fling it in thy face,
Then bear so low a sail to strike to thee.

*King Edward.* Sail how thou canst, have wind and tide thy friend.
This hand, fast wound about thy coal-black hair,
Shall, whiles thy head is warm and new cut off,
Write in the dust this sentence with thy blood:
'Wind-changing Warwick now can change no more.'

(5.5.50–57)

This visceral exchange shrinks the mediacy of language to the point where words actually become identifiable with the physical objects they name. Throughout the trilogy Shakespeare has followed the example of Marlowe in using energetic speech as dramatic equivalents for actions impossible to represent on the stage. But here in the Warwick-Edward confrontation he seems intent on bringing words as close as possible to the actual condition of corporeality. Warwick would fling both his insulting words and his bloody hand into Edward's face, and Edward in turn would express his contempt for Warwick verbally and in words composed from his very life-blood. The goal of both men is a palpable immediacy of expression that would eliminate the between-ness of ordinary communication. For parallels with Marlowe in the dramatic deployment of energetic speech, see Robert Y. Turner, *Shakespeare's Apprenticeship* (Chicago: University of Chicago Press, 1974), 35–66.

10. Burckhardt, 55.

11. See Brockbank's fine essay, "The Frame of Disorder: *Henry VI*," in *Early Shakespeare: Stratford-Upon-Avon Studies 3*, ed. John Russell Brown and Bernard Harris (New York: Schocken, 1961), 93.

# Parrots, Paraquitos, and Poppinjays: Of Birds and Words in *1 Henry IV*

## William Collins Watterson

No bird is invoked more often than the capon in *1 Henry IV*. A rooster castrated to fatten for the pot, it serves as a perfect emblem for gourmandizing Falstaff, aging cock of the walk and self-styled spring chicken: he ruffles the feathers of "Dame Partelet" (Mistress Quickly) in the barnyard of Eastcheap. In sharp contrast to the "starved turkeys" that a carrier transports in his pannier from Robin Ostler's stable, the obese Sir John manages to avoid the slaughter for which he is morally ripe at Shrewsbury, displaying no more valor than a wild duck (as he says of Poins) or the wild geese that he imagines Hal's pitiful subjects to resemble in act 2, scene 4. By playing dead, the "fat deer" counterfeits death and so saves his life, only to be labeled by Poins in part 2 a "martlemas"; that is, an ox too old to survive another winter and one traditionally sacrificed for its meat on the Feast of Saint Martin (November 11). And indeed Hal, as soon as he is crowned Henry V, must cut off Falstaff's ribald influence as of no worth: "item a capon, two shillings, two deniers."

In addition to domestic fowl, estridges, eagles, and other birds of prey, Shakespeare in *1 Henry IV* makes notable use of birds associated with talking and singing to differentiate the moral characters of Hal, Hotspur, and Falstaff.[1] Although we do not hear Warwick's explicit linking of rhetoric to mature morality until *2 Henry IV* (where he tells the King that "the prince but studies his companions / like a strange tongue, wherein, to gain the language / 'Tis needful that the most immodest word / be look'd upon and learnt"[2]), the relationship between articulation and heroism occurs as early as *1 Henry IV* 2.4, where he observes with contempt that Hotspur, a mere warrior, has "fewer words than a parrot." He goes on to make his little satire on Hotspur as *miles gloriosus* an object lesson, "parrot"ing Lady Percy in having her ask her husband "how many hast thou kill'd today," only to "parrot" Hotspur's answer with "Give my horse a drench," the latter turning out to be some plain-dealing medieval John Wayne more interested in the equine than the eloquent. As Hal continues his burlesque, he does have Hotspur get around to answering the question, but he puts laconic overstatement into his mouth to suggest that for Hotspur the only true manliness in speech consists of the quantifying eloquence of action ("reckoning"): "Some fourteen . . . a trifle, a trifle." Later in the same scene, Hal will imagine Hotspur running "a-horseback up a hill perpendicular" and, in a comic image of pure physicality, shooting sparrows out of the air with his pistol.

Hal's self-serving denigrations aside, a case could be made for Hotspur's limited eloquence, though such a case would have to acknowledge that his articulation consists of pithy cliches emanating from chivalric abstractions. Impetuous, explosive, even self-subverting in his discourse, he makes rote and predictable use of personification ("Methinks it were an easy leap to pluck bright honor from the pale-faced moon"), the mannered vocative ("O esperance"), a mechanical kind of quibbling (Lady Percy's urgent "What carries you away, my Lord" is met with the teasing, "Why, my horse, my love, my horse"), and a juvenile taste for crude rhymes ("That roan shall be my throne"). Even his wife recognizes the triviality of his language games ("Come, come, you paraquito, answer me / Directly unto this question that I ask"); and, indeed, compared to the rhetorically protean Falstaff, Hotspur has as little sense of tonal range as a cagebird. In the main aggressive, as he demonstrates in his comic verbal sallies against Glendower, Hotspur stands in marked contrast to Hal and Falstaff as they exchange roles and rhetorical styles in preparation for Hal's interview with the king. While we must no doubt temper Mistress Quickly's admiration of Falstaff's abilities—to break into blank verse spontaneously, to parody euphuism, and to rant in King Cambyses's vein—with an awareness that Falstaff is an essentially opportunistic character, we must also recognize that as rhetorical tutor he plays an invaluable role in educating the Prince in the adaptability necessary for leadership and statecraft. Hotspur, however, remains "unschooled," and so stands as negative exemplum of *virtus* unaccommodated by mastery of the verbal arts. That "policy" in its worst form and semantic subtlety go hand in hand becomes a disconcerting irony in 2 *Henry IV*, where John of Lancaster tricks the rebels shamefully with the literal-minded splitting of a hair.

Although Hotspur "professes not talking" and distrusts the arts of the Elizabethan *homo rhetoricus*,[3] we encounter in part 1 no evidence of his "speaking thick," which "tardiness in nature" Lady Percy alludes to in her poignant elegy in part 2. It would be hard, of course, for an actor to capture convincingly on stage any kind of speech defect (Schlegel's translation of the word "thick" by "stottern" spawned a tradition of stuttering German Hotspurs, though in fact "speaking thick" means only speaking slowly or with hesitation); in any case, nowhere in Holinshed's *Chronicle* is Hotspur associated with verbal deficiency. When the latter lies dying at Shrewsbury, he attempts to prophesy but cannot because the "cold hand of death lies on [his] tongue." I am inclined to accept this last statement not as containing some ambiguous reference to future historical events, as some critics think, but as a capping of the theme of Hotspur's rhetorical incapacity. Verbally explosive, Hotspur can be seen at best only as an eloquent plain-dealer, as a man of action who, paradoxically, remains Shakespeare's most articulate critic of articulation.

In act 1, scene 3 Hotspur himself invokes the idea of mimicking birds when, angry with the king for his refusal to ransom the "revolted" Mortimer, he imagines training a starling "to speak nothing but Mortimer" and then giving the pest to his sovereign in order to pique his conscience. More interestingly, in his famous speech earlier in the scene he rails against a certain lord, "neat and trimly dressed," who appeared at Holmedon to claim important prisoners on the king's behalf. What bothers him most about this glib unnamed dandy or "poppinjay" is his feminine characteristics, his talking "like a waiting gentle woman" and his being "perfum'd like a milliner." Hotspur despises the unmanliness of "bald unjointed chat," and associates fluency with effeminacy, flowery language with flowery perfume ("it made me mad to see him shine so bright and smell so sweet" in Lacanian terms suggests strong unconscious homoerotic attraction masked by negation). That the water-fly has a strong interest in the "slovenly unhandsome corses" which the "untaught knaves" carry by and that he speaks of "good tall fellows" as if they were minions, not soldiers, further outrages Hotspur's machismo, and his mockery of this prototypical Osric entails the express denunciation of prissy adjectives ("*villainous* saltpetre," "*sovereignest* thing on earth," and "*vile* guns" are some of the "lady terms" that irk the warrior, along with the invocation of "parmacity," the latest exotic court remedy for "inward bruises." The latter term, by the way, suggests Hotspur's own sexual repression.). In the Middle Ages a "poppinjay" was a brightly painted wooden parrot used as a target by practicing archers; it is not too much to suggest that Hotspur, in shooting the king's talkative, conceited, and effeminate messenger, is symbolically shooting himself, his alterego of eloquence, effeminacy, and possibly homoerotic desire.

Although Hotspur might well envy the Prince of Wales and his cohorts when they are described by Vernon in their battle attire as estridges or "eagles newly bathed," he sees birds in the main as antiheroic creatures on account of their vocal tendencies. Not only does he distrust articulation, but he also despises music and song. In the Welsh scene Hotspur reviles "mincing poetry" and "ballad mongers," even though "real" men like Glendower and Mortimer appear to have outgrown his fourth-form antipathy to the gentle art of singing. That Hotspur cannot understand Lady Mortimer's Welsh symbolizes the extent to which the higher reaches of language and with them the finer tones of civilization remain incomprehensible to Hotspur, and he seems glad that his wife won't attempt to equal her in musical adroitness. "Tis the best way to turn tailor, or be redbreast teacher," he says, thus trivializing song by associating it with a trade. For Hotspur the falcon is preferable to the robin, and he would rather "prune" himself, as Westmoreland accuses Worcester of doing—that is, trim his feathers like a predator readying for action. A character of repression rather than sublimation, Hotspur sees violence, not art, as the only outlet for his passion.

Despite several references to the cuckoo in *1 Henry IV*, only two are directly related to the language theme. In an image derived directly from the Latin of Pliny the Elder,[4] Worcester sees the rebels as sparrows and the king as an overweening "fledgeling":

> And being fed by us, you us'd us so
> As that ungentle gull the cuckoo's bird
> Useth the sparrow—did oppress our nest,
> Grew by our feeding to so great a bulk
> That even our love durst not come near your sight
> For fear of swallowing; but with nimble wing
> We were enforc'd for safety sake to fly
> Out of your sight . . .
>
> (5.1. 59–66)

Notable here is the way in which Worcester's disingenuous punning places the king in a comically disagreeable light. The adjective "ungentle" calls the usurper's very breeding into question (Shakespeare was fond of making Bolingbroke seem middle-class in manner and aspiration, even though he was a grandson of Edward III), while the primary meaning of "gull" as fool nicely colors Shakespeare's rarer usage of the word as a synonym for "fledgeling." Bolingbroke, devourer in his rise to power, swallows everything, even the respect that the sparrows or lesser nobles accord him, so greedy is he for the crown. "Fear of swallowing" suggests the "nimble wing" patterns of the rebels in flight, darting hither and yon in their efforts to escape the king's wrath.

Henry IV's own invocation of the cuckoo caps the rhetoric theme by tracing Richard's fall to, among other things, excessive familiarity of speech. When he warns Hal of the dangers of becoming "cheap and stale to vulgar company," he employs a tricky simile which argues that compulsive verbiage lacking in gravity of demeanor and firmness of purpose renders one invisible, if not inaudible. Such was Richard's fate:

> So, when he had occasion to be seen,
> He was but as the cuckoo is in June,
> Heard, not regarded . . .
>
> (3.2. 74–76)

Echoing Guicciardini, Machiavelli, and other Renaissance political theorists, Henry deplores levity and simultaneously exalts secrecy in what amounts to a cynical commonplace from the manuals of statecraft.

That Hal has mastered the concept of rhetorical decorum is pointedly illustrated in the only scene in which the king and Falstaff actually appear together. Henry's rhetoric is inevitably formal—as if heavily figured blank verse were the only medium for expression, public or private, though the audience can see how ponderous it is in direct dealings with a son; Falstaff's prose on the other hand is colloquial, supple, and spontaneous, even when it runs to parody as in 2.4. When the king asks Worcester at dawn on the field of Shrewsbury how it is that the rebels have come to this "day of dislike" without actively seeking it, Falstaff interrupts rudely with a joke wholly out of place in grave counsel vital to the state's welfare: "Rebellion lay in his way and he found it." Acutely aware of the impropriety or "cheapness" of Eastcheap banter where England is concerned (or his own political future, for that matter), Hal cuts off his old friend sharply with "peace, chewet, peace."[5] And, indeed, Falstaff does seem like a magpie at this moment, a prating opportunist who can only repeat his mechanical tricks of speech even where they are out of place. Although Hal will let him steal the bright honor of victory over Hotspur like a greedy old chewet attracted to shiny objects, Hal's ultimate rejection of Falstaff is prefigured as the pupil gives his master a first lesson in rhetorical decorum. Whether Hal as Henry V is best seen as Christian humanist or as master of Machiavellian realpolitik I leave it to wiser birds to determine.

## Notes

1. Shakespeare's interest in birds was first documented by Sir Archibald Geikie in *The Birds of Shakespeare* (Glasgow, 1916), but very often, as in *Macbeth*, he weaves images drawn from natural history into larger allegorical patterns that suit his imaginative purpose. As Audrey Yoder claims in *Animal Imagery in Shakespeare's Character Portrayal* (New York, 1947), he employs animals "mainly for purposes of censure or ridicule." She records that the two parts of *Henry IV* are among the very richest plays in the canon for such imagery, with Falstaff as the

central figure of comparison. She stresses Aesop as Shakespeare's principle literary source for his knowledge of animals, though a strong case could also be made for the medieval bestiaries with their moralizing tendencies.

2. 4.4. 68–71. All quotations from the *New Arden* edition of the plays, ed. A. R. Humphreys.

3. Hotspur's rejection of eloquence is un-Elizabethan, though his plain-dealing is consistent with Stoical ideals if not exactly Senecan in its truculence. Othello, Horatio, and Brutus strike me as notable exemplars of laconicism, but in Hotspur's case Shakespeare creates an antiverbal bias that is not so much philosophical as it is bound up in gender stereotype. In diametrical opposition to Richard II, whose rhetorical expansiveness and effeminacy are inextricably bound up with each other, Hotspur, like Hamlet, thinks it unmanly to be eloquent ("like a whore" to "unpack [his] heart with words"). This unfortunate anticipation of modern sex-role stereotyping seems to me peculiarly Shakespearean, and is rare elsewhere in Renaissance literature, where eloquence is exalted as man's most godlike attribute. A detailed study of this topic is long overdue.

4. As T. W. Baldwin demonstrates in "A Note on Shakespeare's Use of Pliny" in *Essays in Dramatic Literature* (The Parrott Presentation volume), ed. Hardin Craig (Princeton, 1935), Shakespeare in 1598 relies for this passage directly on the Latin. Although Shakespeare uses Pliny a good deal in *Othello* (apparently both the Latin and the 1601 Philemon Holland translation), Baldwin concludes that Shakespeare does not rely very heavily on him as a source elsewhere in the canon. Pliny does, however, include in his catalogue of talking birds not only parrots and nightingales, but ravens and starlings as well. Apparently the African Grey Parrot, brought to Rome by Scipio Africanus, stimulated a keen interest in talking birds.

5. Pliny has this to say about magpies, as quoted in the Holland translation by H. W. Seager in his extremely useful and now rare *Natural History in Shakespeare's Time* (London, 1896):

> Pies take a love to the words that they speak; for they not only learn them as a lesson, but they learn them with a delight and pleasure; and by their careful thinking upon that which they learn, they shew plainly how mindful and intentive they be thereto. It is for certain known that they have died for very anger and grief that they could not learn to pronounce some hard words; as also, unless they hear the same words repeated often unto them, their memory is so shittle, they will soon forget the same again.

# A Contemporary Playwright Looks at Shakespeare's Plays

## John Mortimer

I t is a great honor to me to be invited to come from England to give this lecture. The Apple-Zimmerman Fund is a generous endowment for Elizabethan studies at this University, and previous speakers here have included Lacey Baldwin Smith, C. Walter Hodges, and, to my mind the greatest contemporary student of Shakespeare, Professor Sam Schoenbaum. I cannot think why there has fallen on me the honor of being asked to join this most distinguished cast of characters. My only claim to fame, my one proud boast, is that I am undoubtedly the best British playwright ever to have defended a murderer at the Old Bailey, our Central Criminal Court. However, whenever I tell that to the murderers I have defended, they never look particularly encouraged.

With such limited qualification I have, of course, been extremely doubtful as to what I could add to the deliberations of such experts upon the plays of Shakespeare. I have decided that the only thoughts of interest I might have are as a British dramatist who started work in the theater, films, and television some 340 years after Shakespeare's death—a British dramatist, moreover, who was brought up on the plays of Shakespeare much as a later generation was brought up on Ministry of Health orange juice or the works of Dr. Spock.

> Is execution done on Cawdor? Are not
> Those in commission yet return'd?

From my earliest years my father would repeatedly ask me these questions that, at the age of six, I was at a loss to answer. At other moments he would look at me in a threatening manner and say, casting himself as Hubert the jailer and me as the youthful Prince Arthur, about to be blinded,

> Heat me these irons hot; and look thou stand
> Within the arras: when I strike my foot

Upon the bosom of the ground, rush forth,
And bind the boy. . . .

So the words of the plays became a sort of family code and the subject of our jokes. "Is execution done on Cawdor?" was a line of hilarious comedy and "Rushforth and Bind-the-Boy," a firm of dubious lawyers.

From an early age I began to act the tragedies, in an abridged version, for the benefit of my mother and father, at the end of the dining room. Unfortunately, I was an only child and so had to act all the parts. (This gives me an additional qualification: I must be the only Apple-Zimmerman lecturer who has dueled with himself, played a bedroom scene with himself as his own mother, and forced himself to drink his own poisoned chalice.) They were productions that must have been far more enjoyable to perform than to watch.

My father was not musical, and the words of the plays took the place of music for him. He would, in the middle of breakfast, or while taking geranium cuttings, suddenly intone, "Nymph in thy orisons be all my sins remembered," or "Of one whose subdued eyes / Albeit unused to the melting mood, / Dropt tears as fast as the Arabian trees / Their medicinable gum."[1] He would repeat these words of Shakespeare, as other men might hum a favorite phrase from Puccini or melody from *South Pacific*. I, too, have never ceased to be moved by the sheer music of Shakespeare, although today's actors, who race toward familiar quotations in a kind of embarrassed mutter, as though shying at some obscenity, have done their best to teach me otherwise.

When I was a child, my father took me each year to see the plays at Stratford-on-Avon, and he was able to help out the actors by reciting most of their lines quite loudly and a couple of beats before they did. As his eyes failed, he would ask me to keep up a running commentary on the action. We became, I suppose, two of the most unpopular members of the Stratford audience. At night we stayed in the Shakespeare Hotel in Stratford-on-Avon, where the rooms were named after Shakespeare's characters. I remember at an early age standing terrified in "Macbeth" and seeing, reflected in the wardrobe mirror, a terrible hooded figure with spindly legs and a body that seemed to be nothing but a whitish blur. It was surely some ghastly emanation from the cauldron, I thought, and stood paralyzed with fear until I realized that the reflection was me taking off my shirt. I was brought to my senses by a horrendous matrimonial quarrel going on in "Romeo and Juliet" next door.

The point of these random reminiscences is only that I cannot remember a time when my head was not full of pages of Shakespeare, any more than I can now remember not being able to swim. I cannot remember, for instance, not knowing how *The Merchant of Venice* ends, and

I am sure it is hard for us all to appreciate the effect that twist in plotting must have had on its first audience. My feeling for Shakespeare was, perhaps, like a child's feeling toward a half-understood religion or like— even like—the original audiences' at the Globe Theatre to his plays. I was impressed, indeed intoxicated, by the incantations, fascinated by the mysteries, terrified by the ghosts.

It was not until I grew up to be a writer that I was able to understand Shakespeare's extraordinary mastery of that most difficult of all literary crafts, the practice of dramatic writing.

I suppose any consideration of Shakespeare as a worker in the theater must start with him as a man. No one who writes anything about Shakespeare will have failed to receive communications from the Francis Bacon Society. I have, in my life, known many cold-blooded lawyers such as Francis Bacon was, and not one of them would have been capable of writing the plays of Shakespeare. Two facts are beyond dispute, the inscription in the parish church at Stratford, erected in 1623, which likens William Shakespeare of Stratford to Socrates and Virgil, and the First Folio in the same year in which Ben Jonson calls him "The Sweet Swan of Avon." I therefore venture to suggest that we proceed on this basis: If the plays were not by Shakespeare, they were written by someone who lived in the same time and at the same place, and happened to have exactly the same name.

When I started to write some television plays loosely based on the life of Shakespeare, I was told by the late, greatly lamented Professor Terrence Spencer of Birmingham, England, that you could write all that was known of Shakespeare's life on a postcard and leave room for the stamp.

I have since found that this is not altogether true, and that we know as much of Shakespeare as we would of any prosperous middle-class Elizabethan who was never an aristocrat or tried for treason. Shakespeare had too great a consideration for his art, and a determination to practice it, to get into trouble. We know a great deal about Marlowe because he could never keep out of trouble: he was in the middle of every fight, every scandal, every mystery. Shakespeare sat quietly in the corner, I imagine, remembering the dialogue and determined to survive.

The most exciting thing about Tudor society was that it was forever on the boil. Talents shot up out of nowhere and exploded like fireworks. From butcher's son to cardinal, from cobbler's son to poet, or international spy—all in a short lifetime. We have some reason to think that Shakespeare's father may have been illiterate. He certainly used his mark to sign his name. From a barely literate father to a son who made himself master of one of the largest vocabularies in English literature as well as writing some of the world's greatest plays, appears miraculous. He must have had admirable teachers.

But what sort of man was he? He was born an alderman's son, far from the London theater, just as Rudolf Nureyev was born a poor boy in a Siberian town, far from any ballet company, and Kiri te Kanawa in a Maori village across the world far from Covent Garden or the New York Metropolitan Opera. Yet the instinct of the artist, strange and incalculable as the instinct of the homing pigeon or the emigrating swallow, drove these artists inevitably to the place where they could practice their various arts. After an early marriage we lose track of Shakespeare for a number of years, a convenient period in which we can make him anything we want him to be, a lawyer's clerk, a soldier of fortune, or a schoolteacher (if you happen to be a schoolteacher). Because I am a lawyer, I fancy him bored to death in some attorney's office, collecting nothing of value except wonderful metaphors like "My lease in thee is now determinate" or lines like "Let's choose executors and talk of will." He might even have gone to Italy.[2]

It is clear, however, and beyond dispute that Shakespeare became an actor, and then a writer who enjoyed, from his early start with the three parts of *Henry VI*, an enormous popular and box-office success. He was singularly free from that nightmare of the contemporary dramatist, the self-advertising dramatic critic. He seems to have had only one bad notice, when the no-doubt envious Robert Greene called him an "upstart crow, beautified with our feathers, [who] supposes he is as well able to bombast out a blank verse as the best of you and . . . is in his own conceit the only Shake Scene in a country."

Despite this unfavorable notice early in his career, it is clear that Shakespeare went on to make a comfortable living in the theater and was able to buy property and retire early to his hometown, a way of life that the Commissioners of Inland Revenue have made impossible for a dramatist today.

The search for Shakespeare's character behind this bland chronicle of success has been, of course, neverending, and as Professor Schoenbaum has pointed out most entertainingly in his *Shakespeare's Lives,* everyone finds his own Shakespeare. For nineteenth-century romantics he was a simple, handsome country lad who poached deer at Charlecote and grew up to write plays that were really too good for such a vulgar place as the theater. For Oscar Wilde and Lord Alfred Douglas he was a poet of the nineties, in love with a boy actor called Willy Hughes. He may suit us in our modern mood best as the tormented bisexual of the *Sonnets* or the disillusioned pessimist of *Troilus and Cressida* who saw no future after a pointless and all-destroying war. You can, to a large extent, look in the plays and find the Shakespeare you want. If you wish him to be egalitarian and antiestablishment, he will oblige with

Take physic, pomp,
Expose thyself to feel what wretches feel

and

> Handy, dandy, which is the Justice, which is the thief?

If you want him to be an implacable conservative, he will give you

> Oh, when degree is shak'd,
> Which is the ladder to all high designs,
> The enterprise is sick!

and

> Take but degree away, untune that string,
> And, hark, what discord follows!

He can sound a clarion call to free love:

> Therefore despite of fruitless chastity,
> Love-lacking vestals, and self-loving nuns
> That on the earth would breed a scarcity
> And barren dearth of daughters and of sons,
> Be prodigal:

and denounce the pleasures of the flesh with fierce and savage contempt
with

> The expense of spirit in a waste of shame
> Is lust in action.

Is he a humanist, on the side of man against the indifferent gods?

> As flies to wanton boys are we to the gods.
> They kill us for their sport.

Or is he deeply religious?

> Why, all the souls that were were forfeit once,
> And He who might the vantage beast have took,
> Found out the remedy.

So, to a large extent Shakespeare will think, what you want him to
think. But with some exceptions. He will not be mean and he will not be
pompous, or pretentious, or falsely sentimental, and he will not be a
hypocrite.

It is generally supposed that Shakespeare suffered some secret
trauma, some period when fate or his fellows treated him mercilessly,
leaving him filled with bitterness and thoughts of man's ingratitude.

When I wrote my book and television plays about him, I explained his black and bitter period by the fact, clearly revealed in the *Sonnets*, that his fair friend so far forgot his friendship as to jump into bed with his dark mistress. The death of his young son Hamnet at the age of eleven, about the time he wrote *A Midsummer Night's Dream*—a play about a stolen changling child—may have darkened his life. He may have been embittered by death or jealousy; and yet it is often misleading to study a playwright's characters in the hope of finding the playwright's character. The dramatist must perform incessantly and take on a variety of roles beyond the range of even an Alec Guinness or a Peter Sellers.

Shakespeare could turn himself, without effort, into Falstaff and Juliet, Cleopatra and Shallow, Hamlet and Doll Tearsheet. No doubt he had something of all these characters in him, perhaps we all have; and yet there is a danger in identifying a writer too closely with his creations. From a study of John Osborne's excellent plays, works that out-Timon Timon in angry railing against almost everything, you might suppose that Osborne was an embittered, angry, and cynical man.

Those who have had the pleasure of meeting John Osborne have been surprised to find him a gentle, kindly, humorous fellow who often goes to Evensong in his village church and entertains his local vicar to tea. Although Timon railed against the world, it may be a mistake to suppose that Shakespeare was more of a Timon than a Horatio. In fact Horatio and Kent in *King Lear* are the characters he writes most sympathetically: the honest man, the good man, whose life is dominated by friendship to a fallible superior.

There are other contradictions in this character. Like the great majority of English writers, Shakespeare came from the middle class, and yet he wrote almost exclusively of princes or peasants. The middle-class bur- gher, depicted in much Elizabethan drama, hardly appears in his plays. Was Shakespeare, after being pressed into a teenage marriage with an older woman, revolting against the narrow, provincial bourgeois world that was his inheritance? He clearly loved the Warwickshire countryside passionately, and yet he wrote better than anyone of a London tavern and the low life of a city.

The voyage behind that pale, domelike forehead, into the secret thoughts behind those dark eyes, is of endless fascination and must always be attempted. It may be that he even deserved the reputation for sweetness that Ben Johnson gave him, but perhaps his wife would not have agreed.

We think of him now, down the corridor of years, and try to get to know him, but I wonder if even his contemporaries really knew Shake- speare, although they clearly loved him. No doubt he was witty, charm- ing, capable of deep friendship and sudden bitterness, particularly to those he loved. I think we should have liked Shakespeare, surrendered to his charm, listened to his stories of the theater and Warwickshire legends. But he would have left us, even then, with his mysteries intact.

We are on such ground when we join him in his great obsession, mastering what is, as I have said, by far the hardest task a writer faces, the creation of drama. If, in that great invigorating Tudor turmoil, a life could spring from darkness and burst like a firework, illuminating the sky, the great dramatic form which was the Elizabethan theater erupted as quietly, and vanished almost as quickly away. At one moment, it seems, plays were crude pantomimes done on carts in Inn yards; in the next they have achieved the complex subtleties of *Twelfth Night* or *Antony and Cleopatra*. And then, in a few short years, one of the greatest instruments available to writers has vanished. Not much over sixty years from the building of the first regular theater in Shoreditch, the Puritans were in power and passed the laws closing theaters and forbidding public stage plays. The great Elizabethan theaters stood derelict, many of them to be used again only as stables and sheep pens, and actors drifted off to become unsuitable recruits in the armed services or starve. Those who tried to avoid the ban were fined or imprisoned, or whipped as strolling vagabonds.

By some miracle for us, Shakespeare managed to be born in the short life of the Elizabethan playhouse before the Puritans took over and destroyed the drama. There are, it seems, two strands in the British national character; and the playwrights and creators always have to contend with those who regard the theater as a place of sin.

What the Elizabethan theater offered was a freedom in dramatic writing that the playwright did not regain until this century, with the invention of the movies and television, and the return of serious theater to the open, uncluttered stages of Tudor times. Shakespeare had the freedom of the *cine* camera to travel the world, the speed of film or videotape to cut from short scene to short scene without long intervals for changing scenery when the audience has to be plunged into boring, coughing, sweet-paper rustling darkness. He had the radio writer's wonderful opportunity to paint scenery with the two finest materials available: words and the audience's imagination. In fact the Elizabethan theater gave the dramatic writer all the advantages that he was to lose and not recover for another three hundred years.

I think of Shakespeare at the start of his career—faced with a blank stage and a blank piece of paper, equipped with a snatch or two of old history and some fragments of old plays that his task was to cobble into the three parts of *Henry VI*.

He had, of course, no idea that he would manage to survive to write a total of thirty-six or thirty-seven deathless plays: no writer believes he will ever get beyond the work he is engaged on and each has grave doubts if he is going to finish that. He had no way of knowing that he was to enter into the period of the Supreme Tragedies, or the plays of bitterness, ending up with the Great Comedies of Reconciliation. He probably never dreamed that he would end up rich and respected, with a coat of arms and a home in Stratford. He had no thoughts of having university chairs and hotel bedrooms dedicated to him. He felt, I am sure, like any contemporary playwright that any day he might fall a victim to the pox, or the police, or that the theaters might be closed by the Plague, or war, or, what was worse, by the Puritans. Any play he wrote might have been his last, and before death or the Privy Council or those dreaded horrors, the child actors of Saint Paul's, spoiled everything, his concern was to get together, for that yawningly empty platform, some sort of an entertainment.

A stage is an empty space. Put one thing on it—a throne, say, or a bed—and it looks important; add another and its importance is halved. The emptiness of Shakespeare's stage meant that props, even costumes, I suspect, were of minor importance. The power in the theater was the word, and the word was Shakespeare's. In the beginning was the word. That, at least, is one of the opinions in which I find myself in complete agreement with God. I believe the word to be the most important thing in the theater and in television and even in the cinema, but today's dramatist has to fight for his words against the competition of scenic effects, visual excitement, and beautiful pictures. Shakespeare was in a better position because the beautiful pictures could only be provided by his words.

Every working dramatist has learned that the most enjoyable performance of his plays comes at the end of the rehearsal period, when the actors know the words, but before the set has been built, before the costumes have arrived, before the lighting man has got to work and before the makeup (and before, let it be said, the audience is let in). The play always seems to speak, in such final rehearsals, with a particular intensity and conviction, with actors wearing their own clothes and a few props to stimulate but not take over from the imagination. In such final rehearsals we get closer, I am sure, to the theater Shakespeare knew. The word is all.

It is obvious, and has often been said, that Shakespeare was the master stage designer. He could do it with one sentence:

This is Illyria, lady.

And the bare boards of the stage become a sun-drenched sea coast. He could write

> Light thickens, and the crow
> Makes wing to the rooky wood:
> Good things of day begin to droop and drowse
> Whiles night's black agents to their preys do rouse.

And Shakespeare's stage, in the middle of a sunny afternoon, became filled with terrifying and entirely verbal darkness. Today, of course, the director, the designer, and the lighting man would all lend a hand. The stage would actually go dark and the absence of light, as everyone knows, makes words inaudible. Things were better for Shakespeare in this respect: his words were given their due and were the only decor. Do you want a war?

> This battle fares like to the morning's war
> When dying clouds contend with growing light,
> What time the shepherd, blowing of his nails,
> Can neither call it perfect day nor night.
> Now sways it this way, like a mighty sea
> Forced by the tide to combat with the wind;
> Now sways it that way, like the self same sea
> Forced to retire by fury of the wind. . . .

In the movies that would require a location in Yugoslavia, a thousand extras, a couple of hundred technicians, and an army of assistants to call out, "Ready when you are, Mr. DeMille." In today's theater it would still call, perhaps, for strobe lighting, the reverberation of clashing swords, and that health hazard to present-day stalls customers, dense clouds of dry ice to send them coughing out at the intervals. All Shakespeare needed for a battle were words and one man, alone on a daylit platform, sitting on something he pretended was a molehill.

The ability to change scenery with a word gave Shakespeare and his contemporaries a great freedom in time and place that the dramatist has only recently recovered. As with the modern scriptwriter, the world was Shakesepare's oyster: he could cut from Egypt to Rome, from Eastcheap to Harfleur, with the speed of a pair of scissors cutting into film. And the use of voice-over in films and television has made it possible for a dramatist to communicate a character's unspoken thoughts and has restored the soliloquy that the theater lost during the long interregnum of naturalistic drama that followed the Puritan ban on all public plays.

When the Puritans forbade the theater in the streets, they eventually drove it into the drawing room. The picture stage, the box set, gradually led the theater away from poetry and toward naturalism. The three-act play no longer flashed from Rome to Egypt; the curtain fell; and, after a lengthy interval allowing time for a fight for a small warm drink wrenched from a sullen lady in black bombezine in the theater bar, the

curtain rose again on "The same, three months later." Fairies and mon-
sters, battles and executions were driven offstage and took refuge in the
wings.[3]

Perhaps the great theatrical events, during the nineteenth century,
took refuge in the operahouse. There music took over from poetry by
allowing the theater to burst the bounds of naturalism, and characters
could sing out their secret thoughts at the tops of their magnificent
voices and the audience had no difficulty in accepting that no one else on
the stage could possibly hear them. The soliloquy became the aria and,
as a vehicle for a character's inner thoughts, finally the voice-over in
films or television. It is above all, I believe, in his freedom from the
literal demands of naturalism that the playwright of today can feel
closest to Shakespeare and learn most from him.

Shakespeare was also, of course, a master scriptwriter. The author of a
three-act play has to find two good curtain lines to send the audience out
happy. A play split up into a multitude of short scenes depends, like a
good filmscript, on finding the correct way of ending one scene and
starting another, either by linking them with a similar image or by a
ferocious contrast. This is the technique the film writer, whose story
proceeds in short bursts, has to learn, and Shakespeare knew it perfectly. *Macbeth* is full of instances.

The most obvious, perhaps, is the scene of Duncan's arrival and
greeting by Lady Macbeth. At the scene's end the king says:

> Give me your hand:
> Conduct me to mine host: we love him highly,
> And shall continue our graces towards him.
> By your leave, hostess.

And the very next scene starts with Macbeth alone:

> If it were done when 'tis done then 'twere well
> It were done quickly. . . .

Macbeth, whom Duncan spoke of so lovingly, is plotting Duncan's
murder.

Earlier, Shakespeare achieved a similar effect by a cut within a scene.
Duncan speaks of the treacherous Cawdor, on whom execution has been
done.

> There is no art
> To find the mind's construction in the face.
> He was a gentleman on whom I built
> An absolute trust.

And then

      CUT TO
      CLOSE SHOT     Macbeth entering, full of smiles.

The examples, of course, could be multiplied endlessly. But it was the timelessness, the simplicity of the Elizabethan stage, that allowed Shakespeare to cut like a film writer, with savage irony that keeps his audience continually attentive.

Not only the links between, but the juxtaposition of, scenes show what a consummate master Shakespeare would have been of film and television, just as he is of the open stage. And the supreme art of such immediate contrast would have been impossible on the nineteenth-century picture stage.

A scene on the cold, windy, dark battlements, on which walks the restless ghost of a king who cannot sleep in peace, is followed by a huge, glittering court occasion in a room of state. The placing of these two scenes one after the other at the start of the play almost tells us the whole story of *Hamlet*, and it is incredible to me that in a recent London production, where the ghost was reduced to a kind of fit of the collywobbles going on inside Hamlet, the first scene was cut, as though there is anyone alive today who could teach his stage technique to Shakespeare.

The essential trick of such juxtaposition is continual surprise. Everyone has pointed out the way in which the terrible knocking on the gate in *Macbeth* is followed, unexpectedly, by a monologue from a drunken porter. The porter is not very funny; he does not need to be. He is both a marvelous dramatic device, a way of keeping us waiting when it is almost unbearable to wait, and a true echo of the way life suddenly changes its mood at the most unexpected and inappropriate moments.

Such are the matters of technique. But what can a writer say of Shakespeare's characters that could possibly add to the thoughts of those who have made a lifetime's study of his plays? The walls of libraries are lined with studies of the characters. The words written about them, if laid end to end, would no doubt stretch from here to the moon. And yet, reading so much that has been beautifully and intelligently written, it has often seemed to me that something of great importance has been forgotten when the characters in Shakespeare's plays are discussed.

Characters in plays are what they are. They exist to make the plays work. They are an essential part of the artifact, the work of art. They are there to create the conflict, the tension, the drama, the pathos, the tragedy, or the jokes. Their business, their justification is on the stage. Take them off the stage, into the psychiatrist's consulting room, for instance, for a long session on the couch, or put them into the witness box and question their motives, and they become tongue-tied and self-contradictory, lapsing finally, perhaps, into an embarrassed and protective silence. This, I believe, is the reason for the dissatisfaction many academics, particularly former academics, feel about Shakespeare. And it is also the reason why audiences love his plays and writers must learn from them. *Hamlet* is a play that invariably works, even if done by a cast of nervous schoolgirls. Whenever or wherever it is produced it is a box-office success. And yet Hamlet as a man puzzles most of the academic writers who have discussed him. He appears, when closely examined as a human being, contradictory, inexplicable, unsatisfactory even: almost every fault can be found with him as a creation except his ability to produce great drama.

Every writer has had an actor come to him at some stage of a production to say, "Can you tell me why I say this, exactly? What's the motivation?" Every writer has been tempted to reply with the truth: "Your motivation is to get on with the play."

Why does Hamlet hesitate and procrastinate before he swoops to his revenge? A thousand times more words have been written on this subject than Shakespeare needed to write the play itself. Ingenious theories have been advanced, including the idea that Hamlet was a woman in disguise in love with Horatio, or had faked the ghost story as a political maneuver to get rid of Claudius. The late Andrew Bradley devoted many pages to all the possible explanations—that Hamlet was afraid no one would believe him if he denounced Claudius, or that he was deterred by moral scruple from murdering his uncle, or that he was too sensitive to act as an executioner, or that he, perhaps, was too much of an intellectual and thought so carefully that all physical activity became impossible.[4]

At which point it is tempting to imagine a conversation between Burbage and Shakespeare around the coffee machine during the mid-morning break in the rehearsal room at the Globe Theatre.

"What's the matter with me, Will?" Burbage said. "Am I suffering from natural caution or am I too intellectual and profound or I have I got melancholia? I mean, for God's sake, why don't I kill Claudius immediately after I've met the ghost in act 1, scene 4?"

"Because if you did that, dear boy," Shakespeare might well have answered, warming his hands on his paper cup, "we shouldn't have any damned play!"

Now, this may sound an extremely philistine remark and its attribution to Shakespeare, the Divine Poet, almost sacrilege. Such a thought, I dare swear, never entered the mind of Professor Bradley when he set out the various reasons for Hamlet's prevarication under carefully numbered paragraphs. But before I am dismissed entirely as a hack with a forehead villainous low, may I say something about the way in which I think the examination of the characters in Shakespeare's plays, and indeed in any drama, may have been given a wrong emphasis.

In the last century Shakespeare's characters were regarded as heroes, and they seemed to become heroes irrespective of, and perhaps in spite of, the slightly disagreeable fact that they were involved in stage plays. A hero, so the Victorians thought, is more fitted for the library than the stage; and he exists, in his heroic fashion, in a world greater and more prolonged than a temporary evening in the theater. Now a hero is not a hero unless his greatness can be explained. It is true that if he is a tragic Shakespearean hero he has a "fatal flaw," but the flaw itself is of heroic dimensions and must also be attributable to some understandable and heroic quality. Thus melancholy explained Hamlet, ambition Macbeth, jealousy Othello, and so on.

With the passage of time, and the arrival of Dr. Freud in Vienna, men and women began to lose their heroic dimensions. But they still have to be explicable in other terms, by their relations with their mothers, or their jealousy of their fathers, by insufficient weaning, or an infant glimpse of their parents making love. These explanations suit very well realistic or totally naturalistic drama. They come to their logical conclusion in American plays of the 1950s, when every character arrived on the stage fitted with a series of complexes derived from some textbook on psychology. Actors even prepared to take part in such plays by long sessions of talk in the Actors Studio about the early life of the characters they were playing, how much they loved their mothers or were jealous of their fathers or whether they were dropped when young.

The late Noel Coward, when actors asked him what their motivation was, would answer, "Your paycheck at the end of the week," and would counsel them to concentrate on remembering the lines and on trying not to bump into furniture. I do not suppose Shakespeare ever said anything as rude as that to Burbage and it is not necessary, of course, to dismiss all such questions on motivation quite so brusquely. Such questions may be relevant to the characters in the plays of Tennessee Williams or Arthur Miller. They are quite irrelevant when you happen to be dealing with Lady Macbeth.

No doubt in the Actors Studio a long discussion could take place about Lady Macbeth's relationship with the child to whom she had given suck, or of her exact feeling about her father whom, as we know, the sleeping Duncan resembled. Such discussion could take place, but it would be futile. Lady Macbeth does not come as a subject for an essay or a clinical study. She came out of the dressingroom onto a platform one afternoon and there she was—bang!—a character of blazing intensity who needs no explanation, no excuse, except for her huge effect on the drama that she will help to produce.

Or let us take Iago. Iago has every considerable fault and is totally inexplicable—except to actors, who know that he can act Othello off the stage. Iago presented Professor Bradley with enormous problems. Was he possessed, as Coleridge had suggested of "motiveless malignity"? Critics, like lawyers, are anxious to find a motive for everything, and dislike nothing more than an effect without a discernible cause. So Iago is "motivated" by his enjoyment of power. He can be explained. Iago the character has an explanation and so, curiously enough, the play becomes less disturbing and the drama as a whole, may I suggest, is diminished by becoming more rational.

Another question authors are frequently asked by actors is what such and such a line "means." The author who knows his business, as to be sure Shakespeare did, is tempted to answer, "It means what it says. If there were another way of saying it, I should have used it." And again, if the line is learned, and said so it is audible, and the furniture avoided, and the author knows his business, the line will work in the theater, although it may look quite puzzling when taken out and analyzed.

So may I humbly submit, as we say down at the Old Bailey, that, if you are starting out on this voyage of discovery, you experience—above all you enjoy—the works of Shakespeare . . . but perhaps, just perhaps, you do not spend too much time in trying to explain. Perhaps this is because any explanation has to be given in words other than Shakespeare's, and his words are, invariably and after all, the best.

May we take time to consider how Shakespeare, how any good serious dramatist from 1580 to 1980, went to work. He had a theme, no doubt, that he wanted for the moment to express about pride, about ambition, about man's ingratitude, about kingship and the unity of a nation, about mistaken identity, or about the magic of a wood. Such themes can produce either comedy or tragedy. Handled differently, Othello's handkerchief might have been the stuff of farce, and Malvolio's downfall has the whiff of tragedy in it. Given a theme, the playwright needs a plot. This is the most difficult part: Shakespeare often solved the problem by pinching someone else's. When he had thought of his main character, he had to provide other characters who would produce conflict, which, either in comedy or tragedy, is the stuff of drama. When a playwright is working well, his characters assume an existence of their own, take things into their own hands, and surprise him by what they do. No doubt they also surprise a number of academics. But of one thing there can be no doubt. Shakespeare was usually working well.

And one thing also. Just as the scenery for his plays depended on an act of the imagination and was in no way naturalistic, just as his language used everyday speech and played with it, rearranged it, and fired the imagination so that it was in no way naturalistic, just as Burbage's acting no doubt started with life in the court or on the streets, but magnified the gestures, colored the emotions, and raised it at least two feet above the ground—so the people in Shakespeare's plays exist at that level which is best called theatrical.

They are not all explained. A great deal of space is left for us to fill in. They are not painted photographically like realistic scenery. They call for us all, and that is one of their great virtues, to exercise the imagination and leave us free to a large extent—you and me and Coleridge and Professor Bradley—to see in them what we want to see, which is perhaps why audiences have never tired of the plays and why, since he got over his first bad notice from Greene, Shakespeare has been such an astonishingly popular success.

Because with Shakespeare it is not the philosophy or the psychology or the realistic study of character that is important. It is The Play that's the thing. And whatever else happens, the play can be seen to work. And it is the working of the play in theatrical terms that is the element former critics missed. Professor Bradley, whom I have knocked quite enough and may now after so much critical fervor be allowed to sleep well, thought that if he could not explain the characters, if he found them inconsistent, or mysterious, or surprising, Shakespeare had fallen down on his job. But Shakespeare's job was not to explain human nature to Professor Bradley, but to excite and enthrall and intoxicate with drama whoever would be kind enough to pay for a ticket next Wednesday afternoon.

What should we learn from this marvelous collection of plays, those of us who have the honor of carrying on, so imperfectly, the theatrical traditions Shakespeare left us, and work to produce drama either on stage, or on films or television? I would say that we should learn that naturalism is not the last or the only word. That an empty platform and a call to the imagination are worth more than all the elaborate machinery that has never been made to work in London's National Theatre. That stage characters, rooted in real life, can take off and grow and gesture with the greatest theatricality. If their feet start firmly on the ground, they can be made to rise ten feet above it. They exist in a world in which psychological realism is only part of the equation. And we can learn that at the heart of every great play, as at the heart of life itself, is a mystery that each of us must interpret as best we can. And finally we can learn that any character who behaves consistently, according to a logical and reasonable plan laid down by his implacable creator, is very likely to be a crashing bore.

When I undertook the task of writing some television plays about

Shakespeare, I found the most difficult thing to do was to prevent his coming out like Saint Francis of Assisi. Perhaps it was in fact the last revenge of a rival poet, but Ben Jonson's "sweet" Shakespeare has stuck down the ages with a somewhat cloying effect.

Yet this was the man who could also leave his family for many years to pursue, with ruthless ambition, his career in London, who could be torn between a dark mistress and a fair friend, the one producing in him tormented lust, the other some particularly fulsome flattery. He could end up no doubt as a level but hard-headed landlord and man of property.

And yet he appeared, I am sure, as "sweet Shakespeare" among his friends in the Mermaid Tavern. His obsession, I am convinced, was with his work, his ambition was to survive, to keep out of trouble so that he might continue with it for as long as he had the strength and, when he was not writing, to notice, to watch, and to listen to everything. His is a character that, like those of Falstaff and Hamlet and Iago, defies, in the last instance, analysis.

We do not go to playwrights to answer questions about politics or philosophy or religion. If a continuously exciting sense of theatre and an infallible ear for dialogue and stage poetry equipped men to answer us about such matters, we should, no doubt, elect Harold Pinter prime minister and John Osborne Archbishop of Canterbury. We go to playwrights for their art, and when that art is as great as Shakespeare's, it expresses, in terms of theater, the splendors and miseries, the cruelty and mercy, the huge seriousness and enormous absurdity of life itself.

Many will have ideas about who the dark lady was, and who the fair friend, and some of such ideas may well be correct. Many will be able to analyze the plays and their characters with a deeper learning and a greater ingenuity than I could ever command. But however long Shakespeare studies continue, and however many lectures and occasions there are such as this, and valuable they certainly are, they will never be able to pluck the heart out of his mystery. I sincerely hope.

### Notes

1. One great rule for an English barrister is to be polite to solicitors (who bring barristers their work). And whenever he saw a solicitor, my father was wont to say, "The devil damn thee black, thou cream faced loon! Where gottest that goose look?" He thought he was doing a favor to solicitors by improving their education.

2. Anthony Burgess has spoken of the Italian dream of finding half a return ticket to Milan in Shakespeare's tomb.

3. It is true that in Ibsen's plays the trolls and water spirits are haunting the fjord, and that in Chekhov the great tide of history is gradually washing away the

past, but these events are only dimly heard in their drawingrooms. The fairies and revolutions are anywhere but on the stage.

4. Professor Bradley discussed all these possibilities and plumped for the solution that Hamlet was afflicted with a profound melancholy, an *accidie* that paralyzed his will and accounted for four long acts of inactivity.

# Contributors

Rüdiger Ahrens, Professor of English at the University of Würzburg, has taught at the Universities of Hannover, Trier, Erlangen, and at Wolfson College, Cambridge. He has edited multivolume works in Germany on pedagogical and critical approaches to Shakespeare and on English and American literary criticism.

Norman A. Brittin, Hollifield Professor Emeritus of English Literature at Auburn University, has taught at the universities of Southern California, Utah, Washington, Chicago, Puerto Rico, and La Laguna (Canary Islands, where he was Fulbright Lecturer). Former coeditor of the *Southern Humanities Review,* he has published articles in several areas, including Shakespeare, as well as books on Thomas Middleton and Edna St. Vincent Millay.

Michael J. Collins is Dean of the School for Summer and Continuing Education and teaches in the Department of English at Georgetown University.

Ann Jennalie Cook teaches at Vanderbilt University and since 1975 has been Executive Secretary of the Shakespeare Association of America. Apple-Zimmerman lecturer at Susquehanna in 1985, she has written *The Privileged Playgoers of Shakespeare's London* (1981) and the forthcoming *The Bridal Path: Courtship in Shakespeare and His Society.*

Richard Fly, Associate Professor and recent chair, Department of English at State University of New York–Buffalo, is author of over a dozen articles on Shakespeare and of *Shakespeare's Mediated World* (1976). He also edited Scott, Foresman's *The Complete Works of Shakespeare* (3rd edition, 1980).

Werner Gundersheimer, Director of the Folger Shakespeare Library, is a distinguished Renaissance historian and critic.

Jay L. Halio, Professor of English at the University of Delaware since 1968, is author or editor of numerous books and articles on Shakespeare and modern literature. His essay will appear in different form as a chapter in *Understanding Shakespeare in Performance* (1988). He also is editing *King Lear* for the New Cambridge Shakespeare.

C. WALTER HODGES, designer, illustrator, stage historian, and former Wilson Lecturer in Poetry and Drama at Cambridge, has taught at Wayne State and the University of Maryland, and was Apple-Zimmerman Lecturer in 1983. His books include *Shakespeare and the Players* and *The Globe Restored*.

MAURICE HUNT has taught at The College of Marin, Dominican College, Arizona State, and Baylor University, where he is Assistant Professor and Director of Freshman Composition. He has published widely on Shakespeare, including essays in *Shakespeare Quarterly, Bucknell Review, Shakespeare Studies,* and *Modern Language Studies.*

JOHN MORTIMER, British playwright, novelist, barrister, and creator of *Rumpole of the Bailey,* is the author of *Paradise Postponed.* Apple-Zimmerman Lecturer in 1984, he returned as commencement speaker and recipient of an honorary degree from Susquehanna in May 1985.

CHARLES A. RAHTER (1914–1977) was a medievalist and Professor of English at Susquehanna for seventeen years. A graduate of the University of Pennsylvania, he also taught at Douglass College, Rutgers, and Elizabethtown College before coming to Susquehanna. This article is reprinted from an earlier issue of the *Susquehanna University Studies,* of which he was a member of the Editorial Board.

DANIEL W. Ross studied at the University of Georgia and Purdue, was Director of Continuing Education at Brewton-Parker College before coming to Allentown College in 1985 as Assistant Professor of English. He has authored articles on Keats, Conrad, and *Timon of Athens.*

S. SCHOENBAUM, Director of the Center for Renaissance and Baroque Studies and Distinguished Professor of Renaissance Literature at the Univesity of Maryland, was the first (1981) Apple-Zimmerman lecturer at Susquehanna. Author of *Shakespeare's Lives, William Shakespeare: A Documentary Life,* and *Shakespeare: The Globe and the World,* and founding editor of *Renaissance Drama,* he has taught at Northwestern (1953–75) and at the City University of New York, King's College, London, and the University of Chicago. Susquehanna awarded him an honorary degree at its May 1986 commencement.

MICHAEL W. SHURGOT studied at Canisius College and the Universities of Minnesota and Wisconsin, and has taught at the University of Texas–El

Paso, Seattle University, and South Puget Sound Community College. He has published articles on *The Taming of the Shrew, The Merchant of Venice,* as well as works by John Steinbeck and James Joyce.

KAY STANTON received her Ph.D. from Purdue and teaches at California State University–Fullerton. She has published two other articles on *As You Like It,* as well as an article on Milton's sonnets. An earlier version of this essay was delivered at the 1986 World Shakespeare Congress in West Berlin.

GARY TAYLOR, Joint General Editor of the recently published Oxford edition of Shakespeare's *Complete Works,* in which he edited *All's Well,* is also joint chairman of the Institute for Textual Studies at The Catholic University of America.

WILLIAM COLLINS WATTERSON, graduate of Kenyon College and Brown University, has taught at Bowdoin College since 1976. A poet as well as a critic, his work has appeared in *The New Leader, Clio, Studia Mystica, The New Yorker,* and the *Virginia Quarterly Review.*

ELIZABETH WILEY, Professor of English at Susquehanna University, published this essay in *Susquehanna University Studies* 7:3 (1964). A specialist in early American literature, she is completing a concordance to Poe's fiction.

Other Apple-Zimmerman lecturers have been Lacey Baldwin Smith of Northwestern University (1982), Peter Saccio of Dartmouth College (1986), and Trevor Baxter of the Royal Shakespeare Company (1987).

# Index